VALENTINA'S
ITALIAN
REGIONAL COOKERY

ACKNOWLEDGEMENTS

To undertake a project of this kind, which involves so much travelling and being away from home, necessitates an enormous amount of backup from family and friends, especially if you are a mum! To be able to carry out such a project successfully and happily requires the backup of a very tight, professional team of experts. To all of these people, who believed in me enough to give me the support I needed, I am deeply indebted.

The home team: Ben and Jamie, my parents, Jackie, Joan, Diana and Robin. You have all kept the home fires burning so brightly while I have been away, or too busy to stoke them – none of what I have achieved would ever have been possible without you. Thank you.

The away team: Diane Hadley, Clare Brigstocke, Suzanne Webber, Clive Derbyshire, John Rhodes, Rob Franklin, Mike Dauncey, Chris Thomas, Keith Woodward, and Daniel Thistlethwaite. I just wanted to say to you all that I never thought I could do it until you all showed me that I could. Thank you.

P.S. Very special thanks to Rupert at John Frieda who gave me so much confidence.

VALENTINA'S
ITALIAN
REGIONAL COOKERY

VALENTINA HARRIS

BBC BOOKS

The publishers would like to thank the following for their
invaluable assistance: Gianfranco Spaggiani, Italian Trade
Centre, London; Ines Aronadio, ICE Palermo; Paola Greco,
Italian Tourist Office, London; Eleonora Consoli, Catania;
Enio Tonnetta, Trento Tourist Office; Cristina Turchi, Food
and Wine Department, Emilia Romagna region; Pinuccia
and Cesare Gaetani, Aosta; and Roberta Bocchi from
Fidenza.

LOCATION PHOTOGRAPHY: Daniel Thistlethwaite STUDIO PHOTOGRAPHY: Grant Symons
HOME ECONOMIST: Berit Vinegrad STYLIST: Kay McGlone
EDITORS: Sarah Hoggett, Suzanne Webber, Clare Brigstocke

This book accompanies the BBC TV series *Italian Regional
Cookery*, which was prepared in consultation with the
Continuing Education Advisory Council and first broadcast
on BBC 2 from March 1990. The series was produced by
Clare Brigstocke.

Published by BBC Books,
a division of BBC Enterprises Limited,
Woodlands, 80 Wood Lane, London W12 0TT
First published 1990

© Valentina Harris 1990

ISBN 0 563 21470 8 (hardback)
0 563 21471 6 (paperback)

Set in Janson by Ace Filmsetting Ltd, Frome
Printed and bound in Great Britain by Butler and Tanner Ltd, Frome
Colour separations by Technik Ltd, Berkhamsted
Cover and jacket printed by Richard Clay Ltd, Norwich

CONTENTS

THE REGIONS

TUSCANY

Tuscany is the land of my forefathers, and it may be this that makes each return visit like a homecoming, or it may just be that the landscape, the people and the atmosphere are as familiar and comfortable to me as an old armchair. So many English and American migrants set up home here, crowding out the real Tuscans and attempting to adopt a land that never will be theirs, that parts of the region now seem like Surrey. Yet Tuscany is still the most Italian of all the regions – there have been fewer foreign invasions here than anywhere else, and the race and language are almost pure. Italians say that if you want to hear real Italian spoken, you must speak to a Tuscan. Genuine Italian blue blood runs through the veins of the Tuscan nobility, and it is within these circles that my cousins and I grew up, our happy childhood spent in the gardens of our respective villas or in family vineyards and olive groves. What I see now as this invasion of Italophiles is peculiar and alien to the region that is part of my life.

So many books are published about Tuscany and its food; yet, if you know the region, you will be aware that the natives are and probably always will be *'I Toscani Mangiafagioli'* (the Tuscan Beaneaters), and what could be more basic and simple than a plate of simmered beans? The Renaissance was responsible for taking art into the Florentine kitchens, thanks largely to Caterina de' Medici's entourage who were keen to see a twelve-year-old's whims appeased. (After all, most of Europe's political future depended upon keeping her sweet.) So out of the kitchen flowed tagliatelle dressed with rose water and cinnamon; soufflés of every description – with shrimps and asparagus and herbs; and incredibly delicious sweetmeats and cakes.

In contrast to this more refined fare, Tuscan cooking encompasses rustic food such as roast meats, simply cooked over a grill or on the spit; endless different bean dishes; simple vegetable dishes; stews and pot roasts; huge steaks; and full-bodied minestroni along with lots of other thick, nourishing soups. The Tuscan nature is too precise, ironic and down-to-earth to cope with bright colours and flights of fancy. The scent on the air in the region's kitchens is of gently simmering soups and meat sizzling on a wood fire. Even the city food is essentially the food of the farms and smallholdings, of the country villas. In the most elegant of Florentine restaurants your bean soup, your Pappa al pomodoro (a type of tomato soup), or your minestrone will be brought to your table in a modest terracotta bowl, and your vast T-bone steak is quite likely to be cooked over scented embers in the yard behind the restaurant .

Siena is the capital of Tuscan sweetmeat making, with delicious specialities like Panforte, the power-packed cake of dried fruit and nuts blended together with honey; or the light, diamond-shaped, icing-sugar-dusted Ricciarelli cakes, made with almonds.

The Tuscan guest is considered by other Italians to be the most difficult to cook for. An instinctive and uncompromising gourmet, he or she will immediately be able to tell if something has been overcooked or undercooked, and is quite likely to turn his or her nose up at something he or she feels is not up to standard. Anybody would think that Tuscans' culinary repertoire boasted a whole array of complicated, labour-intensive specialities instead of their good, old, steady and very tasty traditional dishes!

Some dishes of the region have interesting stories attached to them. One of these is Arista di Maiale, a dish of roast pork, very highly seasoned with pepper and rosemary, which keeps well for several days and can be eaten hot or cold. It was prepared in honour of the first ecumenical council in Florence to which the Greek Orthodox archbishops were invited. They pronounced the dish *'aristos'* ('excellent') and that is how it got its name.

My home region is one of the loveliest places in the world, with rolling hills, fertile plains and what used to be a perfect, clear blue sea until the local industries polluted it – sadly, the Tuscan coastline is, at the time of writing, the most polluted in Europe. The cuisine of the port towns and seaside villages remains in memory of a time when the sea was alive: for example, there is the sumptuous-looking but actually very simple Cacciucco alla Livornese (a huge fish soup) and the Triglie alla Livornese (red mullet cooked in the classic style of the city of Livorno with garlic, tomatoes and herbs). Then there are the eel specialities of Florence, the *cieche* (new-born eel) dishes of Pisa and the countless recipes for octopus.

From my childhood I remember the long-leaved, wrinkled, black cabbage, the bitter turnips tossed in a pan with deep green olive oil, hard almond biscuits to dunk in glasses of amber-coloured wine at the end of a meal – all these moments an integral part of the heart-shaped region that will always be home to me.

Wines

Chianti wine descends the soft Florentine hills like a smooth-running river; the most perfect of Tuscan unions takes place between the region's food and this world-famous red wine. Its name apparently derives from the word *clangor*, meaning a blast of sound from a trumpet. The Etruscans probably drank this wine, and there are records of its production that go back to the fourteenth century.

Chianti is the collective name given to the wines of the Chianti area, within which the wines are subdivided into various distinctive types. The main ones are: Chianti Carmignano, excellent with all red meats, a fairly elegant red wine from the Albano hill in the province of Florence; Chianti Classico, produced in the area between Firenze and Siena in localities such as Greve, Radda and Poggibonsi, a masterful wine with a majestic, imposing feel about it; and Chianti Colli Aretini, from the province of Arezzo, the best wine to drink with the fine beef produced in the Val di Chiana. The other five main types of Chianti are: Chianti Colli Fiorentini, Chianti Colli Senesi, Chianti Colline Pisane, Chianti Montalbano and Chianti Rufina.

Among the whites, the Elba bianco, from the island which is synonymous with Napoleon Bonaparte, is one of the best, though very slightly fruity. The most noble wines of the entire region are the indisputably sophisticated Vino Nobile di Montepulciano and its cousin Brunello di Montalcino, rich, full-bodied, virile and intense, speaking volumes about the character of the region and perfect with the local roasts. Finally, Vino Santo Toscano, always served with the dry pastries that are such a speciality of the region, a fine amber-coloured dessert wine with an unmistakable nose, tends to be the sort of wine you can't stop drinking once you start!

SICILY

Three volumes of a book twice the size of this one would not accurately cover Sicily and its cuisine. I am always delighted to return to this island, despite the appalling press it gets and all the mysteries and intrigue that blight its reputation. Perhaps I have never appreciated Calabria fully, so deep has been my yearning to cross the straits – to swim if necessary – and return to the island where Etna puffs small grey clouds into that unbelievably blue sky. Who can fail to fall in love with Sicily when she seduces you with lemon groves that tumble down the cliff side to the black volcanic crags below in February? How can you resist her charms when you see the almond trees in full blossom, knowing that the results of this display will soon be transformed into the most incredible array of almond pastries you have ever seen, beginning with *pasta reale* (marzipan) which is shaped into realistic baskets of fruit and vegetables to give as gifts? And nobody in their right mind would refuse a real Sicilian ice-cream: after all, the natives of the island invented it.

The name of the island was formerly Sicania, the original inhabitants being of the Sicani tribe. The Greeks, who colonised it, re-named it Trinacria because of its triangular shape. Less than 2 miles separate it from the mainland, yet its amazing history has turned this island into a nation with its own rules and traditions.

The Phoenicians founded Palermo, the regional capital, which has always been Sicily's most active and populated port. The city has many glorious ancient monuments and, rather like Naples, is divided into luxurious residential areas and squalid back streets. In the surrounding area are many of the island's best-loved beauty spots, but also the amazing Piana degli Albanesi – an Albanian community, set up in 1500 and still preserving its language and traditions.

Baroque Messina sits at the foot of the Peloritani Mountains. Horrendously flattened by earthquakes, it was completely re-built twice and the elegant city is still surrounded by a band of cardboard-and-tin homes where some of the population live in almost subhuman conditions. Within the province is Taormina, a resort built 650 feet above sea level, which overlooks a long stretch of beaches and resorts with the dramatic backdrop of Etna at its shoulder.

Catania, the second-largest city in Sicily, is known as the Milan of the south, because of its active commercial and industrial expansion. Roman and Norman ruins are a constant reminder of the ancient history of this city. In the surrounding area are the attractive little fishing towns of Aci Trezza and Aci Castello, where much of the local swordfish trade goes on.

Unquestionably it was the Arabs' domination of the island that most affected the food eaten there today. Ice-cream was invented to keep the Saracens cool in the desert heat; aubergines, peppers, jasmine and citrus fruits were brought to Sicily from North Africa along with palm trees and cotton. But perhaps most startling is the theory that the Moslems introduced *itriiya*, a form of pasta very close to the varieties we now use. This apparently took the form of hollow tubes curled like a corkscrew – not unlike Neapolitan fusilli. Although pasta in other forms had been around before, this Sicilian/Arab innovation set the trend which has since become legend. It certainly knocks the old Marco Polo story, according to which the famous traveller brought pasta to Italy from China, into a cocked hat!

Sicily produces vast amounts of grain, wine, grapes and olives, olive oil, almonds, pistachios, figs, artichokes, peas, aubergines, peppers and all kinds of citrus fruit, especially lemons. Capers, manna and carob are also produced here, in slightly smaller quantities, as are some special local cheeses. Meat is not part of the economy, nor of the cuisine. There are very few traditional dishes that use meat – who needs meat when you have this wealth of vegetables in almost unbelievable colours and sizes? Etna gives the soil its magical powers: hence cauliflowers as big as a double-sized football, luscious red tomatoes bursting with juice and flavour, and salads that are supremely fresh and delicious.

Put all these vegetables together in colourful combinations or mix them with pasta, add fish and fruit, round off the meal with a choice from the wonderful array of ice-creams, cakes, pastries and sweetmeats that seem to come straight from a Moroccan street vendor's display, and you have the basis of Sicilian cuisine. Add to these elements those extra ingredients that the locals use with such nonchalant ease and style – capers, sultanas, caraway seeds and pine nuts, not to mention the brilliant green pistachio which is the truest symbol of the Sicilian pastry chef. Then add the native love of all things ornate and gilded: the astounding Baroque churches are reflected in the glories of a real cassata; the madness of the Spanish baronets comes to life in a chocolate-covered Caponata (made with octopus, lobster, celery, aubergines and hard-boiled eggs). Put all these things together and you have a vast selection of dishes that span the entire island, from historical Siracusa to busy, modern Trapani; a cuisine that is elegant and crazy, full of strange combinations of flavours and contrasts, over which the experts argue incessantly as to the origin of this or that dish without ever finding the real answer; a cuisine created largely to impress, with wildly extravagant colours and shapes, a patchwork of wit, imagination and history that is unparalleled.

Wines

Although elsewhere used mostly in cooking, Marsala has to be Sicily's most famous wine. Dark brown in colour with a very distinctive flavour of raisins, it was first discovered and exported by an Englishman. The wine takes its name from the port city of Marsala, named thus by the

Arabs because it was the port of Ali – Marsa Ali. On the island Marsala is drunk in little glasses over a game of cards or a conversation. It is offered to visitors and is never absent at the end of a meal, with pastries and cakes – unless the host decides to serve one of the island's other delicious dessert wines: Moscato, Mammertino or Malvasia.

Sicily's huge collection of excellent wines is too vast to cover with any real fairness here, so I'll just list my favourites and urge you to seek them out to taste. Alcamo Bianco, a mother-of-pearl-coloured wine with a delicately aromatic nose and a firm, full bouquet, is the perfect companion for Sicilian fish dishes. The Corvo wines of Sicily are famous worldwide, especially as Italy's national airline serves them during its flights, but not many people are aware that there is also a superb Gran Spumante, a sparkling variety, which is a pale golden colour with a delicate, lingering bouquet. It is perfect on its own or with a vegetable- and fish-based menu. The *amabile* (sweeter) version is excellent with the local cakes and pastries. Among the reds, the ones that stand out for me are the deliciously smooth Eloro Rosso, produced in the Noto area, and the unforgettable Donna Fugata ('runaway woman') from the Ragusa district.

CAMPANIA

*L*aughing Campania, with an *Arlecchino* (Harlequin) on every street corner, the naughty grin of a *scugnizzo* (urchin) as he darts away through streets decorated with multi-coloured lines of washing, the flash of sunlight on the sea lying still in the gulf, tomatoes like rubies in baskets at every market stall: this is a land of passion and joy. Despite all the hardships that destiny has thrown at the inhabitants – earthquakes, eruption of Vesuvius and more man-made disasters – they still come up with that brazen, cheeky grin that somehow makes it all right again. These are not the cunning merchants of Venice, nor the seafaring macho men of Liguria, nor the studious, dry Tuscans. Neapolitans – for all Campanians are Neapolitans at heart – have over the centuries perfected *l'arte d'arrangiarsi* (the art of getting on with it, against all odds). It is this which gives them their spirit and sense of fun, yet allows them to prosper.

Who else but the Neapolitans would have had the courage to try the much-maligned tomato? On its arrival from the New World it was considered either poisonous (an assumption that could have been correct: it does belong to a family of plants of which some are fatally toxic) or worse – the evil apple from the Garden of Eden. It didn't take the wily Neapolitans long to work out that there was money to be made out of this, and soon the tomato was on sale as a powerful aphrodisiac – it sold very well. From the bedroom to the kitchen is a very short distance indeed, and suddenly there it was, married to its eternal companions, *la pasta e la pizza*.

My favourite tomato story is the following one, written by my grandfather's friend, the author Matilde Serao, in 1922.

There once lived a magician called Chico in a tenement building in the back streets of Naples. His neighbours were all typically disreputable: prostitutes, assassins, petty thieves and similar types. Chico aroused the interest of his neighbours because he lived on the top floor, never opened the shutters or windows and was never seen outside. Soon the neighbours began to spy on him through a crack in the shutters. It was obvious that he was inventing something as he shuffled back and forth between his two rooms, muttering to himself. They saw him holding strange instruments and pots of boiling water, and some swore that they had seen red blood dripping from his hands. Chico wandered about, dressed in white, and every day would send his servant out to buy herbs and vegetables from the local market.

The most persistent of the spies was the young girl called Jovanella who lived right next door. One day she was finally able to see just exactly what Chico was up to: he was boiling pasta, and the herbs, tomatoes and vegetables went into a sauce which he poured over the cooked pasta. Jovanella, in typical Neapolitan style, instantly knew how to make the most of her discovery. She raced to the royal kitchens and begged the cook to let her show what she had learned. Before long her fame spread and she became a very rich and popular young woman!

Naples, then, is the heart of all that is Campania, with its soil rich in minerals provided by the volcano, a breathtakingly lovely coastline around Amalfi and Sorrento, the ancient site of Pompeii and all the other historical relics that can be seen here. This is a region with intense religious feeling, verging on the pagan, and however strange this combination may seem, it has always been a part of the local culture. In the country towns any kind of magician or witch can be called upon to distribute potions and spell books, but it is also here that local believers fall into ecstasy before the statue of their favourite saint.

The 1980 earthquake has left many areas still devastated. The mountain region around Avellino was particularly hurt and thousands of people have had to abandon forever the villages where they grew up.

So what keeps body and soul together for these survivors? First and foremost, it is coffee. *Il caffè* is of paramount importance to the Neapolitans; it's something they take very seriously indeed, and they are very choosy about who makes the coffee. They firmly believe that even with the same coffee, same water and same machine, two people can produce completely different results. They have written songs about 'a little cup of coffee' and are quite happy to have a two-hour conversation with you on the subject! Certainly the coffee here is more full-bodied, powerful and rich in flavour than coffee I have tasted anywhere else, and it is several galaxies away from the average cup of instant.

After coffee comes pasta, which, although it has been made all over Italy since the Arabs first introduced it to Sicily during Saracen rule under the name *itriiya*, and was probably being eaten before then in Etruscan and Roman times, was first commercially made in the early 1800s when the first industrial pasta complexes were established at Torre Annunziata, Torre del Greco and Castellamare di Stabia. In those days the long *ziti*, hollow tubes of pasta which could be broken into desired lengths, were hung out on the sails of windmills to dry. The factory where we chose to film pasta-making for the television series *Italian Regional Cookery* was established in 1880 and is also a mill. It was fascinating to watch the entire process, from simple wheat grain to packaged finished product, which took just 90 minutes. The locals enjoy their pasta cooked until very *al dente* (more *al dente* than in any other region: they practically eat it crispy!), preferably dressed with fresh tomatoes that are scarcely cooked at all to retain all their flavour and colour: La Pommarola, they call it.

Pizza vies for position as the culinary king here, and is surrounded by countless legends and stories. Ignore the petrified pizzas discovered at Pompeii, and the ones found in pharaohs' tombs that were dated 5000 BC: pizza as we know it, colourful and covered in tomato topping, came into being after the discovery of America in the 1600s. The original pizza was the Pizza Marinara, which is nothing to do with seafood, and which has always had just a simple topping of tomato, garlic, oregano and olive oil.

Pizza was born on the street – it is the ultimate street food. Nobody knows the name of the genius who first invented pizza; all we know is that he was a Neapolitan street baker who would have been a multimillionaire if he had only patented his wonderful invention. In the USA it is the quickest-growing and most popular fast food, selling more than burgers. All Neapolitan and Campanian food is the food of the people: cheap, colourful and cheerful, and the delicious Ragù of the region (quite different from the Bolognese variety), which once used to be poured over macaroni and sold on every street corner, is no exception.

Mozzarella is another emblem of the food of Campania, in particular the incredibly rare Mozzarella di Buffala, made with buffalo milk, which is made only here. Mozzarella is a firm, chewy cheese which is particularly useful for cooking because it adds a lot of texture to a dish as it melts, but its flavour is rather bland. Sliced up with tomatoes, dressed with oil, basil leaves and salt and pepper, it is a major part of the delectable Insalata Caprese which has become so internationally popular.

The final word on the food of Campania has to be for the delicious cakes and pastries of the region which rival those of Sicily. They form part of this bright and lively parade of specialities that are so well loved.

Here, where the sun laughs down on all life's joys and miseries, where the sea twinkles mischievously at you, summing up the entire spirit of Campania, everything you eat tastes better than you ever thought possible!

Wines

I never think of this region as the one for heavy-duty wines, yet as you move further south they seem to grow headier and heavier, until you reach Calabria where they are almost tangibly thick. There are quite a number of powerful reds, but the only one I have ever enjoyed is the Aglianico d'Irpinia from the inland area where it snows and there are ski resorts, which is somewhere I just don't associate with the region. This 18° proof ruby-red wine has a rounded flavour and is perfect with grilled meats and strong-tasting cheeses.

However, the light whites are my favourites, especially the delightfully joyous, fun-loving Capri with its pale yellow colouring, fresh taste and fragrant bouquet. Lachryma Christi (Tears of Christ) is a lovely wine produced in the Torre del Greco area. It tends to be quite fruity in both the red and white versions, the white being more readily available and popular.

The lovely island of Ischia also provides the region with some good wine. Its red is very special, so light-tasting as to be almost ethereal, and is considered *the* wine to drink with the local speciality of Coniglio all'Ischitana – a rich rabbit stew. The white, very dry and refreshing, is always drunk with local seafood specialities.

The VENETO

The region which surrounds Venice is my favourite of all the northern regions, and that is not because Venice is there like the dream city of a childhood fantasy, but because I feel there a greater sense of history and circumstance than in any of the other regions – Lombardy is too industrialised for me, Piedmont too mountainous and the other regions feel less Italian to someone like me who is so completely in love with the country. But in the Veneto I feel the power of Italy's romanticism.

It would be all too easy to devote this entire introduction to the glories of *la Serenissima* and ignore her region, but I will not give in to the temptation. Suffice it to say that Venice is one of the loveliest places on our planet, a marvellous woven web of 170 canals and waterways which link together the 120 islands criss-crossed by over 400 bridges. The archipelago that is Venice is divided into two parts by the long, S-shaped Canal Grande which winds through the centre and along the two banks of which are situated the city's famous palaces. The heart of the city is the lovely Piazza San Marco, flanked by the Basilica, the church tower and other national buildings which make it so graceful and imposing.

There are six other provinces within the region, which has one of the most changing landscapes in the entire country. Quite apart from the city of Venice and its lagoon, this is a region of unknown villages in soaring mountains, lakes, green valleys and flat monotonous plains peppered with small cities surrounded by industrial complexes; small holiday resorts with every modern facility; rounded hills covered with vineyards and woodland; and the banks of Lake Garda where the mild climate allows a proliferation of olive groves, myrtle and oleander. Near the coast there are areas of reclaimed marshland that has been torn from the water. This landscape of glorious contrasts has only the eternally repetitive church towers as a common feature: in almost every town and village they rise into the sky, each one an almost identical copy of the one in the Piazza San Marco.

In a square area lying between Venice, Treviso, Vicenza and Padua are the villas built here between 1500 and 1700 to provide summer homes where the Venetian nobility could spend time away from the city during the unhealthy and frankly smelly hot season. There are about 2000 of these lovely houses, many of them finer still than the great palaces of Venice itself, adorned with frescoes and intricate plasterwork, masterpieces of architecture. The nobles would arrive by horse-drawn boat along the canals and rivers to hold in the ballrooms and gardens parties and receptions that have been recorded in the history books. Nowadays many of the villas have been abandoned and are falling to pieces through neglect or are used as storage space by local farmers. Some, the more famous ones such as those designed by Palladio, are open to the public and of great interest to tourists. You can still travel along the Brenta Canal by boat from Padua to Venice.

The second most important city of the region is Verona, to me almost as lovely as Venice. It has an antique feel to it, a marvellous collection of ancient, red-roofed buildings spreading out on either side of the Adige River with plenty of lush greenery. Every summer since 1913 the greatest opera singers of the world have performed in the amphitheatre.

The region is so rich in every sense that it is hard to know where to begin describing it. There is every conceivable form of tourism from skiing and mountaineering to seaside resorts to the countless areas of cultural interest, as well as the glorious countryside. It's a region of fishing, agriculture and industry and one in which traditional craftwork is still of great importance. Its cuisine is a delightful collection of country-style dishes mingling with the many treasures from the east which have poured into the flourishing port of Venice for so many centuries.

Risotto is king of the table here, cooked with every conceivable vegetable, fish, meat or a combination of any of them. A risotto prepared by a Venetian cook is a thing sublime – risotto-making is an art form, it must ripple on the top and a little of it has to stick to the bottom of the pot. Only then will you have got it right! The risotto of Venice is worlds apart from the simple rice combinations of Lombardy – the Venetians have far too much artistic flair simply to leave a risotto alone.

It is via the other great symbol of Venetian cuisine, the humble bean, that pasta enters the scene. If it were not for the bean, cooked in the region's wonderfully thick soup called Pasta e Fagioli, it is doubtful whether pasta would have been used here at all. The region has these two dishes – Risotto and Pasta e Fagioli – at its gastronomic base, but then there is so much else! There is the delicious garlic-flavoured salame, the countless duck dishes, the wonderful radicchio from Treviso, the liver that drowns in a sea of sweet onions, the fish of all the rivers and lakes and the sea, the delicate sauces of Byzantine origin, the extraordinary selection of cakes and desserts; and throughout, the addition of eastern exotica such as coriander, cumin, currants and sultanas, pine nuts and orange flower water.

The food of the Veneto speaks volumes about its history. It reminds

Top: What could be more evocative than
the still lakes of Lombardy and their
ancient buildings? *Bottom:* I saw these
two lovebirds in one of the most
romantic places on earth – Positano.

Above: The loveliness of Puglia: th
trulli in all their glory. *Left:* Springt
in Puglia.

you what this city and its region have meant to our civilisation. You cannot fail to be struck by the glories of the Veneto's traditional quintessential dishes, where east meets west in the kitchen.

Wines

In this region of so many riches, three of Italy's most famous wines are produced: Bardolino and Valpolicella, the lively, light reds; and Soave, the universally renowned white. But it does not end here. This is also the birthplace of the delicious Breganze wines: Breganze Pinot Nero, Rosso, Vesapaiolo, Bianco, Cabernet, Pinot Bianco – all superb, and all produced in the hilly area to the north of Vicenza.

However, the most noble of all the local wines are the excellent sparkling ones produced in the Conegliano area. Under the collective name of Prosecco, some of them rival the best French champagnes for quality and consistency. My favourite is the Prosecco Conegliano di Valdobbiadene Spumante, with a wonderfully yellow straw-like colour, an unmistakably winy bouquet and a deliciously dry flavour, although a sweet version is also available. Finally, there is the famous Gambellara, a deliciously light and slightly bitter, golden wine from the Vicenza province; again, it is obtainable in an excellent sweet dessert version.

CALABRIA

*A*s Puglia is the heel, this is the toe of the 'boot', where Italy musters its strength and thrusts out towards the island of Sicily and Africa beyond. Somehow, although I know it is only an illusion, I feel further south in Calabria than I do in Puglia, perhaps because the people tend to be rather enigmatic and other-worldly. In any case, the region has a glorious coastline, with fine resorts like Tropea and Pizzo, but also mountainous areas like the enormous Sila range. Here is where the heady southern red wines and very liberal use of chilli pepper combine to create a stupefying effect over the dinner table. This is a region that has known recent poverty and hunger, clearly reflected in the cuisine – literally everything remotely edible has found its way into the pot, even things which I find frankly nauseating.

The pig rules sublime here: it is killed in the autumn and turned into a hundred different cured meats and sausages to see the family through the winter. Everything that can be preserved is preserved with infinite gusto, which indicates that winters can be hard. Tomatoes are sun-dried, peppers and aubergines preserved in vinegar or oil. Fish of all kinds, from baccalà and stoccafisso to pickled octopus and salted anchovies, are preserved. Huge sausages are preserved in jars of lard to keep them moist, as are olives and capers, cauliflowers and carrots. It all adds up to an amazing riot of colour, put together in a cuisine that is not light or in any way fun but which most of the locals heartily enjoy.

Here too is where swordfish and fresh tuna first enter the scene, to progress across the narrow straits into the kitchens and open-air grills of Sicily herself. Here is where the world's most juicy and erotic peppers and aubergines become part of every meal. Here is where the bowl of oil with crushed chillies floating in it appears on the table next to the salt and pepper, to be liberally sprinkled over the food as we use mustard. The food of Calabria has always had something very faintly Bacchanalian about it for me: there is a hint of peculiar goings-on about the dishes, almost as though they were all prepared for some strange ritual that is always left unexplained. It is gloriously rich food, heavy on the digestion but very pleasing to the eye, a style of cuisine that is not quite Sicilian, yet has elements of Sicilian and Lucanian cooking in it.

However, the seeds of gastronomic revolution have been sown here and changes are afoot. Calabria has long had a reputation for heavy-handed, overflavoured food, and many are keen to alter this as the economy of the region develops and successful businessmen want to take clients out to dine – and to impress them, not give them heartburn! Hence dishes like thinly sliced swordfish in a lemon and oil dressing appear on menus alongside ancient recipes which have been resurrected and updated for modern tastes. There is no need to abandon the old flavours and ingredients which so typify the cuisine of the region, but as we become more health-conscious we all realise that unleavened bread lined with pork fat is just plain bad for you – and it doesn't even taste nice!

It is tremendously exciting to witness change in food habits, to see restaurateurs and chefs take the trouble to think hard about what they are serving while remaining involved in their traditions – which are ultimately much more far-reaching than their bank balance. In Calabria the upmarket restaurants have not gone French or even Lombard; they have remained quintessentially Calabrian, but with a style and flair that was unheard of a decade or so ago.

Wines

The red wine which is wheeled out in Calabria for important guests is the kind which you have to be in the mood for! It is a murky red colour, blows your head off after one glass and makes intelligent conversation absolutely impossible. Local varieties of Ciro, Savuto and Pollino all have this effect on me, although bottled and exported wines of the same name have proved to be excellent table wines, velvety and smooth with plenty of body and very dry. Currently very fashionable in Italy is the delightful Greco di Gerace, with its characteristic orange-blossom nose and (unusually for a local white) its rounded and velvet-smooth taste. It is considered to be a wine to drink thoughtfully between meals! Moscato comes to the fore in Calabria, a rare and delicate dessert wine with a wonderful amber colouring.

EMILIA ROMAGNA

*I*n the second century BC the Roman consul Marco Emilio Lepido had a road built from Rimini to Piacenza. In his honour the road was called Aemilia – hence the 'Emilia' part of the region's name. Romagna used to belong to the Byzantine Empire, and after the unification the whole region was simply called Emilia. In 1947 it was finally given its present double-barrelled name.

Emilia Romagna is surrounded by six other regions, with the tiny Republic of San Marino tucked away between it and the Marche. It is divided into eight provinces. To me it always feels as if it is still divided into two sections, a band of hilly and mountainous, solitary areas contrasting vividly with the bustling, active plains – densely populated, densely cultivated, with every inch of the land put to use. Even the coastline divides into two: the wild and silent areas where the lagoons lie almost still, and the hectic rows of hotels that snake up the long, sandy beach where in summertime you can almost be crushed by crowds of eager holidaymakers.

Bologna is not the region's capital city, yet it is of enormous cultural, commercial and gastronomical interest. *'Bologna la Grassa'* ('the fat one'), they call it, but the city also has another name: *'Bologna la Dotta'* ('the cultured one'). It has an ancient history dating from Etruscan times, when it was called Felsina, after which it was a Gallic centre with the name of Boi, then a Roman city called Bononia.

Bologna is rightfully proud of its fantastic collection of medieval and Renaissance buildings and towers, of which the two most famous are the Torre degli Asinelli and Torre Garisenda. Typical of this lovely city are the wide porticoes which flank the streets. The historic heart of the city has fortunately not been spoiled by Bologna's development as a modern European centre – all the ugliness of modern technology is placed in the suburbs, out of sight of the ancient university buildings. Founded in the eleventh century, this is in fact the oldest university in Europe. The province of Bologna is the largest of the region, with the greatest population. The city is famous for its rich cuisine, which makes the very best use of all the produce of its province.

Piacenza, the ancient Roman city of Platentia, situated close to the Po and to the Lombard border, has been influenced a great deal by the traditions of Lombardy and its position has ensured that it has also become an important crossroads between the two regions, with a major motorway link.

Parma is most famous for its ham, prosciutto di Parma, that is considered to be the best in the world by many experts – though you can get good and bad prosciutto di Parma just as you can good and bad prosciutto from anywhere else: you get what you pay for. Parma is also renowned for an incomparable cheese which is so vital to literally hundreds of thousands of Italian recipes – Parmigiano Reggiano (Parmesan).

Reggio nell'Emilia is the capital of the region. Here, in 1797, the green, white and red flag was first flown when the Repubblica Cisalpina was formed. The flag later came to represent the entire nation. It is this city and province which give Parmesan the 'Reggiano' half of its name.

Modena, the ancient Roman Mudina, is situated between two rivers and has a tower of its own called La Ghirlandina, a fabulous cathedral and one of the largest public buildings in the entire country. Balsamic vinegar, that enigmatic condiment that has recently acquired a slightly yuppie status, is produced here and auctioned annually at Spilamberto di Modena, where a single bottle can be sold for several million lire. A good balsamic vinegar has to be at least fifty years old and sometimes bottles over fifty years old are available. It is made from wine must that is distilled over and over again until it becomes dark and thick and rich – the smell is enough to make you faint! Another product of this city is the delicious Lambrusco, a wine which unfortunately does not travel very well, but here can be drunk as it really is – joyous and bubbling over, like a laughing brook. It is a wine that also goes very well with the overpowering richness of the local dishes.

Modena is also one of the biggest meat market towns in Europe, whether it is meat for curing or for eating fresh. All kinds of meat are produced for this bustling commercial centre: 250 000 head of beef, 17 000 head of pork, 25 000 head of horsemeat are average annual figures. In Forlì, another provincial capital, where the poultry markets are held, annual figures like 314 million eggs, twenty-nine million chickens and eight million other assorted farmyard animals are usual. In just one of the local meat-processing plants which buy their meat from the vast Modena market, a million hundredweight of meat are packed each year. Whatever else you might say about the people of this region, they are not vegetarians.

Ferrara is a graceful medieval city which was the seat of the noble family of d'Este from 1200 to 1500, and most of its fine buildings date from this period. The Renaissance section of the city, built to the design of a single architect, Biagio Rossetti, was called the first modern city of Europe, but I prefer the older parts of Ferrara. The city has maintained its traditional role of active market town, open-armed to receive the many products of its rich, rolling, intensely farmed fields. Ferrara is famous for its wonderful bread, which has a flavour and texture all its own. Before he became completely obsessed with his nation's diet as well as his own, Mussolini commissioned bakers from the city to go to Rome and bake bread for him. They were unable, however, to achieve the same result as in their home region, and it is thought that the local air and water are vital ingredients.

Within the province of Ferrara lies Comacchio, a little town erected on thirteen islets separated by canals and connected by a network of bridges. Saltworks and the intensive cultivation of eels are the principal resources of the town. Eels are to Comacchio what tomatoes are to Naples!

In the Roman era Ravenna was a port city; now it is a little way from the seashore, but is still connected to the sea by a canal which opens out at Porto Corsini, one of the busiest ports on the Adriatic. The city is renowned for its glorious mosaics and lovely churches. Within the province are many of the region's most frequented beach resorts. Others, including Rimini, one of the most famous in Europe, Cattolica, Riccione and Cesenatico, lie in the province of Forlì.

The general impression given by Emilia Romagna is one of immense prosperity. There is so much richness in the land with its endless fields of fruit trees, vast prairies of grain, fields of onions, tomatoes and peas and an excellent selection of wines such as Lambrusco, Sangiovese and

Albana, many of which go on to become brandy, and this variety is reflected in the local cuisine. The fishing industry is also very important, the region being among the top five Italian fish-producing areas. Emilia Romagna has developed culturally too, with important publishing houses, theatres and artistic centres all over the region, even in small towns.

The region has so many products that are world-famous: mortadella, many different kinds of salame, hams, sausages, cheeses, jams, pasta, canned fruit and vegetables, wines, and sugar – just about the only thing it does not produce is olive oil! You get the feeling that food has exploded on to the market here with a vengeance. The entire economy of this huge area revolves around what you eat.

From this cornucopia of offerings, the local cooks have created dishes like tortellini, ravioli, lasagne, cannelloni, tagliatelle and a great many savoury cakes and pies. No other region in Italy offers such a range, and you cannot fail to appreciate how well the natives have used their abundant local produce. The restaurants here are almost sacred national temples for gourmets. They even have a huge range of cakes and pastries and puddings which rivals that of Vienna. It is an astounding gastronomical Mecca, blessed with millions of flavours – and an equal amount of calories!

Wines

If you can drink the local Lambrusco, you will discover something very different from the fizzy drink that, sadly, is exported. Real Lambrusco is a wine which commands respect. There are five varieties worth a mention: Lambrusco di Parma (Parmigianino), Lambrusco di Sorbara, Lambrusco Grasparossa di Castelvetro, Lambrusco Reggiano and Lambrusco Salamino or Santa Croce. The story goes that the wine originated from vines brought from Provence when a French princess came through the region on the Via Emilia on her way to marry a local nobleman. As part of her dowry she carried vines called Lambruscu that were planted here and from which was developed the well-known wine that is now very much a part of the local scene.

Sangiovese is the famous red which marries so well with the region's cuisine. Rich and robust, it blends perfectly with the weightier local dishes. The very best bottles are to be found in the hilly areas between Imola and Rimini (one good reason to go to Rimini), especially at Predappio.

Superb whites are also produced here, far too many to list individually. My personal favourite is the deliciously light Pomposa Bianco from the Comacchio area, a golden wine that is a must with local fish dishes. Albana Dolce, from the provinces of Ravenna and Bologna, is an ancient dessert wine, apparently drunk for many centuries and enjoyed by the Empress Galla Placidia.

PUGLIA

*I*t is not always to Italy's advantage that it is so long and narrow in shape. The problems arising from a country not having a heart at the centre are exposed most visibly in this huge southernmost eastern tip of the country which forms the heel of the 'boot'. Puglia is vast, with wide expanses of plain where nothing but grain grows, and then equally enormous expanses of olive trees. I had never seen so many olive trees growing in one place before I witnessed those of Puglia, so it came as no surprise to me to learn that the region supplies most of the olive oil available in Europe, the 1985 frosts having destroyed virtually all the olive trees elsewhere.

Yet, despite the grain, despite the olives and despite the equally vast wine production, the region remains principally one of shepherds. Their primary concern is for their herds. You will see flocks of sheep under the millions of olive trees, gambolling merrily in lush fields and penned up on farms where intense breeding programmes are in full swing.

Puglia's primary problem has always been and always will be a shortage of water. The landscape changes very little as you travel through the region: there are few mountains of any relevance and the countryside is mostly flat and smooth, with areas of stony soil contrasting with the more fertile zones.

Where it is very stony the locals have, for centuries, made a virtue of necessity by piling the stones into sections of their fields and using them to build their traditional *trulli* – peculiar conical buildings which they use as homes, animal shelters, tool sheds and so on. One *trullo* I visited was huge – in fact, it was made up of many separate *trulli* blended into one farm. Every time a new field is ploughed and de-stoned, a new *trullo* is built. The locals have been doing this for many hundreds of years and it seems to me as though they will go on doing so forever, especially as *trulli* have recently been declared national buildings and are now government-subsidised.

Puglia is divided into five provinces: Bari, Lecce, Foggia, Taranto and Brindisi. Bari is the regional capital and the attractive old quarter of its city seems stuck in a romantic time-warp, with winding narrow streets where women sit and prepare the local pasta called orecchiette (little ears). This area has for many years been justly famous for its seafood.

Because of its central position and the natural dynamism of the city, Bari is doubtless responsible for the recent advances the region has made. The city has been a commercial centre throughout its existence; it has an active port which carries goods and passengers to and from Greece, Yugoslavia and the Middle East. An annual business fair is held there, la Fiera del Levante, which is second in national importance only to the Milan business fair. Bari is also one of southern Italy's most lively cultural centres and is home to many of the thriving local businesses. Within its province lies Bitonto, the ancient Greek settlement of Bytonton, now producing much of the region's best olive oil, as well as almonds and vines. The area of Alberobello, within this province, is where you will see most of the region's *trulli*.

Brindisi is where we all used to head for when we set off as eager teen-agers for the Greek islands: the ferries leave for Corfu and beyond about every four hours or so. The ancient Romans used this port for their travels round the Mediterranean, so it enjoys a very long tradition as a seafaring city. I remember the streets filled with dazzling-white-suited sailors and the air filled with the uncompromising smell of ships. The petrol refineries which have mushroomed around the city have drawn people away from the countryside and the local farming is in decline. Inland, Fasano rises up in an area thickly cultivated with almond trees, vineyards and olive groves. In other areas of the province, fruit and tobacco are also grown successfully.

Foggia is where the *tratturi* (sheep trails) from the Abruzzi and Molise eventually stopped, the *transumanza* (annual migration) ending at the city's great livestock market, which meant reaping the rewards of hardships endured on the long journey south. Nowadays it is an important fruit and vegetable market town, the only local industries of any relevance being the pasta factories. Within the province lies the Tavoliere, the largest plain in mainland Italy. This prairie is partly cultivated and partly pastureland. Foggia sits in the centre of the Tavoliere, a proud city which has been almost completely reconstructed after the horrendous bombings of the Second World War. In the province are also situated the fantastically beautiful resort area of the Gargano, the Daunian Mountains and the lovely Tremiti Islands.

Lecce is unquestionably the loveliest of all the cities of Puglia. It is built of ochre-coloured stone and the light here is particularly lovely as it is reflected off the buildings, which are largely Baroque in style. Lecce is so far away from everything, so much a city on its own, that it retains a very graceful, relaxed and aristocratic atmosphere which, sadly, has been lost elsewhere. Whenever I go there, I feel that this must be what all the Italian cities I have visited used to be like.

Taranto is a city that I find disconcerting. It is full of chaos, with small oases of organised and stylish Italian-ness, yet there is a horrifying petrol refinery stuck right in the middle of the huge port, and when I visited the city close to the time of writing I was shocked and distressed by the warships bobbing about in the harbour right next to innocent fishing boats. Taranto is a great traffic snarl-up, with an unbelievably hot climate in the summer and a mild one in winter. I travelled around quite a bit within its province and was amazed at how unpopulated and lovely the rural areas are. In particular I was fascinated by the hundreds of largely abandoned *masserie* (walled farms), where the echoes of times past were almost tangible in the heat and among the nettles running riot. I think it will be discovered soon, just as Tuscany was, but before life can flourish here they must have water, and water is what they don't yet have. Within the province Martina Franca is in a fertile area producing excellent grapes, including the widely exported Uva Regina which is on every British supermarket shelf in late summer.

I love Puglia dearly but, my goodness, do they eat a lot of offal there! By the third day of my recent visit I was definitely going off the idea of any more lambs' innards cooked on a spit. Orecchiette pasta, made of kneaded flour and water, is everywhere. Chilli reigns supreme – locally it was once thought to ward off or cure diseases such as malaria, cholera and others. I personally loathe the stuff, so I was delighted to discover that the regional fondness for salads and vegetables guaranteed their appearance at every meal. This is a region where the flavours are strong and as yet mostly unsophisticated, loved by the natives but slightly worrying for the visitor. The wines are immensely strong and heady – locally they say that the wine 'cuts your legs away' and I do know what they mean!

Seafood here is delicious, especially the mussels, which are famous all over Italy. Outside Taranto a marine biologist showed me how the mussels are purified and I felt immediately happy about the safety of eating them. Water is brought into the purifying plant from several hundred miles out at sea, processed with ultra-violet light to sterilise it completely and then the live mussels or oysters are put in tanks overnight to filter in the clean water. By morning they are as pure as the water was. The locals cook them in all kinds of delicious dishes, or you can eat them raw with just a squeeze of lemon if you are very brave.

Wines

Until very recently the wines produced here were used solely as Vini da Taglio – blended with wines from other areas to give potency and flavour. Large amounts are still sent to other parts of Europe and re-bottled as the euphemistically labelled 'table wine'. Now, however, at long last, Puglia is producing many wines that can be considered as real wines in their own right. The Pugliese wine industry is absolutely booming, and I wish it every success. Among my special favourites which are quite widely obtainable are Ostuni, available as either red or white and generally considered an excellent all-round wine to be drunk with all meat or fish dishes; and San Severo, probably Puglia's most famous white, a fine, delicately flavoured wine with a lovely, pale straw colouring.

The ABRUZZI

T he region of the Abruzzi, due east of Lazio, is the nearest you get to real mountain conditions in the south of Italy. You can ski here – there are several well-equipped resorts such as Campo Felice – and the region enjoys a lively tourist trade in both summer and winter. As you drive up through the mountains and zoom out of long tunnels into the dark light of snow-laden skies, you get the impression of changing landscape, but the climate, atmosphere and local temperament seem to alter even more. It is like falling asleep and waking up in the Alps!

The main city of the Abruzzi is L'Aquila (the eagle): sitting on the mountain top and mistress of all she surveys. You simply cannot help being touched by this town's magnificence – it has a history that encompasses important religious events and extraordinary mystique and magic. There is a small square at the far side of the city where ninety-nine spouts have been spurting clear mountain water for 200 years. Intensive research has not been able to establish where the water comes from; it is simply there and has always been there, but no scientist or geologist has been able to trace its source. The ninety-nine spouts are symbolic of the ninety-nine castles that used to stand on these mountain tops, many of which are still there, although in varying stages of decrepitude.

Higher up the mountain on the other side of the town is the splendid Basilica di Collemaggio, which is famous not only for its artistic glories but also because it is the only cathedral with a holy door (a door through which a Pope has passed immediately after being crowned) outside the Vatican. In a time of great unrest for the area and indeed for the entire Roman Catholic world, Celestino V was crowned Pope here in 1294, shortly after he had begun work on the cathedral. He was later made a saint, St Peter Celestine, for all the good works he did as peacemaking Pope. His mausoleum is situated to the right of the cathedral's altar.

The region itself is divided into four provinces, L'Aquila, Teramo, Pescara and Chieti. Within the province of Aquila lies Sulmona, an ancient city at the foot of the imposing Maiella mountain – a local saying is *'Oh, per la Maiella!'* ('Oh, by gum!'). For many decades Sulmona has been famous for its small factories that produce exceptional sugared almonds and sweets. Of these the most impressive is Pelino's where you can witness local brides, usually accompanied by three-quarters of their family, selecting their sugared almonds and choosing the way in which they will be distributed on their wedding day.

Within the province of Teramo there are several small fishing ports and seaside resorts, but most of the province is modern and semi-industrialised, processing the produce flowing in from the rich countryside surrounding it. One crop grown extensively in this province is liquorice, destined for pharmaceutical companies which make great use of the root.

Pescara is the most densely inhabited and dynamic province of the region. Although L'Aquila is the regional capital, it is Pescara that has all the activity of a real city, with an airport, canal port, fly-overs, skyscrapers and all the other trappings of urban life.

Situated on a hillside densely covered in olive trees, half-way between the mountains and the sea, Chieti is so old that, according to legend, it was founded by Achilles himself. Historical research has shown that it was actually a Roman city. The suburbs of the city are sprawling out so that Pescara and Chieti are gradually edging towards each other. Within the province are two fishing and resort towns of some importance – Francavilla al Mare and Ortona.

Traditionally this has been a region of sheep farmers. In L'Aquila in particular fortunes have been made off the backs of enormous flocks of sheep. The insides of some of the local houses are stunningly lovely, with domed, frescoed ceilings and impressive decorated archways. The traditional transfer of flocks and shepherds to warmer pastures, crossing the Molise to end their journey in Puglia during the cold season, has almost disappeared. Nowadays the local sheep farmers prefer to use buildings and central heating to keep their animals healthy and warm.

The Abruzzi National Park, a huge wooded area that used to be the royal family's hunting land, was established in 1923. It spreads itself out across three provinces, L'Aquila, Frosinone in the Lazio and Campobasso in Molise. Here wild animals live in happy freedom, including wolves and golden eagles. The Gran Sasso is much more than just a mountain; it's a range of very lovely mountains and flat plains, popular with ramblers. One of the higher areas, called Campo Imperatore, is a much-loved ski resort.

In the Italian catering trade they say that if you have an Abruzzese in your kitchen your restaurant will never fail. The natives of this region are renowned for being excellent and well-organised cooks, with a charming disposition to boot. At the exceptionally beautiful restaurant called Le Tre Marie in L'Aquila, you can sample the truth of this belief – the food is just wonderful and the building itself is a national historic monument which, by law, can never be anything other than a restaurant. There is a perfect balance here between traditional, rustic recipes and sophistication which results in delicious dishes that nourish and soothe. Surprisingly, although the region borders on the Lazio, Marche and Molise, its recipes are not apparently influenced by any of these. Because the Abruzzi is a largely prosperous region with large, isolated, mountainous areas, customs, traditions and habits have evolved here that are its exclusive preserve.

Chilli is used here, though rarely in doses that take your breath away as in Molise or Calabria. Deliciously warming soups are made, many of them with spells woven into the recipe itself. Some recipes, for example, specify in which direction you must stir, in what order the ingredients should go into the pot, or that ingredients should be picked by moonlight. Excellent fruit and vegetables are grown. The local cooks are expert at cooking tender lamb that has been fed on the juicy mountain grasses, usually over a scented wood fire. They have wonderful cheeses and fantastic cured meats to see them through the winter. All the skills and traditions which these mountain people link to eating and drinking come together in the *panarda*, a traditional banquet, where the courses never number less than thirty. It is absolutely forbidden to stop eating if you are the guest at a *panarda* – it is your duty to see it through until the end!

Wines

The rolling and dipping, never dull landscape of the Abruzzi has yielded a selection of really excellent wines, of which the Montepulciano d'Abruzzo is the most famous. This is the perfect companion for the Abruzzi's delicious pasta dishes. It is a ruby-red wine with a delicate nose and a smooth, dry flavour. It is fairly alcoholic at 18° – so be careful! A less heady and more accessible red is the light and delicious table wine called Marsicano Rosso. Among the whites the one which stands out above all others is the dry and rounded Trebbiano, the best of which is produced in the province of Chieti.

THE SAFFRON OF L'AQUILA

In Aquila province they grow the only *zafferano* (saffron, the pistils of the plant *Crocus sativus*) produced in Italy. This is back-breaking work, with very small returns, although six million lire's worth of saffron is used in Italy each year. The ground-level flowers have to be picked before dawn, and several hundred flowers are needed for just 1 gram of saffron – yet all the growers seem to think it's worth the effort, just to be the best! In a tiny, dusty, dark room I saw three young girls, saffron farmers' daughters, who sat round a Heath Robinsonian machine packaging the threads and the powder, mostly by hand. The local farmers have banded together into a co-operative in order to keep the saffron industry going. The co-operative's chief, Silvio Sarra, has even enlisted an aunt of his to make a liqueur with saffron – it is 37° and mindblowingly yellow!

Saffron was first brought to L'Aquila, to the village of Navelli, from Spain by a local priest who was sent there during the time of the Spanish Inquisition. To everyone's astonishment, the crocus grew very well in this valley. It grows all over the Asian continent too, but the air currents round the plant cause considerable variations in its quality. A sample taken to the Botanical Gardens in Rome did not grow at all, nor will saffron grow elsewhere in Italy.

In the East, saffron is employed as a fabric dye and also as a powerful medicine. It must be used with great precision and care. Five grams of it will send your blood pressure soaring, but it is known to lessen the cholesterol levels by diluting blood fats. It will ease swollen gums, period pains and other menstrual problems because it is an anti-inflammatory drug. One sachet added to a cup of coffee is a stimulant, but one sachet divided between five cups of coffee is a relaxant. At the time of writing a medical expert in Parma is studying the extensive historical evidence of the medicinal use of saffron.

SARDINIA

A lthough situated quite close to Sicily, Sardinia, Italy's other large island, has almost nothing in common with her cousin. The Sicilians have always grabbed the bull by the horns and lived their lives with extraordinary vigour and energy. The Sardinians' way of life is not like this: these are gentle sheep farmers who are extremely proud of their island, a little arrogant at times and, some say, difficult to communicate with. They have a sense of honour which is just as powerful as the Sicilians', but it makes things happen very differently.

The best time to see Sardinia is during the spring, when the balmy air brings the wild flowers into bloom. Even the soft, sandy beaches become carpets of colourful, scented flowers. In springtime the island is green and lush; by midsummer it has a rather ragged, burned-out, brown look which sends visitors to the beaches to be lapped by turquoise-blue, crystal-clear water – close your eyes and you could be in the Seychelles.

Yet this is not traditionally a land of sailors – the natives seem almost afraid of the sea because out of it, over the centuries, have arisen the pirates and savage invaders who gradually pushed the timid population further and further inland to live in the caves and remote hilltop villages. From this history has emerged a cuisine that owes nothing to the sea, the national dish being sucking-pig or new-born lamb cooked on an open fire. The Sardinians enjoy countless rabbit, game and offal dishes. They have made their own pasta here for centuries, little hand-worked shell shapes prepared with flour and water called malloreddus. Their huge stuffed ravioli, like folded handkerchiefs, are filled with everything from potatoes and cheese to spinach and eggs. They produce excellent cheese which is well known and sought out all over Italy. But fish does not traditionally feature. Fish and seafood came into the picture when 'the millionaires who came from the sea' (such as the Aga Khan) discovered the wild loveliness of this island, with all its perfect natural bays and harbours. Then the cooks turned their attention to the sea, and now you can enjoy a whole host of delicious shellfish and fish – lobsters such as you have never tasted, juicy sea bass, succulent red mullet, huge mussels and sea urchins. Even more unusual fruits of the sea are cooked into delicious antipasti: ever tried deep-fried sea anemone?

This is quite a serious-natured island. The holiday spirit does not seem to have shaken off the years of oppression and the locals tend to cling to their traditions and customs. Many women still wear their local costume every day and will be buried in it.

The cooking of Sardinia seems to reflect the sobriety of the island – until you get to the cakes, where an explosion of marvellous designs and incredible technique bursts on to the table in a blaze of flavours and textures. The bread of Sardinia deserves a special mention too, in particular the paper-thin *carta da musica* (music sheets) which are made in many layers. This bread is more like large crackers – very crisp.

One cooking smell will haunt you for weeks after your first visit to this beautiful island. It is *mirto* (myrtle), the local herb which is used in copious amounts. Chickens are literally wrapped up in it, then cooked on a spit or in the oven. Roast sucking-pig is flavoured with it, and the local after-dinner tipple is a liqueur made of myrtle. If I were to choose one emblem to sum up the food of Sardinia, apart from its wonderful cakes, it would have the incomparable scent of myrtle.

Wines

My most loved white wine, Torbato, comes from Sardinia, light and refreshing with great depth of flavour and character. Serve it chilled with fish and seafood. Torbato is also produced as a delicious dessert wine, very similar to good-quality Malaga wines from Spain. Anghelu Ruju (Red Angel), one of Sardinia's most famous wines, is an aristocratic dessert wine – ideal with the phantasmagorical collection of little cakes. Cannonau is the Sardinians' own favourite wine in either its intense red version or the more delicately flavoured rosé. Mandrolisai is the wine with the prettiest name I have ever come across: it tastes rather like it sounds, lively and bright – perfect with pasta dishes or grilled meats.

Nuragus is the wine named after the ancient Nuragic civilisation which left the countryside of Sardinia littered with strange rock formations with imposing and mysterious towers situated at one end, that are presumed to be settlements. This fine white has lately been improved considerably, thanks to up-to-the-minute techniques. Vermentino is another excellent white produced in the Gallura area, really delicious and perfect with fish. This is another wine that is also produced as a dessert wine, when it acquires a very high alcohol level.

LIGURIA

The corner of this planet which will always be home to me is the part of Tuscany which borders with Liguria, where the sweeping beaches of sand become rocky coves and deep blue depths topped by white-tufted waves. I have always loved Liguria, almost as much as I love Tuscany, perhaps because they are so different. Liguria is alive, vibrant and colourful – a shimmering silver sea, purple bougainvillaea bursting from a front doorstep, golden wine from the vines that cling relentlessly to the hillsides.

Ligurian cuisine, quite literally, uses everything that grows under its sun – just about the only thing which has not been used in some local recipe is the fabulous carnation, which is exported from here to the four corners of the world. There's garlic, borage, basil and every other herb: herbs even end up being mixed into the local pasta dough! The region produces fantastically light, smooth, green olive oil, and many experts claim that it is the best available variety for use raw, as in salads. Pizza is cooked here, but as there is no mozzarella, the Ligurians have invented a whole range of pizzas, including the most famous of them all, the delicious Pizza all' Andrea, as invented by the great admiral, Andrea Doria.

Perhaps the most typical and traditional feature of this cuisine, however, is the extraordinary selection of fish dishes, for Ligurians are, above all else, a seafaring people. For the sailors and fishermen the Burrida, the Cappon Magro and the Torta Marinara have been created. Fish in Liguria is used in pasta sauce, salad, soup, stew, and as the filling for ravioli. And never will you taste such perfect wine to accompany this collection of fish dishes, starting with the wines from the Cinque Terre, five little villages constructed out of the rock face near Porto Venere which have become internationally famous. It used to be hard to reach Cinque Terre in any way except via water, and during harvest time you will see the little wooden boats transporting huge buckets of golden grapes to the cellars for pressing. Nowadays the newly built roads and funicular railways have brought a more modern but no less quaint feeling to the local trade.

It was the English who first discovered the loveliness of this region – for them the Italian Riviera was once *the* place to pass the winter. Indeed, the region has a very mild climate: protected from the cold northern air currents by its band of mountains, it basks in the beneficial warm winds coming in off the sea. Even in very harsh winters snow and ice are a rare occurrence, and the climate is very much like that enjoyed south of

Above: Apples of Alto
Adige against the loveliness
of the Dolomites.
Left: Fodder for a hungry
rabbit!

Above: Cherry picking in a Pugliese May.
Left: Golden peaches to celebrate summer.

Naples. In the 1930s the northern Europeans descended upon the Riviera to escape their own cold winters, many of them building fabulous villas overlooking the sea, others populating the local luxury hotels. The Russians were so enamoured of the Riviera that they even had an Orthodox church built for themselves in Sanremo. Hans Christian Andersen wrote quite a lot of his work here, or from notes he made here. Certainly, it would be hard to imagine how he could write his famous descriptive passages in his native Scandinavia when what he is describing sounds so obviously Mediterranean: 'The coast was in splendour. All along the roadside, there grew huge plants of aloe, the most vivid colours alternated with one another amongst the mountain tops. The trees themselves were like huge baskets of fruit.'

But that golden era has gone. The local casinos, such as the one at Ospedaletti where the foreign visitors would all gather, are in ruins, and many of the villas are crumbling away among the cobwebs. The mountains and hills of inland Liguria have become almost deserted as, over the centuries, more and more people have been drawn towards the busy ports and industries which have sprung up along the coast. The impression given here, on the outskirts of the coastal cities, is that there is a desperate scramble for every inch of available space, whereas the mountains are silent and still, with abandoned farms and wide, rather sad, open spaces. This has always been a land of sailors, fishermen and merchants – four-fifths of the entire population of Liguria lives along the 205-mile coastline, which is 1¼ miles wide at best! Inland, the only settlements which survive are those which have some sort of local industry.

After the Second World War, Liguria was submerged by a wave of immigrants from Sardinia and southern Italy, many of whom have taken over the farms and agriculture of the region from the locals, who have turned to industry, tourism and commerce. Gastronomically, it is interesting to note that the Sardinian cuisine more than that of the south has influenced Ligurians. There are very definite similarities between the dishes of Sardinia and those of this lovely region, shaped like a smile.

Genoa is one of the most important ports in Europe, and certainly the most important in Italy. In the Middle Ages it was a marine republic in its own right. It is a wonderful city, with ancient slums, rich merchants' houses and villas, and the new modern section surrounding these. It is built like an amphitheatre, stepping down towards the port (actually four separate ports) where all the products required for the Lombard and Piedmontese industries are brought in from abroad – metal, crude oil, cotton, wool, grain and so on. The only problem facing Genoa's commercial expansion seems to be lack of space – you feel crowded from the second you step off the boat!

A little further along the coast lies La Spezia, a vibrant, young city, built around the original military arsenal here. Imperia, the main centre for the olive oil industry, has several very important olive oil plants. Imperia province is also where Liguria's famous flowers are grown and exported. The other main city of Liguria is Savona, which once used to rival Genoa in importance as a trade centre of the nation. This port serves the industries of Turin and is still a major commercial city, though at the same time preserving some of its old charm.

To me, however, Liguria's tiny port towns are of more interest – places like Portofino, Portovenere, Paraggi and Camogli, where every year in May they hold a huge street party during which fried fish is eaten. In these towns you will see charming houses painted in tones of ochre and burnt orange, usually with green shutters. In a small quayside café here, or on an abandoned mountain farm, you will be able to feel the real Liguria, and know what it was that drew all those northern visitors here to pass their winters over fifty years ago.

Wines

Pigato is my favourite Ligurian white wine. It is exceptionally wonderful, perfect for hot summer days with its faint almond scent, shiny yellow colour with green flashes and dry, very fresh flavour. Locally it is drunk with the fish soup called Ciuppin. The Cinque Terre wines are the most famous of the Ligurian whites: they come from Vernazza, Monterosso, Corniglia, Manarola and Riomaggiore and are delicate and fresh – just right for drinking with all the lovely fish dishes. A pale red wine of some note called Barbarossa, with a similar delicate flavour to that of the whites, is good to drink with roast chicken or other light meat dishes.

UMBRIA

The small central region of Umbria has an intense atmosphere all its own. You become aware of the change as soon as you cross the border from Lazio or Tuscany. It is incredibly beautiful, with a serene, peaceful light: I always feel as if I am standing in a huge cathedral when I visit the region. Here also you can marvel at the glorious Duomo of Orvieto, and the equally stunning Duomo of Spoleto. Everywhere there is a feeling of grandiose, deeply religious fervour which fills me with a sensation of rather serious joy.

There are two main cities in Umbria, dividing the land into two corresponding provinces. Perugia is one of these and is without a doubt one of the most interesting and beautiful cities in Italy. It has had three separate faces: the Etruscan one when it was the residence of an Etruscan prince; the medieval one, when it flourished as a commercial centre, dominating almost the entire region; and the modern one, efficient, clean and businesslike, with a very active university campus and flourishing chocolate, pasta, clothes and wool industries. The many medieval and Renaissance buildings that remain bear testimony to the city's glorious past.

East of Perugia lies Assisi, whose sanctuary is so heavy with atmosphere that it seems locked in a time warp – the huge basilica was consecrated in 1253 and it feels as though nothing has changed since.

Within the province of Perugia, at opposite ends of the Umbrian Valley, are situated Foligno and Spoleto. The latter was once famous because of its position at the foot of Monteluco (the Sacred Mountain), formerly inhabited by many anchorites, hermits and saints. Nowadays it is renowned for its ambitious Festival dei Due Mondi (Festival of the Two Worlds), which takes place here every summer with days and nights of entertainment and cultural activities from ballet and theatre to concerts and exhibitions.

Going down the valley, following the River Tiber, you pass through Città di Castello, Umbertide, Deruta, Marsicano and eventually reach ancient Todi – a lovely little town gathered protectively around its central Piazza del Popolo. In the north of the region, isolated between two mountains is Gubbio, where one of the finest public buildings in Italy can be admired: the Palazzo dei Consoli. It is in the woods of these mountains that St Francis talked to the wolf. (St Francis went on to become the patron saint of Italy.)

Moving towards the boundary with the Marche you come to Norcia, which is famous for three different reasons. Thirteen centuries ago, twins were born here who became very well-known and important saints: St Benedict and St Scholastica. The fabulous black truffle of Umbria grows in profusion here; and the black Umbrian pig is also bred here. So renowned have the Umbrians become over the years for their skill in preserving pork and making sausages that in central Italy the word *norcineria* has come to mean a shop where such goods are on sale, and a *norcino* is a person who works with pork.

South of Norcia is the little town of Cascia where St Rita was born; a sanctuary is built there to her memory. You cannot get away from religion in Umbria!

In complete contrast to Perugia and her provincial towns, Terni is a completely modern settlement, re-built after severe bombing in the Second World War. It is one of central Italy's main industrial centres and as such is as noisy and busy as Perugia can be peaceful and serene. Yet Terni's main provincial town is Orvieto and you couldn't imagine a more abrupt contrast. Orvieto rises up on its rocky hill like a medieval skyscraper, essentially a very pretty town, full of wonderful buildings and producer of an excellent white wine. Two of Italy's most famous and important mineral water springs, Sangemini and Aquasparta, are within the province of Terni, lying to the north of the city.

Gastronomically, cured pork and black truffles are the region's main highlights. It is quite an experience to watch a local cook nonchalantly chop up truffles rather as others chop parsley! Excellent olive oil is also produced here, and chocolates and sweets of various kinds, as well as a limited but very special collection of wines. This is a cuisine with no fuss or frills – it's just good and tasty. It seems that the serious streak which you can feel in the atmosphere of Umbria is reflected in its cuisine: food to feed the body and the soul, but not the imagination.

Wines

Trasimeno, Italy's fourth-largest lake, is at maximum about 20 feet deep. It is prevented from becoming stagnant by an underwater tunnel system which keeps the water flowing through a series of artificial torrents. This remarkable system was first introduced and built by the Romans and is now in use once more. But that is not all: the lake even has a series of wines named after it. Colli del Trasimeno Rosso has a wonderful scent of violets, a deep garnet-red colour and a harmonious, balanced flavour. It is a table wine, perfect with the local roasts and truffle dishes. The white version, Colli del Trasimeno Bianco, is good with the local freshwater fish and light fried foods; it has a lovely straw-yellow colour and is based on Tuscan Trebbiano grapes.

Orvieto wine has been famous all over the world for several decades. It has a delicious, delicate bouquet and a dry flavour with a slightly bitter finish. The very old-fashioned version, called Abboccato, which used to be drunk with the local sweetmeats and chocolate, is going out of fashion now. The very best is the Orvieto Classico, produced in somewhat limited quantity by very antiquated methods.

FRIULI VENEZIA GIULIA

*F*riuli Venezia Giulia is the most eastern of all Italy's regions, with a very strong Middle European atmosphere about it. After the Second World War, much of the vast area called Venezia Giulia was handed over to Yugoslavia, leaving Italy with Gorizia and Trieste and a much smaller section of land. This was lumped together with Friuli to create a completely new region. And yet it is still very much Yugoslavian, very non-Italian in so many ways; it is hard for the visitor to come to terms with being in Italy, but harder yet for those living there who, until very recently, were of a different nationality. The region still touches Austria as well as Yugoslavia, and in the areas closest to the border the common language is not Italian but German or Slovenian. In the suburbs of Trieste, which is just within the frontier, and in the mountain villages of the Carso schools hold classes in the pupils' mother-tongue.

The region is divided into four provinces, its capital being Trieste. The skyline of this beautiful city is dominated by its lighthouse, erected in 1927, 223 feet high and visible from a distance of thirty-two miles. For many centuries Venice prevented the expansion and development of the port of Trieste because it represented a threat to the former's dominance of the seas. It took the power of the Austro-Hungarian Empire, which turned the city into a free port at the beginning of the eighteenth century, to release it from its chains, thus opening up an outlet for a vast expanse of land. Trieste developed very quickly and became one of Europe's most important commercial ports.

Out of its reclaimed marshes, Trieste has created space to construct a vast and very active industrial belt. Its tiny province, the smallest in Italy, consists of a small strip of land in between the Yugoslavian frontier and the coast. Here there is a very pretty little fishing port called Muggia, situated in a lovely area given over to the cultivation of fruit trees and vines. On the coast the bay of Sistiana is a most attractive beauty spot, popular with visitors.

Gorizia came to life two centuries ago with the institution of Trieste as a free port. It is a tranquil, green-filled city with just a few industrial and commercial centres. In the tiny province are Gradisca and Grado, both well-known resort centres.

Udine is one of the prettiest cities, graced by several lovely buildings and carefully laid out to make the most of its position. It has stood here, as the original capital of the area called Friuli, since the Middle Ages. Its province is almost entirely mountainous, taking in the little town of San

Daniele where the most exceptional prosciutto crudo is cured. The entire province of Udine was badly affected by the earthquakes of 1976. One of the most interesting small towns of this province, set among the mountains of the Carnia, is Palmanova, built in 1593 by the Venetians as a protection against Turkish invasion from the east. It is surrounded by walls and bastions which form the shape of a nine-pointed star.

Pordenone and its province have developed so quickly in the last thirty years that the city has been called the Milan of Friuli, a mushroom city. It is modern, successful and industrialised. Within the province, at Spilimbergo, there is a famous school where the techniques of mosaic-making are taught.

The region is renowned for its wonderful wines and its potent grappa, for its excellent pork and beef and dairy produce. But there are also many superb fish dishes from this region, and pale, creamy polenta, cooked slightly wetter than usual, is enjoyed with fish stews and casseroles. Much use is made of spices and dried fruit in conjunction with pasta, polenta and rice to create some rather sweet-tasting first courses and soups. Don't make the mistake of assuming that they are eaten at the end of a meal – every region has its traditions and sweet pasta dishes are just part of Friuli Venezia Giulia! Spices like cumin, poppy and fennel seeds are an obvious legacy of the Slavic cuisine, as is the use of yoghurt and rye bread. But the gnocchi and ravioli with sultanas and chocolate blended with spinach and potatoes have much more intricate origins. Not to be forgotten is the selection of game dishes, using venison and birds from the mountains. Unforgettable, and to me reminiscent of the best Viennese cake shops, is the region's list of wonderful local cakes, puddings, fritters, sweet breads, sweet polentas, tarts and strudels. You get the impression that they have a sweet tooth here! The cuisine of Friuli Venezia Giulia is a small collection of dishes using the best local ingredients, mixed with large helpings of history and tradition.

Wines

There are many wines produced in this small region – far too many to list individually. Those from the eastern hills are better known and better quality than those from the west. One very rare wine in particular deserves a mention: C.O.F. Picolit. It is generally considered to be the Italian equivalent of Château d'Yquem and should be drunk on its own, without food. A sweet, noble wine with a delicate bouquet, it has a lovely golden colour. My own favourite wine from this region has to be C.O.F. Pinot Grigio, with its unmistakable bouquet of wild flowers.

Collio, the area to the west of Gorzia, produces just as many wines as the eastern area. You can recognise instantly which area a wine comes from by the name on the label which will begin with 'C.O.F.' ('Colli Orientali Friulani') or with 'Collio', followed by the name of the wine. Collio Tocai, a very good white, is especially well known and perfect as an aperitif or with fish. Tocai is drunk a great deal all over the Venice area of north-east Italy and is completely different from sweet Hungarian Tocay.

BASILICATA

Basilicata is an arid, burned-out region. To look at it you'd think it had nothing except burning heat: scorching, blasting heat of the sort which sucks the lifeblood out of everything. You can see why the Fascists liked to banish their undesirables down here – it is a land forgotten by God, unloved by man. The soil is poor and stony, the mountains solitary and distantly remote, and although the region opens out on to the sea on both the southern and the western sides, there are no ports of any relevance here. The only stretch of fertile soil is to the north, where the ashes of a dead volcano, the Vulture, have left the soil rich in minerals. The lower sections of the slope are covered in vineyards and olive groves. As you climb higher, these give way to oaks, ash trees and horse chestnuts. On the lower hills, stretching down towards the gulf of Taranto, an occasional pine tree will quietly remind you that these hills were once covered in woodlands, before they were stripped in a desperate attempt to create more fields for crops and to build ships for English shipyards! The plains represent about one-tenth of the region and were until very recently a malaria-ridden swamp, now reclaimed and transformed into more fertile countryside. Although the region is rich in rivers, all of them tend to be torrential, sometimes flooding over neighbouring fields, destructive and violent, then dry as a bone and useless during long, rainless periods. The inland areas of Basilicata suffer from harsh, cold and rainy winters, and the rest of the region never really recovers from the completely dry, breathtakingly hot summers.

This is one of the least populated regions of Italy, where the rural population prefers to live in large villages rather than in isolated farms and houses. Basilicata has for many centuries lived in complete isolation, and the resulting misery has very much encouraged emigration. They say there are more Lucani (natives of Basilicata) living about the rest of the world than within the confines of their own region.

Two principal cities form the two provinces of the region, Potenza and Matera, of which the latter is the more interesting. The original city began as three Neolithic villages built in a triangle around a well. Until man became a hunter, the three villages were the region's only settlements. Two of the villages were then abandoned and all the inhabitants moved into the third. This is now one of the oldest cities in the world, having never been uninhabited. From the late Neolithic era until 1860 it existed without any problems, passing from the Longobards to the Byzantines to the Normans, twice to the Saracens when it was sacked and destroyed, and finally becoming independent under the Aragonese. When the local brigands entered the scene in 1860, this peaceful city had become a Piedmontese province. Until then the natives had been happily independent, constructing boats for the English, producing goods for other nations and pursuing local crafts. All this was stopped by the Piedmontese – including commercial activity carried out in local convents. Convent land was sold off and the local agriculture was destroyed. This caused the countryside to empty and the people crowded into the city, built out of the rock face with one home on top of another – a human anthill.

By the mid-1950s all kinds of problems had arisen in Matera. There were grave sanitation difficulties and overcrowding had caused crime to escalate. A special international body was set up to study this serious state of affairs, recognising the city's importance as the only perfect spontaneous urban development in existence. The inhabitants of Matera were moved into hastily built apartment blocks. A plan for improvements was drawn up, but failed; the people were not returned to their homes. The old city was thus left abandoned for thirty years, but at the time of writing the plans are being re-studied and new attempts being made to bring the city back to life. Matera must be inhabited in order to survive, yet who would choose to live there nowadays, in cramped conditions with poor plumbing and no open spaces?

In the eighth and ninth centuries hermits and monks came to live in the caves of Matera and built no fewer than 117 churches into the rock face. There are even convents cut into the rock itself, where nuns carried out their holy duties. The paintings and decorations in the churches and monasteries contain elements of oriental Byzantine and Latin art and reflect other influences of unknown origin too.

In 1450 many Albanian immigrants took refuge in Matera. An area was set aside for them and they are still there, speaking Albanian, eating their traditional dishes, wearing their national costume and continuing to live their lives according to their own beliefs.

It is very difficult to do justice in words to the 'Sassi' (the ancient city of Matera) and even photographs don't show its special quality. I urge you to go and see for yourself, because it is totally unique.

Potenza, the region's other principal city, is completely different. One of the highest settlements in Italy, it sits on a plateau at the centre of an agricultural area with a few local industries of minor importance. To the north of the entirely mountainous province is the agricultural centre of Melfi, which was the residence of the Norman kings in the eleventh and twelfth centuries. Potenza always seems to have the highest summer temperatures and lowest winter temperatures in the whole of Italy. The earthquake of 1980 destroyed large areas of this province, especially those where sheep farming was the main source of income; it does, however, boast one of Italy's loveliest seaside resorts in Marina di Maratea.

Despite all the problems which the region faces, the food of Basilicata is varied and delicious, and the tradition of 'making do' with nothing is certainly true here. The chilli pepper reigns absolutely supreme, perhaps because it was the old-fashioned cure for malaria and other ills such as worms and cholera. The exceptionally wonderful, nourishing bread of Matera is famous throughout Italy, and the lamb and mutton stews are delectable. I enjoy Basilicata's food as long as I steer clear of the chilli, which is not easy! The flavours of the region's cuisine tend to be quite strong and intense: there is nothing delicate about it.

There are exceptional cheeses, wonderful fruit like oranges, nectarines and cherries, a good selection of cured meats, and dishes like fried onions flavoured with chilli and capers to eat with great slabs of bread. Incidentally, the local bread is made in huge loaves because it was baked in a central oven, payment was made per number of loaves, not by weight, and therefore the loaves were made as big as possible in order to save money!

This is, on the whole, simple food, in which the chilli features strongly and imagination definitely plays a starring role. Pignata is a delicious local dish which typically illustrates the ingenuity of the poor cook: chunks of lamb are put in an earthenware pot with vegetables and herbs and chillies, then the pot is sealed tightly with a large lump of bread dough and the dish baked in the centre of a wood fire. The dough makes the pot into a rudimentary pressure cooker.

Wines

The wines of the deep south are extremely alcoholic and intense, but in Basilicata you can come across some delightful rosés that are very drinkable. The most famous of the local bottled wines is Aglianico del Vulture, an extremely heady, heavy, violet-smelling, garnet-coloured wine. Two local whites of note are the Malvasia del Vulture and the Moscato del Vulture. The former is delicate and almond-flavoured, excellent with fish or cheese and vegetable dishes. The latter is a lightly foaming dessert wine, delightful with the rather heavy local pastries.

TRENTINO   ALTO   ADIGE

Trentino Alto Adige was the very last of the regions of Italy to become unified. It was the 'dagger in the heart' – a long, knife-shaped region, remaining obstinately Austrian until 1918, when it finally became part of Italy. The region is divided into two provinces, Bolzano and Trento. It is an autonomous region with special laws and separate administrations. The landscape is almost completely mountainous with great soaring peaks punctuated by rich, green valleys and hills where bubbling streams and silent rivers run through the countryside. This is a very beautiful region in which the Dolomites provide an ever-changing, colourful backdrop to the fir trees and isolated castles perched on rocky crags.

Within the confines of the region live two very different populations. In the province of Trento, Italian is spoken; in Bolzano, German; and even a third language exists – in parts of the Dolomites they speak a language called Ladino, which is derived from Latin but different from Italian. Trento is a lovely city, with its proud castle and graceful Duomo blending into the skyline. Surrounded by green trees and hills, the towns in its province are mostly tourist resorts or small agricultural centres.

The city of Bolzano (Bozen in German) lies on the banks of the River Isarco. The old part of the city is especially attractive, with narrow, winding streets and wide porticoes. Bolzano province is largely a holiday area for skiing or simply enjoying the glorious mountains. The area is extremely rich in natural beauty and there is an almost inexhaustible variety of things to see and do, but then the locals know how to make the very best of their natural riches. Hence there is a very good road system, an efficient hotel network, excellent trails for ramblers, every variety of ski lift, chair lift, funicular and other ways of getting up the mountains. The region is a paragon of organisation and efficiency second to none, a tribute to German precision. But you tend to feel the lack of Italian passion.

As far as food is concerned, the Germanic influence is very strong. In the Bolzano province in particular, the dishes all have German names such as Spaetzle, Kartoffel-Krapfen and Sheiterhaufen. Dumplings feature most strongly, along with sausages of a very different sort from the kind you find further south, served with mounds of Sauerkraut and horseradish sauce. Goulash, potatoes, cabbages and turnips all come into their own. It is good, honest, tasty, cold-weather food, guaranteed to warm you up and keep hunger at bay.

In the Trento province the food is a little less Austrian, with a strong influence of Venetian cooking too, but somehow the Venetian subtleties go almost unnoticed under the rather heavy-handed smothering of Teutonic flavourings.

Wines

What the region lacks in terms of sensual, imaginative, passionate food it makes up for a thousandfold with its wines. What a marvellous selection of fruity, full-bodied whites there is – and with names like Trentino Riesling, Trentino Traminer and Trentino Casteller, you can be sure that they will be many times removed from the drier, more sour-tasting wines of the south. Especially famous, and rightly so, are the delicious local Spumanti, in brut, riserva, secco, semi-secco and extra versions – there is something to suit every pocket and every palate. There is also excellent red wine to be had here, in particular the wonderful Trentino Marzemino or the Valdadige Rosso, both fine table wines.

There are far too many wines to mention by name, but every corner of the region seems to produce one that is special in its own right. My own favourite is the lively red Colli di Bolzano (Bozner Leiten) and the delicious Santa Maddalena (Alto Adige) which blends so well with the local cured meats and game dishes. An average of fifty-five wines are usually listed for the region, which gives you a fair idea of the quantity.

LAZIO

Being the region surrounding Rome through twenty-three centuries of history cannot have been easy, yet it is very easy for the tourist to ignore the small towns set in the beautiful rolling countryside of Lazio and concentrate instead on the glories of the capital. However, Lazio is a wonderful region in its own right, very Roman yet lacking the chaos, traffic problems, pollution and noise of Italy's metropolis. The region was given its name long before the foundation of Rome, but then this name referred only to the small territory to the south of the Tiber which was inhabited by the Latini tribe. It is now much larger and divided into five separate provinces: Rome, Frosinone, Latina, Viterbo and Rieti.

The entire region of Lazio is like a mosaic made up of different colours and textures, with landscapes that are in contrast with each other. There are brown, dry, naked mountains like those found in the Abruzzi, and green, lush mountains similar to the Umbrian slopes. To the north the long plain ends up as the Maremma and suddenly becomes Tuscany. To the south the coastline gradually turns into the rocky bays and cliffs which are a sneak preview of the Campania coast. The region has islands – Ponza, Zannone, Palmarola and three others that are mere dots on the map, sitting just outside the Gulf of Gaeta. It has lakes, most of volcanic origin, all of them beautiful – Bolsena, Vico, Bracciano, Albano, for example. There are abandoned villages stranded in arid, lonely countryside, then areas of enormous agricultural development, with intensive farming and extremely fertile fields, criss-crossed in every direction by irrigation canals. There are historical ruins at every turn, and brand-new, modern cities and towns that have appeared in the last few decades. Yet although Lazio has all this to offer, the tourist usually turns to Rome, overlooking her region and everything it represents.

La Campagna Romana, the glorious band of fertile countryside which surrounds the capital, has since very ancient times been a source of wonderful agricultural produce both for Rome itself and for the rest of the region. It has also inspired painters, photographers and writers, who have been able to see the stunning beauty of this land. From La Campagna all manner of superb fruits and vegetables pour into the local markets – each stall is a work of art in itself. Unquestionably, the fruit and vegetables of the area are the most important element in the local cuisine. On the whole the dishes of this region tend to be full of very strong flavours, quite greasy and heavy – not food for the faint-hearted!

There have always been flocks of sheep in the lush fields on the out-skirts of Rome, and once the fields reached as far into the city as Testaccio. On this hill, which is, believe it or not, a Roman rubbish tip where masses of broken pots and amphorae were dumped by hordes of slaves, sheep formerly grazed quite happily. Then, in the 1870s, it was decided that this was a perfect site for the new slaughterhouse: near the river, enabling the easy removal of rubbish; near the pastures, and out-side the main city so that the risk of disease was kept to a minimum. Here it still stands, the municipal abattoir, now abandoned and empty, but used occasionally for concerts and exhibitions. The tradition of meat has carried on here, however: in this area of Rome you will find all the best restaurants which cook the offal dishes that are so much a feature of Roman cooking, and the local butchers' shops sell a huge range of offal which you will not find elsewhere in Rome. Once the area was a work-ing-class quarter and most of the people who inhabited its blocks of flats were connected in some way with the slaughterhouse or the meat trade generally. Now it is an up-and-coming, trendy place to live, all of which helps to keep alive the specialities of Roman cuisine and the character of the area.

This cuisine is known as *'la cucina del quinto quarto'* ('the cooking of the fifth quarter'), which refers to the fact that while the Pope, cardinals, kings and princes could afford all kinds of luxuries, like proper meat, fat fish and juicy vegetables, the people, the working classes, ate scraps: they made their dishes, their specialities, out of everybody else's rubbish. If a dish was divided into four parts, then the poor got the fifth quarter – i.e. the non-existent part! The heart, guts, liver, kidney, tails, ears, teats, lungs, testicles and other assorted parts of the animal that were thrown out at the abattoir were gathered up and turned into traditional Roman dishes like Coda alla vaccinara, Pagliata, Coratella and many others. The rotting bits of beef gathered off the floor of the slaughterhouse were used to make La Garofolata, a beef stew that tastes of nothing but cloves, thus covering up the rancid smell and flavour of the meat.

Arzilla is a muddy-tasting fish, ignored by most fishermen, pulled free of the net and left to the seagulls. Scavenging Romans would take the discarded fish home and turn it into La Zuppa d'Arzilla, now one of Rome's most classic dishes. The irony of this is that these very dishes have now acquired snob value and are eaten by the elite at extortionate prices in the local restaurants, many of which have given in to the call for luxurious surroundings which retain a certain quaintness. You won't find tourists in these restaurants (unless they are French); Italian gourmets go to dine here, knowing they will always be able to enjoy the traditional dishes.

Out in the provinces, however, the people have been farmers and peasants for many centuries and were never forced to go through other people's rubbish – they grew what they needed to eat. So here you will find chicken eaten in large quantities, rabbit and a certain amount of pork, all served with the popular local vegetables: peas, artichokes, salads like puntarelle, peppers, broad beans, broccoli and cabbages of many different kinds, as well as the carefully picked wild vegetables, gathered at the roadside by people who know what they are looking for. Snails are popular also, probably because they too were free, but the most traditional local dish is Abbacchio, a young lamb cooked with plenty of olive oil, garlic, anchovies, rosemary and other herbs – definitely not a light and delicate meal.

The entire range of Roman and Lazio dishes is typified by the generous use of herbs, oil and garlic, with plenty of onion and anchovy too. Take, for example, the salad of fresh, raw onions, dressed with mashed anchovies, olive oil, salt, pepper and vinegar; or the mashed lard flavoured with onion, celery and parsley which serves as a base for almost all Roman soups and many of the full-bodied pasta sauces. Pasta itself, of course, features very strongly among the local specialities, but it is almost always the good, thick, chunky varieties like bucatini, ave marie, rigatoni, conchiglie and similar shapes that are most popular. Out in the provinces you are more than likely to come across polenta, served with a stew of tasty, full-bodied sausages. The thing to remember is that there are very few dishes, like Gnocchi alla Romana for example, that are not overpoweringly virile and full of lusty, liver-saturating flavour: so be prepared!

Wines

The most famous wines of Lazio must be those from Frascati. There are many new wines currently emerging from the Castelli area of Rome (Frascati is one Castelli village) and they are arousing considerable interest among wine experts. Aprilia is another source of excellent wines in the region: Merlot di Aprilia, Sangiovese di Aprilia and Trebbiano di Aprilia are all worth trying.

However, the most interesting of all the wines of the Lazio is Est! Est! Est! because of how it got its name. All bottles of this wine carry the story on the label, so you can confirm that what follows is true!

There was once a German cardinal called Defuck, who was travelling through Lazio on his way either to or from the Vatican. He was accompanied by his faithful servant Martino, whose job it was to go ahead and test the local inns to see which one had the best wine, a drink to which his master was especially partial. When he found a good inn with good wine, Martino would write '*EST*' on the door so that Defuck would know which inn to enter when he eventually caught up with his servant. ('*Est*' is Latin for 'It is'; the complete phrase would be '*Vinum est bonum*' – 'The wine is good' – but Martino used a shortened form.)

In one particular village, called Montefiascone (a *fiascone*, incidentally, is a large *fiasco*, or wine bottle, but it was here that Defuck met with disaster, so the other meaning of the word can be applied), Martino became so excited by the local wine that he wrote '*EST! EST! EST!*' on the doorway of a house. His master obviously agreed in full, because he died there from overdrinking and is buried in the village graveyard. The present-day wine from Montefiascone is supposed to be of equally excellent quality.

MOLISE

*M*olise has a sad atmosphere to which I am sensitive from the moment I cross its border. For centuries the region has been no more than a thoroughfare, a passing-through place between the Abruzzi and Puglia, a region without an identity of its own because it has never had anything which anybody else particularly wanted or needed, a land plagued by the problems of poor, stony soil and malaria-ridden swamps. Yet there is a serene beauty about Molise that is hard to find in any other part of Italy; the only place where I have ever seen or sensed any similarity is Eire, among the bogs and the dry stone walls.

Each year, in the winter months, the rich sheep farmers of Aquila and the other towns of the Abruzzi used to send their shepherds and flocks off to Puglia, to warmer climes and lusher grass, following the well-worn *tratturi* (tracks), a tradition known as *la transumanza*. While the shepherds were away, their families were cared for by the owners of the flocks. The progress of the shepherds and flocks was overseen by higher-ranking shepherds on horseback, who were there to make sure that their subordinates didn't slaughter lambs or sheep along the way for food or barter. These rivers of sheep and people would snake their way south, crossing Molise and collecting a few of the local flocks *en route*.

Molise has an unfortunate climate of harsh winters, with snow some-times lasting right into June, and summers that are searingly hot and completely dry. It has a poor road system, an under-developed tourist trade, virtually no industrial development and the agriculture is held back by the very nature of the soil itself, which is so stony that modern farming methods are impracticable. Yet the people are trying very hard to improve all this: they are eager to develop their tourist trade and are very keen on their local gastronomy. Their warmth and enthusiasm, and the way in which they treasure what little heritage they have, make them extremely likable.

While visiting the region to research this book, I met an expert on the local food, Anna Maria Lombardi, who, with her friend Rita Mastropaolo, has written a two-volume book on the cuisine of Molise which was a total revelation to me. I never imagined that there were so many specialities from this little-known and understood region. Some of their recipes have been reproduced in this book by kind permission of the authors. However, one thing I did know was that Molise has been famous for many decades for the excellent quality of its pasta. I visited one of the local pasta factories and sampled for myself this fine product: its fame is well deserved.

Although Molise has many traditional dishes, by the very nature of its being a thoroughfare between Abruzzi and Puglia they are mostly ones which can be found in either or both of those regions. Great use is made of chilli peppers, lamb and mutton, ewes' milk cheeses, *lampascioni* (wild onions) and orecchiette and cavatelli pasta – this is where the cuisine of Italy begins to be truly southern. However, the region has almost no dishes that are unique; most are very similar to those from the rest of the south.

Wines

Traditionally Molise has produced vast quantities of wine which it has sold to the Abruzzi. The wines of this region have always tended to be light and graceful, with none of the intensity of flavour and high alcohol content of the wines of Puglia or the deeper south. Molise has been well known for its perfumed whites, light reds and delicious table wines of a deep pink colour. Two centuries ago it was the most important wine-producing area in the kingdom of the south. The tradition of wine pro-duction has been updated and renewed and Molise is still producing much excellent wine, plenty of it sophisticated and elegant, but unfortunately very little of it known outside the country. Even within Italy itself it isn't easy to find a wine expert who is up to date on the wines of Molise, although those of the Abruzzi are very well known.

The following are just a few of the new-generation, modernised Molise wines which I have been lucky enough to try and which I hope will be available in your local off-licence. Rocca del Falco exists, like most Molise wines, in dry white, dry rosé and dry red versions, all from the Tappino valley and all delicious. Another truly wonderful wine, from one of the largest producers in the same area and also obtainable as a red, white or rosé, is Serra Meccaglia; and there is a superb Vernaccia too – a light, sherry-type wine to be drunk with antipasti or as an aperitif. There are many other wines bottled in Molise, but limitation of space prevents me from covering them here and they are not readily available in the UK. However, should you visit the area while on holiday in Italy, do look out for the local wines and support the region where they try the hardest.

The MARCHE

*I*f Umbria has a sombre, serious atmosphere, reflected in its rather sensible, no-fuss dishes, the Marche, next door, offers a total contrast. This region is joyful, brimming with the holiday spirit: in the Marche they love singing, dancing, music and laughter.

This glorious region is divided into four provinces: Ancona, Pescara and Urbino, Macerata and Ascoli-Piceno. About one-third of the Marche is mountainous, although the peaks are not as high as those in the north. Nevertheless, they are more than hills; they are fairly steep and slope down towards the seashore, leaving only a thin strip of plain.

Ancona derives its name from the Greek word meaning elbow, because it is situated on the point where the coastline forms a natural elbow shape. The inland towns of the Marche are all agricultural market towns where the produce of the countryside is processed. The coastal towns have flotillas of fishing boats and are also seaside resorts, although here and there factories and industrial complexes have sprung up alongside the hotels and beaches. Ancona itself is one of the most important Adriatic ports, but much of the old city was damaged in the 1972 earthquake. Within the province of Acona lies Iesi, which is famous worldwide for the delicious wine known as Verdicchio.

Ascoli Piceno, where most of the buildings are constructed of the local stone, Travertino, which is similar to marble, is a particularly beautiful city. The resort town of San Benedetto del Tronto seems to have forgotten its history and is a very modern, well-equipped, seaside holiday town, with an impressive row of palm trees along the seafront, leading to the port of Ascoli. Urbino, on the other hand, is a city which has been locked in a time warp for several centuries. It is one of Italy's major cultural centres, boasting many beautiful historical monuments. This is Raphael's birthplace, a perfect medieval town with history pouring out of every brick. It is also a university city of some importance and great popularity.

The final province is that of Macerata, a largely fourteenth-century city with the modern town sprawling outside the old city walls. The loveliest spot in the whole region lies in this province at 1970 feet above sea level. It is Cingoli, known as 'the balcony of the Marche'; from this point you can enjoy a glorious, far-reaching view.

For me, however, the real beauty of the region lies in its mountains, where you can enjoy the peace and quiet of wonderful scenery and soak up the splendid hospitality. They really love their food here, and whatever else might happen, they will never go hungry. They have an obsession with stuffing food: nowhere else have I eaten a dish of stuffed olives followed by a chicken stuffed with olives. There exists a modest cured pork industry, and the local prosciutto crudo (prosciutto di Carpegna) is especially good. Several versions of baked, stuffed pasta dishes are popular, cousins of the original Bolognese lasagne. Porchetta, the whole sucking-pig roasted and eaten cold inside crisp rolls, so much loved and enjoyed in Rome and all over the Lazio, actually originated in the Marche and tastes better here than anywhere I have eaten it. This is also the main region for table olives: there are huge succulent ones to serve as part of an antipasto or to use in cooking, but very few are pressed to make oil. Particularly special is the Zuppa di Pesce as made in Ancona, the only place in Italy where it is traditionally made with saffron. As the region comes third in the national stakes, after Sicily and Emilia Romagna, for the amount of fish caught, there are lots of wonderful fish and seafood dishes in its cuisine.

The Marche does not boast a large selection of specialities compared with some regions, but what it does have is well flavoured and offered in generous quantities, always with the infectious sense of joy that is so much a part of the land and its people.

Wines

There are not many wines that can be attributed to the Marche, but the few there are have always been of excellent quality. The most famous wine is the aforementioned Verdicchio di Iesi, unmistakable in its amphora-shaped green bottle. It's a delicious, green-golden, dry white wine, excellent with all antipasti and fish dishes. A sparkling form, which is normally drunk with desserts, and a still higher-quality version called Classico are also available. Other favourites of mine from the region include: Rosso Piceno, a ruby-red wine with a fine, dry flavour that is perfect with roast meats; and Verdicchio di Matelica, a rarer wine than the Verdicchio di Iesi, more delicately flavoured and sophisticated.

PIEDMONT and VAL d'AOSTA

*P*iedmont owes its name to its geographic position, being *ai piedi dei monti* (at the foot of the mountains), and has been so called since the Middle Ages. Because it borders on both France and Switzerland, it is sometimes difficult to believe that you are still in Italy. Val d'Aosta sits within the confines of Piedmont, even though it is an autonomous region in its own right.

Piedmont

Piedmont is a very mountainous region, crossed by the Alps on three sides, with a sharp incline down to the plains where huge industrial complexes and modern cities sprawl. A notable aspect of the landscape is the canals which irrigate the fertile arable fields in the higher plains. The longest, measuring 50 miles, is named after the region's favourite son, Cavour, the first Prime Minister of Italy, who proclaimed the first King of Italy to be Vittorio Emmanuele, King of Piedmont.

The political importance of this region to the country as a whole cannot be ignored. It was here that the plans for unification were laid and debated. The elegant townhouses of Turin, with their smart drawing rooms, could tell you a thousand stories if they could only speak! The region's people are known for their great patriotism and strength of character, and it is probably because of these qualities that Piedmont has always been a leader. French was the official court language here until the middle of the tenth century, and the influence of neighbouring Savoy is very obvious in the local food.

The best time to visit Piedmont is in the autumn, when all the colours and flavours and smells of the region come to life. Piedmont is famous, as is Val d'Aosta, for its wide variety of wild mushrooms, its wonderfully rich red wines and its sublime white truffles – especially in the area around the town of Alba. This is a region which draws you into the great outdoors, to ramble the gentler hills or ski on the snowy peaks. It is somewhat awesome, with its mountains soaring up into the sky above you, its cities so smart and elegant, the people tending to be polite but a little cool.

Piedmontese cooking very much reflects the flavours of the autumn: mushrooms, game, truffles, grapes and game all feature very strongly. But there are also the endless rice fields in the Vercelli and Novara provinces. Here is where the *mondine* work – women who are employed during the summer months to hand-weed the fields. The rice fields have found their way into the history books: in 1859 the flooding of the Vercelli rice fields prevented the advance of the Austrian army. It is generally believed that rice was introduced into Europe by the Arabs in the eighth century, and into Italy in the thirteenth century by the Aragonese.

The Langhe area is where most of Piedmont's culinary glories originate. These include the aforementioned truffles from Alba and also strawberries, wonderful wines and excellent beef.

White truffles are extremely expensive, costing more than their black cousins from Umbria, but they are a real luxury, there is nothing more delicious and they are so versatile. Pigs or white dogs are used to seek them out, preferably at midnight, when their smell is strongest. There is great competition amongst truffle hunters for these elusive tubers. They grow underground in wooded areas and a good-sized one is about as big as a large egg. You can shave a white truffle over scrambled eggs, toasted cheese, risotto, meat or pasta dishes.

Val d'Aosta

The Val d'Aosta can be traced back to the twenty-fifth century BC when the Romans built a city here on the site of a conquered fortress after defeating the Salassi. They named the new city Augusta Praetoria, in honour of their Emperor Augustus, and the present-day name is a derivation of this.

It is the smallest region of Italy, with the highest mountains in Europe. French is officially recognised as the second language, and the locals speak their own patois. French is obligatory in all the local schools.

On the whole this is a holiday region – people come here to enjoy themselves, and a relaxed feeling permeates all aspects of life in Val d'Aosta. The people here are jolly and friendly, used to dealing with visitors – because visitors are the lifeblood of their region.

Aosta is the main city, but it is important above all for its position on the main route linking France, Italy and Switzerland. Here it is even harder to believe that you are really in Italy.

In food terms the region is famous above all else for the delicious cheese called Fontina which is produced here. A marvellous fondue, called Fonduta, is made locally using this cheese blended with butter and eggs.

Wines

The wines, as already mentioned, are few but very special indeed. Barbera, with its intense ruby colour, is a very well-known Piedmontese wine. It has a bouquet reminiscent of violets and a very strong, lingering flavour. It is excellent with specialities of the area such as *bollito* (a selection of boiled meats) and with game dishes.

Barolo is probably one of the most famous of all Italian wines. It starts off with a deep ruby colouring which tends towards orange as the wine ages. It too has a violet scent, but a very characteristic, smooth, velvety flavour with its famous *goudron* of tar. It is important to let this wine breathe for at least one hour before drinking it, especially if it is an old bottle. It's excellent with game and all red meats. Barolo improves with age and is generally considered to be at its peak after 10 years. Recent developments in the production of this noble red have improved its quality enormously. Barbaresco is the other important red wine of the region and it too is improving with each vintage.

Dolcetto is generally considered to be more of a table wine; in other words, a wine which can be drunk throughout a meal. It's garnet-coloured, dry and clean-tasting. Gattinara is another intense-flavoured red which is drunk with red meat or game and can be recognised by its raspberry nose. My favourite is Grignolino, a pale ruby-red wine with a delicate rose nose, and a pleasing dry flavour. I like to drink it fairly young, with all kinds of meat, egg and cheese dishes.

Finally, of course, there are the delightful Spumanti that are made locally, the most famous of which is Asti Spumante, available in sweet and dry versions and now enjoyed all over the world.

LOMBARDY

*I*n the sixth century AD the original Lombards (or Longobards, so called because of their long beards), a wild and raucous bunch from the area we now know as West Germany, descended upon Italy. They dominated a large area, part of which bears their name today.

Lombardy is so wide and vast and flat that to Italians of other regions is seems endless, with its elegant poplars standing silently in the swirling, blinding, treacherous fog. There are rice fields which reflect the sky like still mirrors, and convents and monasteries tucked away in the hills which surround the lovely lakes of Maggiore, Como, Garda, Lugano and Iseo, where the nuns and monks still distil and sell mysterious liqueurs. There are mountains as well as hills, but the slopes are less harsh and steep than in other areas, with wide, soft valleys.

Milan, the main city of the region, is where most of Lombardy's population lives – over 1 700 000 people. It has always been a great city. In Roman times it was called Mediolanum and was an important centre; in the Middle Ages it gained in power and importance. During the Renaissance my own ancestors, the powerful Sforzas, fought with the Viscontis for the domination of what had become a *signoria* (duchy). A fine castle in the city centre bears my family name, and there is an interesting story connected with it about this feud.

The story goes, according to my family sources, that the Sforzas had gained possession of the castle, but the Viscontis were still powerful in Milan. So the Sforzas invited them to dinner in the castle's banqueting hall, which is lined with tapestries. Behind each tapestry the Sforzas hid one of their own, armed with a dagger. The Viscontis, suspecting nothing, sat down to dine, convinced that the invitation was a gesture of genuine friendship. Immediately the Sforza men leaped out from behind the tapestries and cut their victims' throats, throwing the bodies out of the window to the dogs below. Apparently, dinner resumed without them! (There is no historical basis to this story – it is only a family tale!)

As far as today's food is concerned, Lombardy does not, unlike the other regions of Italy, have any one dish that you immediately identify with it. Rice, for example, is eaten widely, but there are areas where they won't even contemplate the thought of Risotto. The same goes for pumpkin, and for Casoûela or one of the other lugubrious dishes which were planted here by the Spaniards under their intensely religious domination; again none of these applies to the region as a whole. There is a huge selection of specialities here – excellent beef and dairy produce;

superb cheeses, such as Gorgonzola, Grana Padano, Taleggio and Mascarpone; exquisite fruit and vegetables; wonderful cakes like panettone; and strange peculiarities like Mantua's pumpkin ravioli and Cremona's Mostarda di frutta – pickled fruit in mustard essence which is served with a mixture of boiled meats called *bollito*. The natives adore all kinds of cured meats and sausages. They eat polenta in parts of the region, rice in other parts and delicious green pasta in others. The food of Lombardy encompasses the very best of the cuisine of northern Italy, bringing together a little of each of the four regions which surround it.

Lombardy is a rich region, with many great commercial and industrial centres. The average Lombard treats himself or herself well and expects good quality in everything. You will, therefore, find it hard to eat badly here – even the humblest fast-food joint sells food that is imaginative, varied and fresh. There is also a strong immigrant population – men and women who have come from the south to work in the big, sprawling factories – and there is no doubt that this has influenced the cuisine of the region over the decades. Lombardy is where Italy begins to feel as if it really is part of Europe rather than a Mediterranean country.

Wines

Well worth a mention are the excellent wines of Lombardy. Many of my favourite red wines come from this region that is almost a country in its own right. A top-of-the-range red is Grumello from the Valtellina area which is ruby-red in colour tending towards garnet, and has an unmistakable bouquet and a corresponding velvety, harmonious flavour. Generally considered to be a superior wine, excellent with roast meat and game, it is probably the most famous and valuable of all the Valtellina wines, especially after five or six years.

Inferno (hell) is a tonic and digestive wine of a similar colour to Grumello. This is also perfect with roast meat and game dishes, but it stands on its own for its unique flavour of strawberries.

My special favourite, however, is Sassella, a wine of great historical note – it was drunk by the Emperor Augustus and by Virgil, who mentions this in his 'Georgiche'. In a class of its own, it is a deep ruby red tending towards brick as it ages. With its dry, lively flavour and vivacious nose, it is the wine that is drunk with roasts in the Valtellina area.

Lombardy also produces excellent sparkling white wine which can rival any champagne. Franciacorta Pinot Spumante comes in brut, rosé and pas dosé versions; it is delightfully light and bubbly with a fresh flavour tending towards the pleasantly sour and cleansing.

ANTIPASTI

LENTICCHIE all'OLIO
Lentils with Olive Oil

This very simple dish was actually served to us as a side dish in a small roadside trattoria in the Abruzzi. Lentils are used a great deal in the cooking of this region. The local lentils are tiny and dark brown, full of flavour. This dish is served throughout southern Italy and can also be prepared with other pulses.

SERVES 6

11 oz (300 g) brown lentils, soaked overnight in cold water

½ teaspoon salt

6 tablespoons olive oil

½ red chilli pepper, de-seeded and very finely chopped

2 cloves garlic, peeled and finely chopped

2 tablespoons chopped parsley

Drain the lentils, wash carefully and cover with fresh water. Simmer, covered, for about 1–2 hours or until the lentils are completely soft. Mix the salt, oil, chilli, garlic and parsley together. Spoon the hot cooked lentils into 6 soup plates, then cover with the oil mixture and serve at once.

NOTE

If preferred, you can omit the chilli and/or the garlic and dress the lentils with just oil and chopped parsley.

LA PARMIGIANA di MELANZANE di NELLO

Nello's Baked Aubergines with Tomato and Mozzarella

Last May we were invited to lunch at Nello and Vera Oliviero's lovely villa overlooking the bay of Positano, on the gloriously romantic Amalfi coast near Naples. We could not have dreamed of a more perfect setting: the villa is right at the top of the cliff, reached only by a winding pathway. Here, amongst all kinds of flowers and shrubs, surrounded by lemon trees heavy with fruit, we stood on the terrace and looked down to the beaches and across the blue water into the distance.

Nello and I were to cook his version of Parmigiana di melanzane together on this very terrace, but sadly he was ill that day and could not cook. Vera stepped in for him and between us we prepared this sumptuously rich, lavish dish of layered aubergines with tomatoes, mozzarella and basil – plus, of course, the Parmesan cheese which gives the dish its name. My thanks go to the Oliviero family for being such wonderful hosts, for letting us into their home despite Nello's illness, for cooking us such a lovely lunch, and for teaching me how to make this dish!

SERVES 4

about 10 fl oz (300 ml) oil

2 aubergines, cut lengthways into slices ½ inch (1 cm) thick

8 fl oz (250 ml) cold basic tomato sauce (see page 284)

4 oz (100 g) mozzarella cheese, sliced

4 oz (100 g) Parmesan cheese, grated

about 12 fresh basil leaves

Pre-heat the oven to gas mark 5, 375°F (190°C).

Heat the oil and fry the sliced aubergines in it until golden brown. Drain them very thoroughly on kitchen paper.

Cover the bottom of an 8 inch (20 cm) baking dish with about 2 tablespoons of tomato sauce. Arrange a layer of aubergines on top, making sure they all point in the same direction. Cover with a layer of mozzarella, a layer of tomato sauce, a layer of Parmesan cheese and a few torn basil leaves. Repeat with a second or third layer, depending upon the size of the aubergines and the shape of the dish. Finish off with a thickish layer of tomato sauce and plenty of cheese and basil. Bake in the oven for about 20–25 minutes. Serve cold or just warm.

FRITTELLE di MELANZANE
Aubergine and Pecorino Fritters

These very Eastern-tasting fritters, made with aubergines and sultanas, flavoured with grated pecorino cheese, oregano, and nutmeg, come from Sicily. Like so many Sicilian dishes and specialities, this seems a rather odd combination of ingredients which looks as if it won't work when you see it on paper, but works extremely well on the tastebuds! All over the south of Italy, and particularly in Sicily, there are countless recipes for aubergine dishes. The vegetable was introduced to the island by the Arabs, along with oranges, lemons, cotton, palm trees, dates, jasmine and many other items which tend nowadays to be regarded as inimitably Sicilian.

MAKES ABOUT 24 FRITTERS
2 lb (900 g) aubergines
salt
3½ oz (90 g) sultanas
3 eggs
3 oz (75 g) sweet pecorino
  or Parmesan cheese,
  grated
large pinch dried oregano
generous grinding of black
  pepper
¼ teaspoon grated nutmeg
3 tablespoons plain white
  flour
3 tablespoons stale white
  breadcrumbs
oil for deep-frying

Slice the aubergines into thick rounds, place them in a basin and fill to the top with cold water. Add 2 pinches of salt and place a plate on the top of the basin to keep the aubergines submerged. Leave them for 1 hour. Cover the sultanas with cold water and leave them for 45 minutes.

Bring a large pan of salted water to the boil. Drain the aubergines and slide them into the boiling water. Cook for 5 minutes, then drain them again. Leave until cool enough to squeeze dry in your clenched fist. Then chop them coarsely with a sharp knife or *mezzaluna* and put them into a large bowl.

Separate 2 of the eggs and set the whites aside. Add the yolks, the cheese, oregano, pepper, nutmeg and a large pinch of salt to the aubergines. Strain and dry the sultanas, then add them to the mixture. Mix everything together until well blended, then shape the mixture into 24 round and flattish balls.

Beat the reserved egg whites with the remaining whole egg. Coat the aubergine balls in flour, then in the beaten egg mixture, then in breadcrumbs.

Heat about 4 inches (10 cm) oil in a 12 inch

(30 cm) lidded pan until a small piece of bread dropped into it sizzles instantly. Fry the fritters in batches of 6 or 8 until crisp and golden all over, scoop out with a slotted spoon, drain carefully on kitchen paper and serve hot or cold.

POLPETTINE alla CONTADINA
Fried Bread Balls

This is a recipe from a delightful restaurant run by Signor Ritella in the ancient city of Matera. It underlines the importance of bread in very poor cuisine such as that found in the deep south: when there was nothing else to eat, the people turned to bread as their staple diet. The bread of Matera is famous all over the country for its excellent quality.

SERVES 4–6

1 lb (450 g) slightly stale bread, crust removed
12 fl oz (350 ml) cold water
2 tablespoons chopped parsley
2 cloves garlic, peeled and finely chopped
4 oz (100 g) pecorino *or* Parmesan cheese, grated
6 eggs
1 teaspoon fine salt
½ teaspoon pepper
oil for deep-frying

Soak the bread in the water for about 15–20 minutes until completely soft. Drain it, squeeze out the excess water with your hands and put it in a bowl. Add the parsley, garlic, cheese, eggs and salt and pepper and mix them all together very thoroughly. Using your hands, shape this mixture into balls each about the size of a golf ball.

Heat the oil until a piece of bread dropped into it sizzles instantly. Fry the bread balls for 1–2 minutes or until crisp and golden-brown. Scoop them out with a slotted spoon, drain them on kitchen paper and serve piping hot.

SALUMI

The word *salumi* refers to all kinds of cured or preserved meats. A shop which specialises in selling these items is called a *salumeria*. Salumi include all kinds of salame, ham, and various other types of sliceable prepared meats such as Cotechino and Zampone.

Here is a brief list of some of the more common varieties you are likely to come across and how to recognise them.

SALAME: This is a dark red, firm, air- and salt-cured sausage with a thick rind. When it is sliced into rounds, you will see that it has spots of white fat blended into the meat.

There are several different types of salame, from the tiny little Cacciatorino to the huge, fat Finocchiona. You can buy salame ready-sliced and vacuum-packed at all large supermarkets.

PROSCIUTTO CRUDO: This is often mistakenly called Parma ham. It is, in fact, air- and salt-cured leg of pork, which is then sliced very thinly. When you want to buy raw, air- and salt-cured ham, simply ask for prosciutto crudo, unless you especially want ham from a specific area. The paper-thin slices of ham are dark red to pale pink in colour with a wide strip of soft fat down one side. Prosciutto crudo is only given the name Parma ham if the pig used to make the ham has eaten the whey left over from making Grana cheese: Parmigiano Reggiano or Grana Padano. As long as the pigs have been fed this substance, they can rightfully be said to be Parma ham pigs and the

ham will be branded accordingly during the curing process. The Langhirano valley, in the province of Parma, is particularly suitable for the curing of prosciutto crudo and therefore a great deal of it comes from this area. However, this type of ham is also produced in neighbouring regions. Extremely good prosciutto crudo is produced in San Daniele in Friuli, and at Carpegna in the Marche.

PROSCIUTTO COTTO: This is cooked, ordinary pink ham, very like British ham. Often, the hams that are not perfect in shape, and therefore rejected for prosciutto crudo, are used to make this type of ham.

MORTADELLA: This is a very large, soft, cured sausage, made with minced and seasoned cooked pork. It tends to be quite greasy and bland and has large spots of white fat throughout each slice.

BRESAOLA: Cured, salted beef. Dark red in colour and very lean, it is always served sliced paper-thin and coated with olive oil as it tends to be rather dry.

COPPA: This is best described as a cross between prosciutto crudo and bacon. Made from various pork offcuts, it is rounded in shape and tends to be marbled with fat. I call it 'poor man's prosciutto' because of its texture, but it does have a fantastic flavour.

PANCETTA: This is Italian bacon, made with the belly of the pig. It is a great deal fattier than English bacon and is usually cubed for use in cooking. Unlike prosciutto crudo, it is not normally eaten raw.

GUANCIALE: This is a different kind of Italian bacon, made from the cheek of the pig (*guancia* is the Italian for 'cheek'). It is only very slightly different from pancetta, and is almost always used for cooking purposes only. Both types of bacon can be smoked or unsmoked.

SERVING SALUMI

All kinds of salumi, except when used in cooking, are usually served as an antipasto. You can serve a selection of them with olives, sun-dried tomatoes, pickles and bread. Bresaola is excellent on its own, sprinkled liberally with best quality olive oil, lemon juice and black pepper. Some people also like to cover it with finely chopped onion. Prosciutto crudo is most commonly served with melon, although figs or pears are equally traditional and make delicious partners too. Recently people have begun serving this type of ham with more exotic fruits such as avocado, pineapple, mango or kiwi, all of which are prefectly acceptable if you like the combination of flavours. Salumi are a very easy and trouble-free way of starting a meal in a very authentically Italian style.

COTOLETTE di CAVOLFIORE
Cauliflower Fritters

This is a delicious change from smothering a boiled cauliflower in a cheese sauce. It is wonderful with other fried dishes or on its own as a perfect antipasto. The dish comes from Turin in Piedmont, where I have enjoyed it many times.

SERVES 4

8 fist-sized florets of
   cauliflower
salt
8 walnut-sized chunks of
   cheese (mozzarella,
   gorgonzola or anything
   which will melt and go
   gooey)
3 eggs
6 tablespoons fresh
   breadcrumbs
oil for deep-frying

Boil the cauliflower in salted water for about 4 minutes until just tender – remember: it must *not* be mushy! (One of my pet hates is mushy cauliflower!) Drain and dry carefully.

When cool enough to handle, insert a piece of cheese inside each floret, pushing it amongst the stalks to prevent it falling out. Beat the eggs with a pinch of salt. Put the breadcrumbs on to a plate. Heat the oil until a piece of bread dropped into it sizzles instantly. Dip each floret into the egg, then into the breadcrumbs, and deep-fry until crisp and golden. Drain on kitchen paper and serve at once, piping hot.

SUPPLÌ alla ROMANA
Wild Mushroom and Mozzarella Rissoles

Real shades of my Roman childhood here! These rissoles are often called Supplì al telefono in Rome, the gooey centre of melting mozzarella representing the telephone wires. They can be bought from the many tavola calda establishments which serve hot, ready-made food. I think they taste even better made from left-over Risotto. Delicious and simple, they are excellent party food as they are just made to be eaten with your fingers. You can serve them with a tomato dipping sauce (see page 284) if you wish.

SERVES 4

18 fl oz (500 ml) cold water
1 × 7 oz (200 g) can tomatoes, de-seeded and chopped
4 oz (100 g) butter
11 oz (300 g) Risotto rice
4 large eggs, beaten
2 heaped tablespoons grated Parmesan cheese
salt and pepper
1 teaspoon lard *or* pork dripping *or* vegetable oil
¼ onion, peeled and chopped
2 chicken livers, chopped (optional)
1 oz (25 g) prosciutto crudo *or* ordinary ham, chopped
1 oz (25 g) dried porcini mushrooms, soaked in water for 15 minutes
1 teaspoon tomato purée, diluted with 4 tablespoons hot water
4 oz (100 g) mozzarella cheese, cut into small dice

Pour the cold water into a saucepan, add the tomatoes and about 3 oz (75 g) of the butter. Bring to the boil, and tip in the rice. Stir and cook for about 18 minutes or until tender, but don't let it overcook. Drain, remove from the heat, then stir in half the beaten eggs and the Parmesan cheese, and season to taste. Tip the cooked rice on to a platter, spread it out and let it cool completely.

Meanwhile, fry the onion, chicken livers (if using) and prosciutto or ham in the remaining butter and lard, dripping or oil for about 5 minutes. Strain the mushrooms, squeeze them in your hands to remove all excess water and add them to the mixture. Cook for 3 minutes, then add the diluted tomato purée, stir, season and cover. Simmer slowly for about 20 minutes, then remove from the heat.

Take a spoonful of rice and form it into a large egg shape, using your hands. Hold it in your left hand and make a hole through it with the index finger of your right hand. Into the hole, insert a little of the mushroom mixture, and a few pieces of the mozzarella. Cover the hole up with a little more rice. Pat into a nice shape, then roll each one in flour, then in the remaining beaten egg, then in breadcrumbs. Continue until you have used up all the ingredients.

3 tablespoons plain flour
3-4 tablespoons stale
 breadcrumbs
oil for deep-frying

Heat the oil until a small piece of bread sizzles instantly when you drop it in. Fry the rissoles in batches until they are crisp and golden. Drain on kitchen paper and serve piping hot.

NOTE
This is good as a vegetarian dish, omitting the chicken liver, prosciutto and lard or dripping.

CARCIOFI RIPIENI al FORNO
Baked Stuffed Artichokes

Another recipe from the Ritella Restaurant in Matera. This one is for delicious stuffed artichokes with a filling of bread, eggs, cheese and capers. They make a fantastic starter for any meal and look very impressive.

SERVES 6
12 medium artichokes,
 cleaned and prepared
 (see page 231)
a little lemon juice
7 eggs
3 lb (1.5 kg) stale white
 bread, grated
4 oz (100 g) pecorino *or*
 Parmesan cheese, grated
large pinch pepper
1 tablespoon capers, rinsed
 and dried
1 teaspoon fine salt
2 tablespoons chopped
 parsley
2 cloves garlic, peeled and
 very finely chopped
2 fl oz (50 ml) olive oil
5 tablespoons cold water

Pre-heat the oven to gas mark 3, 325°F (160°C).
 Cut the stalks off the artichokes and discard. Pull the artichokes open so that they form little cups and leave them floating until required in water to which you have added a little lemon juice.
 Beat together 5 of the eggs and mix with the bread, cheese, pepper, capers, salt, parsley and garlic to form a smooth dough. Drain the artichokes and dry them carefully with kitchen paper, then fill each one with some of this mixture. Arrange them upright in an ovenproof dish. Pour the olive oil on and around them, then beat the 2 remaining eggs and pour them on top. Pour the water around the base of the artichokes. Bake for about 1 hour. Serve very hot.

MOZZARELLA *in* CARROZZA
Crispy Fried Mozzarella

Hot, crisp-fried mozzarella encased in egg-soaked bread and flavoured with anchovies, oregano and tomatoes – a delicious afternoon snack or first course. Although this dish is originally from Campania, it is very popular all over Italy. Traditionally the best mozzarella comes from Campania, although excellent varieties are also made in the Abruzzi and the Lazio. Sadly, buffalo mozzarella, with which the dish was originally made, is becoming more and more rare and is very expensive.

SERVES 4

4 anchovies preserved in salt, cleaned and boned, *or* 8 canned anchovy fillets, drained
8 medium-thick slices best-quality sliced bread, crusts removed
8 ½ inch (1 cm) thick slices mozzarella cheese
3 very ripe fresh *or* canned tomatoes, peeled and de-seeded
1 teaspoon dried oregano
pinch salt
pepper
3 eggs, beaten
oil for deep-frying

Cut each anchovy in quarters lengthways or, if using canned fillets, cut the fillets in half lengthways so that you end up with 16 strips of fish. Cut the slices of bread in half to create 16 oblongs. Take 8 slices of bread and cover each one with mozzarella, anchovy and tomato and sprinkle with oregano, salt and pepper. Cover with the remaining oblongs of bread to make 8 sandwiches.

Lay the sandwiches in the beaten egg and press down so that they are completely covered. Leave to soak for about 1 hour, turning them over occasionally. Heat the oil until a piece of bread dropped in sizzles instantly. Fry the sandwiches until crisp and golden on both sides, drain carefully on kitchen paper and serve piping hot.

Bagna Caoda (page 72)

Delectable Parma ham being nurtured
like a baby for 15 long months.

OLIVE RIPIENE
Stuffed Olives Fried in Breadcrumbs

This delicious dish of huge green olives, with a meaty filling and crisp breadcrumb coating, is typical of the joyous region of the Marche. Here, everything stuffable will be stuffed to bursting; and whatever you eat will be washed down with a river of delicious local wine, like the famous Verdicchio. Only in this corner of the country are you likely to be served olives stuffed with chicken – and then a chicken stuffed with olives for your next course! If you wish you can serve the Olive Ripiene as a vegetable dish to accompany meat.

SERVES 4–6

2 oz (50 g) minced beef *or* chicken *or* veal

2 eggs, beaten

1 heaped tablespoon grated Parmesan cheese

1 tablespoon bone marrow *or* lean back bacon, very finely chopped

large pinch ground mixed spice

60 huge green olives, stoned

2 tablespoons plain white flour

3 tablespoons stale breadcrumbs

oil for deep-frying

lemon slices to serve

Mix together the minced meat, half the beaten egg, the cheese, bone marrow or bacon and mixed spice. Use this to stuff all the olives carefully. Roll the stuffed olives in flour, then in the remaining beaten egg, then in the breadcrumbs.

Heat the oil until a small piece of bread dropped into it sizzles instantly. Fry the stuffed olives until golden brown and very crisp on the outside. Drain on kitchen paper and serve hot with slices of lemon.

PÂTÉ di OLIVE NERE
Black Olive Pâté

This intensely flavoured olive spread first became popular in the southern immigrant areas of Piedmont, and it was the incomers who first introduced the idea to the rather straight-laced natives of Turin. It has since become a firm favourite in even the most aristocratic families! It makes a delicious snack to savour before a meal and is traditionally served with ice-cold, fairly acidic white wine to offset the slightly cloying flavour of the olives. It is important to use juicy olives with plenty of flavour in this recipe – not the bitter calamata olives. In the summer months, many people add aubergine pulp to the mixture (see Variation below).

SERVES 8

8 oz (225 g) black olives

grated rind and juice of ½
  lemon, strained

1 large tablespoon best-
  quality olive oil

2 oz (50 g) softened butter
  (preferably unsalted)

¾ oz (20 g) very fresh white
  breadcrumbs

pinch salt

generous grinding of black
  pepper

If the olives are not stoned, remove the stones with an olive pitter or very sharp knife. Chop them as finely as possible using a *mezzaluna* or a sharp knife, then put them through a mincer two or three times using the finest blade. Alternatively, whizz them in a food processor for about 30 seconds at high speed. When you have a smooth purée, stir in the lemon juice and the olive oil, then the butter and breadcrumbs, and finally the grated lemon rind, salt and pepper. Do be generous with the pepper! Stir and stir, until you have a very light, almost fluffy texture with no lumps. Taste and adjust the seasoning – you may like to add more lemon juice. Spoon into small individual bowls and refrigerate for a minimum of 3 hours before serving.

To serve

Serve with thin slices of bread, lightly toasted then coated with just a sheen of olive oil, applied with a brush.

VARIATION

Instead of 8 oz (225 g) olives, use 4 oz (100 g) olives and 4 oz (100 g) aubergines. Purée the olives as above. Slice the aubergines and grill them until dry and papery. Push them through a sieve or blend in the food processor to a smooth purée. Mix with the olive purée and proceed as above.

BRUSCHETTA al POMODORO
Garlic Bread with Tomatoes

This is an exceptional dish, found on the menus of most Tuscan trattorie. It looks very pretty and tastes delicious. You must use fresh, ripe, luscious tomatoes and the best-quality olive oil. Although fresh basil works best, a generous pinch of dried oregano or mixed herbs is also an excellent finishing touch.

SERVES 4

1 lb (450 g) fresh ripe tomatoes
3 tablespoons olive oil
8 fresh basil leaves, torn into small pieces *or* large pinch dried mixed herbs *or* dried oregano
salt and pepper
8 thick slices white bread
2 cloves garlic, peeled

Dip the tomatoes into boiling hot water for just a few seconds, remove and peel quickly. Cut them in half and remove the seeds, then cut into very small cubes. Toss them with the olive oil, fresh basil or dried herbs and season with salt and pepper to taste. Toast the bread lightly on both sides and rub it on both sides with garlic. Spoon the tomato mixture over the warm bread and serve.

INSALATA di RISO NOVARESE
Novara Rice Salad

This is a lovely rice salad with optional truffles! Other ingredients include lemons, anchovies, white wine and garlic. Many people object to the combination of truffle and lemon, claiming that the delicate flavour of the truffle should be protected from something as harsh as lemon juice. I think they marry very well indeed in some dishes and this is one of them. It is a recipe from Novara, in whose province stretch endless rice fields.

SERVES 4

11 oz (300 g) long-grain rice (preferably Novara)

salt

9 tablespoons olive oil

1 glass dry white wine

1 × 4 oz (100 g) white truffle, sliced into thin slivers *or* 4 oz (100 g) button mushrooms, thinly sliced

4 anchovies preserved in salt, cleaned and boned, *or* 8 canned anchovy fillets, drained

juice of 2 lemons

1 clove garlic, peeled and crushed

1 handful of parsley, chopped

Pre-heat the oven to gas mark 4, 350°F (180°C).

Toss the rice into a large pan of salted, boiling water. Cook for 8 minutes, then drain. Using about 1 tablespoon of the olive oil, oil an ovenproof dish large enough to take all the rice with some extra space for swelling. Tip the rice into the dish, pour the wine over it and place in the oven for approximately 15 minutes or until tender.

As soon as it is cooked, take it out of the dish and spread it out on a work-surface or tray to cool, forking it up to separate the grains. Put it into a bowl and stir in 2 tablespoons oil to dress it. Arrange the rice in layers in a deep dish (such as a soufflé dish or deep terracotta casserole) with the truffle or mushrooms and set aside. The reason for layering the ingredients in this way, even though they will eventually be mixed, is to ensure that the flavour of the truffle or mushrooms is evenly distributed.

Cut the anchovies into small pieces and put them with the remaining oil and garlic in a small saucepan. Heat the oil gently, mashing the anchovies carefully. Remove from the heat when the anchovies are completely disintegrated, allow to cool, then sieve. Stir in the lemon juice and parsley. Pour this over the rice, mix it all together and serve cold but not chilled.

CAPONATA

Aubergine and Olive Salad

From the elegant Conti restaurant, in Reggio Calabria, comes this delicious recipe for Caponata. Signor Conti himself has very kindly allowed me to use his recipe.

This combination of ingredients is typical of southern Italian cooking. The result is a dish which has varying levels of flavour and a great deal of interesting texture.

SERVES 6

2 lb (1 kg) aubergines, cubed

salt

3½ fl oz (100 ml) olive oil

1½ oz (40 g) onion, chopped

9 oz (250 g) assorted pickles (such as onions, peppers, gherkins)

1 oz (25 g) capers, rinsed and dried

6 celery leaves, chopped

2 oz (50 g) green olives, stoned

1 tablespoon granulated sugar

1 wine glass red wine vinegar

2 tablespoons pine kernels

Cover the cubed aubergines with salt, put them in a colander in the sink and leave them to drain out their bitter juices for about 1 hour (longer if possible). Then wash and dry them thoroughly.

Divide the oil between two deep pans. Fry the aubergine cubes in one pan. In the other fry the onion, pickles, capers, celery leaves and olives over a low heat for about 15 minutes. When the aubergines are soft and well coloured, remove them from the oil and let them drain on kitchen paper. Add the sugar and vinegar to the onion mixture, let the fumes of the vinegar evaporate and then stir in the aubergines and the pine kernels. Serve warm or cold.

INSALATA CAPRESE
Capri Salad

Everybody's favourite! My friend Vera Oliviero and I prepared this on the terrace of her glorious villa overlooking the bay of Positano. You are unlikely to find the delicious pink tomatoes that she used anywhere other than in the Positano area – apparently the volcanic soil gives them their strange colour and texture. They were the most delicious tomatoes I have ever eaten. As a substitute, use beef or marmande tomatoes, or organically grown tomatoes – they taste more like Italian ones! As for Vera's husband Nello's amazing basil, it was exceptionally perfumed! You must be sure to use really fresh mozzarella in this recipe. Press it gently between your finger and thumb: if it's fresh it should be very soft and wet. The salad was originally created on the island of Capri, which is how it got its name.

SERVES 4

2-3 large tomatoes

5 oz (150 g) very fresh
   mozzarella cheese

1 large handful fresh basil
   leaves, torn and whole

olive oil

salt and pepper

Wash the tomatoes and cut them into thickish slices. Slice the mozzarella into similar-shaped pieces.

Arrange the tomato and mozzarella slices alternately on a platter, working round the edges in a circle. Fill the centre if you have enough slices left over.

Scatter with the basil, then dress with oil and salt and pepper to taste. Serve at once, or after no more than 30 minutes.

GATTÒ SANTA CHIARA
Santa Chiara's Savoury Cake

The name of this delicious, savoury cake comes from the days when it was prepared by the nuns of the Santa Chiara Convent near Naples. Serve it just warm in thin slices, perhaps with a dish of olives and dried tomatoes, for your guests or family to nibble on over a glass of cold white wine, while they wait for the main part of the meal. It also makes a delicious afternoon snack. Incidentally, Santa Chiara is also the patron saint of television!

SERVES 6

9 oz (250 g) plain white flour plus extra for dusting

1 oz (25 g) fresh yeast *or* ¼ oz (7 g) Easyblend yeast *or* ½ oz (15 g) dried yeast

4½ oz (120 g) unpeeled potatoes

salt

4 oz (100 g) prosciutto crudo, in thickish slices

2 oz (50 g) lard *or* butter, cut into small pieces

5 oz (150 g) mozzarella cheese, diced

If you are using fresh or dried yeast, put 4 tablespoons of the flour into a small bowl and add the yeast. Mix together with enough warm water to make a very wet, soft batter. Cover with a napkin and put in a warm place to rise for 30 minutes or until doubled in volume. If you are using Easyblend yeast, simply mix it into all the flour – no liquid is needed.

Boil the potatoes in salted water until tender. Cut the prosciutto into finger-sized strips. Put the dry flour on the table, make a hollow in the centre with your fist and add a pinch of salt. Drain the potatoes, peel them and mash them into the hollow in the flour.

Add the risen flour and yeast mixture and knead the flour and potatoes together with three-quarters of the lard or butter and another pinch of salt. Slap and knead energetically until everything is well blended and the dough is very light to handle. Add the mozzarella and the prosciutto and knead for a further 10 minutes.

Grease a 10 inch (25 cm) cake tin with the remaining lard or butter and flour it very lightly, tipping it upside down to remove excess flour. Put the kneaded dough in the tin and place it somewhere warm to rise for 1½–2 hours. It should double in volume. Bake it in a pre-heated oven at gas mark 4, 350°F (180°C) for 40 minutes or until golden brown.

BAGNA CAODA
Piedmontese Hot Oil, Garlic and Anchovy Dip

Traditionally, this classic Piedmontese dip is served in a terracotta pot placed over hot embers, preferably oak, to keep it hot. All this is much too complicated for the average household, so I recommend you use a fondue set instead, or alternatively some kind of heating tray with a night light set underneath. It is served with a selection of vegetables which are dipped into the bubbling garlic and anchovy mixture and eaten at a leisurely pace.

For decades, the dip was made with walnut oil, which is now a rare delicacy in Piedmont. To recapture that ancient flavour, try crushing a few shelled and peeled walnuts in the olive oil. There are several variations on this dish: some people add wine to the bubbling oil, whilst in the Alba area if there happens to be some Bagna left at the end each person will break an egg into the mixture and scramble it over the heat to finish the meal.

This delicious version was prepared for me by Franca Caccia. Although she uses almost the same ingredients as everyone else, her method is quite definitely her own – obviously developed over years of experience! Franca lives near Alba, the centre of the Langhe, where the white Piedmontese truffle and the vast range of delicious Piedmontese wines come from.

SERVES 4

The vegetables
Jerusalem artichokes, peeled
cauliflower florets
red and green peppers, cut into strips
crisp white cabbage leaves
turnips, peeled, boiled and cut into strips
potatoes, peeled, boiled and cut into strips
carrots, cut into strips
button onions, peeled and lightly boiled
fennel bulbs, quartered

globe artichokes, prepared as explained on page 231 and served raw or cooked

The dip
5 fl oz (150 ml) olive oil
3 cloves garlic, peeled and thinly sliced (more if desired)
1½ anchovies preserved in salt, cleaned and boned, *or* 3 canned anchovy fillets, drained
1 heaped tablespoon unsalted butter

salt to taste
½ tomato, peeled and
chopped (optional)
3 tablespoons cream
(optional)

Prepare the vegetables and arrange them on a platter in an attractive pattern.

Heat the oil until sizzling hot, then add the garlic. Fry the garlic until golden, then add the anchovies and lower the heat. Cook slowly until the anchovies have dissolved into the oil, then stir in the butter and add salt to taste. If you wish, add ½ chopped tomato and 3 tablespoons cream, stir and heat through briefly. Serve very hot.

MUSCIOLI ARROSTO
Stuffed Mussels

This recipe, in which the mussels are stuffed with chopped prosciutto crudo, breadcrumbs and tomato, is from the Marche.

SERVES 4–6
2½ lb (1.25 kg) mussels,
  scrubbed and cleaned
2 oz (50 g) prosciutto
  crudo, finely chopped
1 handful of parsley,
  chopped
3 tablespoons fresh
  breadcrumbs
4 tablespoons passata
salt and pepper
8 tablespoons olive oil

Pre-heat the oven to gas mark 6, 400°F (200°C).

Steam the mussels in a large pan for about 8 minutes and throw away any which have not opened.

Remove all the mussels from their shells and keep half the shells (choose the prettiest ones!), discarding the rest. Arrange 2 mussels in each half shell and put them all into an ovenproof dish.

Mix together the chopped prosciutto, parsley, breadcrumbs and passata. Season with salt and pepper and mix thoroughly.

Spoon enough of this mixture into each half shell containing the mussels to fill it completely. Trickle the oil all over the dish and place in the oven. Bake for about 8 minutes, then serve at once.

FRUTTI di MARE GRATINATI
Grilled Seafood

This is one of my favourite ways of eating seafood, and even people who don't like other seafood recipes normally like this one. It was given to me by Signor Balducci, the charming chef at the Hotel Riva del Sole, just outside Bari. You don't need to limit yourself to the varieties of seafood I've suggested: you can use any combination you like.

SERVES 4

16 large fresh mussels
8 large oysters
4 fresh razor shells
20 large fresh baby clams
4 scallops
4 tablespoons fresh
  breadcrumbs
4 tablespoons grated
  pecorino *or* Parmesan
  cheese
3 cloves garlic, finely
  chopped
3 tablespoons chopped
  parsley
5 tablespoons olive oil

Carefully clean and scrub all the shellfish. Steam them very quickly in a large pan for 5–8 minutes to open them. Take them off the heat and allow to cool at once so as not to overcook them. Discard any which have not opened. Remove them from their shells and arrange them in an ovenproof dish in a single layer. Mix together all the other ingredients except the olive oil, cover the top of each piece of seafood with this mixture, then drizzle olive oil all over the top. (Be generous: this recipe mustn't be allowed to go dry.) Place the dish under a medium grill for 5 minutes, then serve at once.

RAW SEAFOOD

Eating raw seafood, bought from street vendors or personally fished, has always been popular in southern Italy, though since the last cholera scare has been traced back to raw mussels, it has become less so. If you like the taste of raw fish (as in Japanese cooking), all kinds of shellfish, sea urchins, whitebait and small squid can be sampled in fishing-port towns like Taranto and Bari, served to you simply with a cleansing squeeze of lemon.

INSALATA di MARE ADRIATICA
Adriatic Seafood Salad

This scrumptious fresh seafood salad is another recipe from the jovial Signor Balducci, chef at the Hotel Riva del Sole near Bari. As in the recipe for grilled seafood, you can use any type of seafood you like. However, please do be sure to include squid because it gives the salad its traditional chewiness. The mussels and clams, which filter about 17 or 18 gallons of water a day, are left overnight to filter in flavoured water which gives them an especially nice taste.

SERVES 4

20 fresh mussels, scrubbed
  and cleaned
40 fresh baby clams,
  scrubbed and cleaned
1 bay leaf
1 lemon
7 oz (200 g) fresh or frozen
  squid, cleaned and cut
  into neat rings or strips
salt
6 oz (175 g) fresh prawns
4 large fresh Mediterranean
  prawns
6 tablespoons olive oil
3 tablespoons chopped
  parsley
freshly ground black pepper

Leave the mussels and clams overnight in a bucket of water with 1 bay leaf and half the lemon (reserve the remaining half).

Boil the squid in salted water for about 25–30 minutes or until tender.

When it is almost time to eat, steam the mussels and the clams for about 8 minutes, discarding any that do not open. *Never* eat a mussel that has been forced to open; if it does not open naturally then it was not meant to be eaten!

Wash the prawns carefully and cover with cold water. Bring to the boil and cook for about 1 minute, then drain and cool almost completely before shelling.

Remove the mussels from their shells and put them in a warmed bowl with the prawns and squid. Mix them all together. Squeeze the juice from the reserved lemon half and add it to the seafood with the oil, parsley and pepper to taste. Add salt after mixing and serve whilst just tepid.

CROSTINI di POLLO e FEGATO
Chicken and Liver Crostini

This recipe is one of my own and comes from Tuscany. Many variations are to be found in different parts of the region but I always come back to this one. Crostini are simply pieces of bread covered with a delicious savoury topping – ideal with a pre-dinner glass of wine.

SERVES 4

½ onion, chopped
1 carrot, chopped
1 stick celery, chopped
1 tablespoon finely
   chopped parsley
3 tablespoons olive oil
1½ oz (40 g) unsalted
   butter
1 chicken liver, trimmed
   and washed
4 oz (100 g) calf's liver,
   trimmed and washed
2 tablespoons dry white
   wine
1 heaped tablespoon
   tomato purée diluted
   with about 4 tablespoons
   hot water
salt and pepper
1 oz (25 g) capers, rinsed
   and finely chopped
4 or 8 thin slices crusty
   white *or* brown bread

Fry the onion, carrot, celery and parsley in the olive oil and half the butter. Cook until the onion is soft, then add the chicken and calf's livers. Stir and add the wine. Allow to evaporate for 2–3 minutes, then add the diluted tomato purée. Season with a little salt and pepper, add 2–3 tablespoons water, cover and simmer for about 20 minutes.

Remove from the heat, lift the livers out of the sauce and mince or process them until smooth. Return the liver purée to the pan and stir in the rest of the butter and the capers. Heat through and remove from the heat, but keep warm.

Spread the bread generously with the liver mixture and serve at once.

SOUPS

ZUPPA di VALPELLINE
Valpelline Soup

Valpelline is a valley in the most northern part of Val d'Aosta, halfway between Aosta and the Swiss border. This soup is a real winter warmer, with a wonderful texture and flavour, almost a meal in itself.

SERVES 4

8 thick slices hearty brown
  or rye bread
1 small green cabbage,
  shredded
2 oz (50 g) pancetta *or* pork
  dripping
8 tablespoons meat jelly
  from the bottom of the
  dripping jar (pork or
  beef)
large pinch ground mixed
  spice
4 oz (100 g) fat prosciutto
  crudo, cut into paper-
  thin slices
5 oz (150 g) Fontina *or*
  mature Gouda cheese,
  thinly sliced
2 oz (50 g) unsalted butter
1½ pints (900 ml) best-
  quality beef broth (see
  page 289)
salt

Pre-heat the oven to gas mark 3, 325°F (160°C).

Toast the bread lightly and place 2 slices at the bottom of a deep ovenproof pot, preferably terracotta or cast-iron. Put the rest of the toasted bread to one side until required.

Put the cabbage and pancetta or pork dripping into a saucepan and braise until the cabbage is fairly tender and well coloured.

Cover the bread in the bottom of the pot with a little meat jelly, then a pinch of spice and then a layer of cabbage. Cover the cabbage with a layer of prosciutto crudo, then a layer of cheese slices. Repeat the process until you have used everything up, finishing with a layer of cheese. On top of the cheese dot the butter. Then pour the broth over the whole thing, plunging a long knife or spatula down through the layers so that the liquid penetrates properly. Bake for about 1 hour. Serve very hot.

RIBOLLITA alla PISTOIESE
Alvaro's Ribollita

Ribollita is one of those sturdy Tuscan soups that were part of my upbringing. When I was a child, it was one of the things I disliked eating the most, and I was threatened with all kinds of punishments unless I finished my plateful. When my friend Alvaro Maccioni suggested we make it together, my first reaction was one of horror – I was transported back to scenes of silent childhood rage in which I used to eat the soup as slowly as possible in the hope that somebody would give up the fight and let me off (they never did!). I soon realised my fears were unwarranted. Ribollita is delicious, nourishing and very easy to make. Basically, it is a thick vegetable soup with chopped stale bread and white beans, but the addition of virgin olive oil transforms it completely. What a pity I never appreciated it until now: what a lot of wasted years!

This is one of those very flexible recipes where you can use whatever is available in approximate quantities. The total weight of vegetables should be about 3 lb (1.5 kg) when raw, but the types of vegetables and the amount of each are entirely up to you.

SERVES 4 *(generously)*

9 oz (250 g) stale country-style white *or* brown bread (the harder the better)

salt and pepper

2 tablespoons olive oil plus extra to serve

3 carrots, scraped and coarsely chopped

2 medium potatoes, peeled and cubed

2 cloves garlic, peeled and chopped

2 onions, peeled and sliced

1 small spring cabbage, shredded

any other leaf vegetables of your choice

Slice the stale bread as thinly as possible. Season it with salt and pepper and 2 tablespoons olive oil and arrange in the bottom of a large tureen.

Put all the vegetables and the sausages into a large saucepan with the water and season to taste with salt and pepper. Cook for about 1¼ hours over a medium to low heat, covered, adding more water if necessary.

Remove the sausages and keep them warm on a plate. Stir the beans into the vegetable soup. Taste and add salt or pepper as required. Heat through, then pour the soup over the bread. Arrange the sausages on top, then cover and let the soup rest for at least 15 minutes. Serve tepid with a small jug of olive oil so that each person can drizzle some over their serving of soup. You can also serve grated Parmesan cheese if you wish.

1–4 Italian sausages
  (available from most
  good Italian
  delicatessens) *or* strong-
  flavoured English
  sausages (preferably
  hand-made)
about 2 pints (1.2 litres)
  cold water
1 × 5 oz (125 g) tin white
  beans (butter beans,
  haricot or cannellini)

ZUPPA alla BOLOGNESE
Bolognese Soup

The gastonomic capital's very own soup is based on best-quality mortadella and fresh eggs, to make a very nourishing and unusual dish.

SERVES 4
3 oz (75 g) mortadella
4 eggs
4 oz (100 g) Parmesan
  cheese, grated
4 oz (100 g) semolina
pinch grated nutmeg
pinch salt
3½ oz (90 g) butter,
  softened
2 pints (1.2 litres) chicken
  or beef broth (see page
  289)

Pre-heat the oven to gas mark 4, 350°F (180°C).
  Mince or process the mortadella finely.
Separate the eggs and set the whites aside. Beat the yolks in a bowl, add the cheese, 3 oz (75 g) of the semolina, the nutmeg, salt and about 3 oz (75 g) of the butter. Mix together very smoothly. In another bowl, beat the egg whites until stiff, then fold these into the mixture.
  Use the remaining butter to grease an ovenproof dish large enough to take the mixture. Pour in the mixture and level the surface with the back of a spoon. Sprinkle the rest of the semolina on the top and bake in the oven for about 10–15 minutes or until firm.
  Remove from the oven and cool. Cut into neat cubes. Heat the broth to boiling point, then toss in the cubes. Cook for 5 minutes, transfer to a warmed tureen and serve.

JOTA

Sauerkraut and Barley Soup

Jota was once the staple daily diet of the inhabitants of the Carso mountain villages around the lovely city of Trieste. This was an area where genuine hunger and poverty was a reality until very recently. A book published in 1898, called Guida alla Carnia, *tells of how, in an enormous area covering most of the mountain and its valleys, Jota was almost all there was to eat.*

There are countless versions of this soup – with meat and without, with barley or with beans or both – but the basic theme is always the same: a nourishing, thick and satisfying meal, made from a few readily available ingredients.

Here is my favourite version of Jota (which also happens to be the simplest!), adapted from a very old recipe from Gorizia. Sauerkraut is about as German-tasting as anything you can get, showing this region's very strong Austro-Hungarian influences. To this basic soup, you can add chopped radicchio, celery, lettuce or pork. Serve it with plenty of rye bread and butter.

SERVES 6–8

5 oz (150 g) smoked
   pancetta *or* smoked
   streaky bacon, chopped
1 large onion, peeled and
   finely chopped
1 handful parsley, chopped
6 fresh sage leaves, chopped
3–4 cloves garlic, peeled
   and chopped
1 oz (25 g) unsalted butter
4 oz (100 g) pork dripping
   or fat cut from a joint of
   pork, chopped
7 oz (200 g) dried beans
   (such as borlotti or
   cannellini), soaked
   overnight in cold water,
   boiled for 5 minutes and
   drained

Fry the pancetta or bacon, onion, parsley, sage and garlic in the butter and dripping or pork fat until the onion is soft. Add the beans, barley and stock. Bring to the boil and add the potatoes, cover and simmer for about 2 hours or until everything is very soft and almost disintegrating. You may need to add a little more stock or water as the soup cooks if it appears to be thickening too much. Stir in the sauerkraut and season to taste. Return the soup to the boil, give it one last stir and serve.

Frutti di Mare Gratinati (page 74)

Top: Sunset, and the fishermen set off
for a night of work. *Bottom:* Fontina –
the cheese of the mountains.

7 oz (200 g) pearl barley,
    soaked overnight in cold
    water and drained
4½ pints (2.5 litres) meat
    stock (see page 293)
2 medium potatoes, peeled
    and cubed
7 oz (200 g) sauerkraut
salt and pepper

MINESTRA di RISO e FEGATINI
Chicken Liver and Rice Soup

*This delicately flavoured and nourishing soup often crops up at country
wedding feasts in the small towns and villages along the banks of the Po.
Many households use very fine tagliatelle instead of rice, which gives the
soup a completely different texture. You could also substitute small seed-
shaped pasta for an equally good effect.*

SERVES 4
1¾ pints (1 litre) meat
    broth (see page 289)
8 oz (225 g) long-grain rice
4 chicken livers, trimmed,
    washed and finely
    chopped
1½ oz (40 g) unsalted
    butter
1 handful parsley, chopped
1 handful very mature
    Parmesan *or* Cheddar
    cheese, freshly grated

Bring the broth to the boil, then slip in the rice.
Stir, return to the boil and simmer for about 15
minutes or until tender. Meanwhile, fry the
chicken livers very lightly in the butter for
about 5 minutes. Remove from the heat and
keep warm. When the rice is tender, stir in the
warm chicken livers. Remove from the heat and
rest for 3–4 minutes to allow the rice to absorb
the flavour fully. Stir in the parsley and the
cheese and serve at once.

VARIATION
If you are using small pasta or fresh tagliatelle
instead of rice, they will take less time to cook.
The cooking time of dried pasta will vary
according to size and brand (check the packet),
but the tagliatelle should take no more than
1–2 minutes.

MINESTRONE alla LIVORNESE
Livorno Minestrone

The word minestrone *actually means 'big soup' – in other words, one which contains lots of different ingredients and is power-packed for larger appetites! This particular recipe comes from the bustling port of Livorno, where ferries and cargo boats come and go amongst the everlasting atmosphere of rich medieval history, and where the surrounding fertile countryside yields much of the wide variety of vegetables that are required to make it. Use fresh beans if at all possible.*

SERVES 6–8

1 lb (450 g) fresh *or* 8 oz (225 g) dried cannellini *or* borlotti beans

¼ savoy cabbage

5 oz (150 g) fresh spinach

6 leaves Swiss chard *or* dark green lettuce leaves

2 oz (50 g) prosciutto crudo *or* unsmoked fat back bacon

1 oz (25 g) parsley, finely chopped

1 clove garlic, peeled and finely chopped

1 carrot, scraped and cut into thin strips

1 onion, peeled and thinly sliced

1 courgette, cut into thin strips

1 potato, peeled and cut into thin strips

1 stick celery, cut into thin strips

2 strips belly pork, cubed

1 tablespoon tomato purée, diluted with 1 ladleful very hot water

If you are using dried beans, cover them with cold water and soak overnight. Then drain and wash them. Boil them twice for 5–10 minutes, draining and washing them in between each boiling. Then cover them in fresh cold water, cover them tightly and simmer for 1 hour or until tender. If you are using fresh beans, shell them, cover with cold water and simmer for 1 hour or until tender.

Wash and trim the green vegetables, then shred them all together. Place in a saucepan with a little water and cook until just soft. Remove from the heat, cool and then squeeze dry in your fists.

Chop the prosciutto or bacon and place it in a big cast-iron pan with the parsley and the garlic. Fry together gently for about 5 minutes. (You don't need to add extra oil – the fat from the prosciutto is enough.)

Add the green vegetables to the prosciutto, parsley and garlic, stir together, then add all the other vegetables, the belly pork and the beans. Stir in the diluted tomato purée, all the stock or broth and simmer for about 2 hours, covered. Check the seasoning and add salt if required.

After about 2 hours, add the rice, stir well and continue to cook for about 15–20 minutes or until the rice is tender. Remove from the

3½ pints (2 litres) meat
   stock or broth (see page
   293)
salt
9 oz (250 g) long-grain rice
2 heaped tablespoons
   grated Parmesan cheese

heat, stir in the Parmesan and serve hot or cold, but not chilled.

La MINESTRA di LENTICCHIE di CONCETTA
Concetta's Lentil Soup

In Campobasso, regional capital of the rather remote region of Molise, there is a tiny back street trattoria owned and run by a lady called Concetta Cipolla. In a very small kitchen, dominated by a vast fireplace, Concetta prepares lunches and dinners for up to 160 people! One of the most memorable things I have ever eaten there is this delicious lentil soup.

SERVES 4
7 oz (200 g) brown lentils,
   soaked in water
   overnight, *or* red lentils
2½ fl oz (65 ml) olive oil
1 clove garlic, peeled and
   crushed
salt
croûtons of bread fried in
   olive oil to serve

If using brown lentils, remove and discard all those which have come to the surface of the water during the night and rinse the others in clean cold water. Put the soaked lentils (or the unsoaked red lentils) in a saucepan with the oil, garlic, salt to taste and about 3½ pints (2 litres) cold water. Bring to the boil and simmer very slowly for about 1½ hours or until the lentils are almost disintegrating. Serve the soup very hot, with croûtons of bread fried in olive oil if you wish.

ZUPPA di FAGIOLI alla FIORENTINA
Florentine Bean Soup

This is the authentic bean soup recipe from Florence. The Tuscans have been renowned for centuries for their great love of bean-eating! With the leftovers of a bean soup such as this one, you can make the famous Florentine speciality Ribollita (see page 78). The soup is placed in a wide ovenproof dish, covered with thinly sliced onions, coated with a sheen of olive oil and heated in the oven until the onions form a perfect golden crust.

SERVES 4

2 lb (1 kg) fresh *or* 1 lb (450 g) dried cannellini *or* borlotti beans
5 large cloves garlic
2 large onions, peeled and chopped
8 tablespoons olive oil
1 carrot, scraped and chopped
1 leek, chopped
1 stick celery, chopped
1 large ripe tomato, peeled, de-seeded and chopped
1 ham bone
2½ pints (1.5 litres) water
salt
½ teaspoon beef extract
10 oz (275 g) dark green cabbage leaves (in the absence of black Tuscan cabbage, alas!), washed and cut into large pieces
1 sprig fresh rosemary
pinch dried thyme
4 slices coarse white bread
5 tablespoons grated Parmesan cheese

If using dried beans, soak overnight and boil twice for 5–10 minutes, washing in between each boiling. Drain.

Peel and chop 2 of the garlic cloves and fry with the chopped onions in 3 tablespoons of olive oil for 5 minutes. Add the rest of the chopped vegetables and the ham bone, the beans and 2½ pints (1.5 litres) cold water. Add a pinch or two of salt and the beef extract. Cover and simmer for about 1 hour or until the beans are tender.

Remove the ham bone and 1 large ladleful of whole, cooked beans. Liquidise or sieve the rest of the soup. Return the whole beans to the soup with the cabbage. Continue to simmer gently until the cabbage is tender.

Meanwhile, pour the remaining olive oil into a small saucepan and heat it gently with the rosemary, thyme and 2 more of the garlic cloves, unpeeled but crushed. After 10 minutes or so, strain the oil into the soup and heat it through for 3 minutes, stirring constantly. Toast the bread in the oven. Peel the remaining garlic clove and rub each side of each slice of bread with it. Place the bread in the bottom of a warmed soup tureen. Pour the soup over the bread, sprinkle with Parmesan cheese and serve at once.

MINESTRONE D'ORZO alla TRENTINA

Trentino Barley Soup

Barley is used extensively in the cooking of the Trentino region and this rich soup is cooked in various ways all over the region. Like most of the local dishes, it is designed for cold, snowy weather and for feeding large appetites, further sharpened by outdoor activities.

SERVES 4

8 oz (225 g) pearl barley

3½ pints (2 litres) cold water

½ teaspoon beef extract

1 onion, peeled and chopped

1 sprig each fresh marjoram, parsley and rosemary, chopped

5 tablespoons olive oil

1 very meaty ham bone

1 very large potato, peeled and cut into chunks

1 very large carrot, scraped and cut into chunks

salt

6 tablespoons grated Parmesan cheese

Wash the barley, put it into a pan and cover with cold water, bring to the boil and add the beef extract. Cook slowly, uncovered, for 2 hours.

After 2 hours, fry the onion and the herbs in the olive oil for 5–6 minutes, then stir this into the barley. Add the ham bone, potato, carrot and a little salt and simmer for 1 hour. Remove the ham bone and transfer the soup to a warmed tureen. Sprinkle with the cheese and serve.

MINESTRA di PASTA e CECI
Pasta and Chickpea Soup

This is a typical 'lean day' dish from the Lazio, served traditionally on Christmas Eve, saint's day eves, Fridays, Lent and similar occasions when the eating of meat was forbidden for religious reasons. Despite the recent more relaxed attitude towards eating habits and religion, the soup remains extremely popular.

SERVES 4

8 oz (225 g) dried chick-
   peas *or* 14 oz (400 g)
   canned chickpeas
1 large sprig fresh rosemary,
   leaves removed and
   finely chopped
1 very large clove garlic,
   peeled and finely
   chopped
3½ fl oz (100 ml) olive oil
1 tablespoon tomato purée,
   diluted with ½ wine glass
   hot water
8 oz (225 g) dried pasta
   (fettuccine or linguine)
salt

If you are using dried chickpeas, soak them overnight in cold water. Drain and wash them, then place them in a heavy-bottomed pan with approximately 2½ pints (1.5 litres) cold water. Cover, bring to the boil and simmer for about 2½ hours without ever lifting the lid. If you are using canned chickpeas, drain and rinse them, then cover with 1¾ pints (1 litre) cold water and simmer for 1 hour without lifting the lid. The chickpeas should be almost falling apart.

In a small saucepan, fry the rosemary and garlic in the olive oil for about 6 minutes. Add the diluted tomato purée and continue to simmer. As soon as the chickpeas are cooked, stir the rosemary and tomato mixture into the pan. Make sure you have plenty of liquid: if the soup seems thick, add more water. Bring to the boil and add the pasta. Cook for about 4 minutes or until tender. Season to taste with salt and serve.

NOTE
No cheese is served with this soup, but sometimes a small jug of best-quality olive oil is offered so that each person can pour a little on to their portion.

MINESTRONE con la ZUCCA
Pumpkin Minestrone

In Mantua, they have always had a reputation for being great eaters of pumpkin. In this recipe, brilliant orange pumpkin is combined with rice and milk to make a bright, warming and nourishing soup.

SERVES 4

14 oz (400 g) pumpkin, peeled, de-seeded and cut into chunks

salt

1¾ pints (1 litre) milk

1½ oz (40 g) long-grain rice

4 fl oz (120 ml) chicken stock (see page 292)

1½ oz (40 g) very fresh unsalted butter

7 tablespoons grated Parmesan *or* grana cheese

Boil the chunks of pumpkin in salted water for about 10–15 minutes, then drain and liquidise to a smooth pulp in a liquidiser or food processor. Return to the saucepan and stir in the milk. Bring to the boil, add the rice and the chicken stock, stir and simmer for about 15–20 minutes or until the rice is cooked. Remove from the heat and stir in the butter, then stir in the cheese and serve immediately.

ZUPPA di FUNGHI CALABRESE
Calabrian Mushroom Soup

The rugged mountains of inland Calabria yield vast quantities of delicious wild mushrooms of many shapes and sizes. In this recipe, they are turned into a delicious soup, poured over a thick layer of coarse toasted bread and covered with a fine layer of freshly grated cheese. Any kind of mushrooms can be used, but the more flavoursome they are, the better the soup will turn out. Do not use porcini (Boletus edulus), as they will overpower any other flavour.

SERVES 6

1¾ lb (800 g) assorted fresh
  mushrooms, brushed
  clean
salt and pepper
1 tablespoon lard *or*
  chopped bacon fat
2 fl oz (50 ml) olive oil
1 medium onion, peeled
  and finely sliced
2 large cloves garlic, peeled
  and crushed
1 heaped tablespoon
  tomato purée, diluted
  with 4 tablespoons warm
  water
1¾ pints (1 litre) cold
  water
1 handful parsley, finely
  chopped
4 slices coarse bread *or* 8
  large slices cut diagonally
  from a French stick,
  lightly toasted
3 tablespoons freshly
  grated pecorino *or*
  Parmesan cheese

Lay the mushrooms out on a wide platter and sprinkle with salt. Heat the lard or bacon fat and olive oil and fry the onion and garlic for about 6 minutes, or until transparent. Then add the diluted tomato purée and stir thoroughly. Add the mushrooms and stir, then pour in the water. Season generously with pepper and bring to the boil, then stir in the chopped parsley and remove from the heat. Lay the toasted bread in the bottom of a warmed soup tureen, pour the soup over the bread and sprinkle with the cheese, then serve at once.

NOTE

If you don't want to salt the mushrooms to make them exude their juices, the flavour will not change, but the texture will be slightly different.

ZUPPA alla GENOVESE
Genoese Borage and Lettuce Soup

Equal quantities of borage and fresh lettuce combine to make a soup with a perfect summery flavour. This Ligurian soup is perfect for showing off the intensity of the fresh local herbs. All Ligurian dishes feature herbs: even the traditional trenette (thin ribbons of pasta) are studded green with chopped herbs mixed into the dough. Wild or cultivated herbs work equally well – but if you are going to pick wild herbs, please make sure you know which are the edible ones!

SERVES 4

11 oz (300 g) borage, washed and trimmed

11 oz (300 g) cos lettuce leaves, washed and trimmed

salt and pepper

3½ tablespoons olive oil

1 onion, peeled and finely chopped

1 handful mixed fresh herbs, finely chopped

pinch ground mixed spice

3 large eggs, beaten

3 heaped tablespoons grated Parmesan cheese

2 pints (1.2 litres) best-quality chicken broth (see page 289)

Bring a saucepan containing enough salted water to cover the borage and lettuce to the boil. Plunge in the borage and lettuce and cook for 1 minute, then drain and rinse in cold water. Squeeze it in your fists to remove all excess liquid, then chop finely.

Heat 3 tablespoons of the oil in a deep pan and fry the onion and herbs for 5 minutes. Stir in the chopped lettuce and borage, season with salt, mixed spice and pepper. Cover and cook very gently for 30 minutes. Turn the mixture out into an oiled heatproof bowl and allow to cool completely.

Mix the eggs and cheese together, then pour them into the bowl. Stir everything together very carefully, then place the bowl in a deep saucepan containing hot water. The water should come three quarters of the way up the outside of the bowl.

Place over a medium heat and cook for about 10 minutes or until the eggs have set. Take off the heat, remove the bowl from the saucepan and allow to cool. Turn out the contents of the bowl and slice into little-finger-sized strips. Bring the broth to the boil, then slip in the strips. As soon as the broth returns to the boil, serve the soup.

BORAGE

Fresh herbs, particularly basil and borage, are widely used in Liguria. Sweet basil is pounded to a paste with olive oil, pine kernels and Parmesan cheese to make the world-famous Pesto; and it is used in many other local recipes. The lesser known herb, borage, is also used a great deal. It has a fairly mild flavour which blends especially well with vegetables and in soups. Borage is also chopped very finely and kneaded into hand-made pasta for a delightfully speckled effect.

ZUPPA di FINOCCHI SELVATICI
Wild Fennel Soup

Despite its title, this deliciously refreshing Sardinian soup works equally well with cultivated fennel. It's a baked soup, with a delicate flavour, which makes it rather unusual.

SERVES 4

1 large handful wild fennel
  or 4 bulbs cultivated
  fennel with as many
  leaves as possible
salt
24–30 × 1 inch (2.5 cm)
  cubes white crustless
  bread
5 oz (150 g) unsalted butter
4 oz (100 g) stracchino *or*
  Bel Paese cheese, thinly
  sliced

Pre-heat the oven to gas mark 4, 350°F (180°C).

Wash and trim and finely slice the fennel, cover with cold water, add a large pinch of salt and cook on top of the stove for about 10 minutes or until tender. Don't drain. Fry the bread in about two thirds of the butter until crisp and golden. Use half of the remaining butter to grease an ovenproof dish large enough to take the fennel and the cheese. Arrange the fried bread, cheese and fennel in layers in the dish. Pour the water from the fennel over the top, dot with the remaining butter and bake in the oven for 20 minutes. Serve directly from the dish.

ZUPPA di ORTICHE
Nettle Soup

In the Molise, where I found this recipe, they consider young nettle stalks to have a flavour superior to that of asparagus! This is a delicate soup, made in the springtime when nettle stalks are at their most tender. (Be sure to wear gloves all the time you are handling the raw nettles!) A similar soup is made in Campobasso in the winter months, using tender cardoons as an alternative.

SERVES 4

1½ lb (750 g) stinging
   nettles (stalks only)
2 oz (50 g) pancetta *or*
   unsmoked streaky bacon
1 medium onion, peeled
   and finely sliced
6 tablespoons olive oil
8 oz (225 g) fresh ripe *or*
   canned tomatoes, peeled,
   de-seeded and chopped
salt
1¾ pints (1.2 litres) water

Put on a pair of thick gloves, remove all the leaves from the nettles and throw the leaves away. Remove the strings from the nettle stalks as you would with celery or string beans. Chop the stalks finely and weigh them again to be sure you have the correct amount – you should have about 1½ lb (750 g). Wash and dry them.

Fry the pancetta or bacon and the onion in the oil until the onion is soft and the pancetta or bacon nicely browned.

Add the tomatoes and stir. Simmer for about 10 minutes, then add the chopped nettle stalks and enough boiling water to cover them. Simmer, covered, for about 30 minutes, adding boiling water every now and again and stirring frequently to blend the ingredients thoroughly. You can purée the finished soup in a liquidiser or food processor if you wish. If you do, heat it through again before serving. Transfer to a warmed soup tureen and serve.

ZUPPA di CARDI AQUILANI
Cardoon Soup

Cardoons that come from Aquila are famous throughout the entire country for their size and quality. They appear to be somewhat hard to get hold of in the UK (I wonder why? The climate is so perfect for them!), so large crispy fen celery is one substitute, or Jerusalem artichokes, or half celeriac and half Jerusalem artichokes. I have seen cardoons growing in herbaceous borders in the UK, but why not in the vegetable patch? They are such a delicious and versatile vegetable.

SERVES 4–6

1 × 2 lb (1 kg) cardoon *or* 2 lb (1 kg) celery *or* Jerusalem artichokes *or* celeriac
juice of 1 lemon
salt and pepper
11 oz (300 g) veal, finely minced
10 oz (275 g) Parmesan cheese grated
3 large eggs, beaten
6 tablespoons sunflower *or* mildly flavoured olive oil
4 tablespoons unsalted butter
4 oz (100 g) chicken giblets, trimmed, washed and chopped
½ glass dry white wine
½ teaspoon tomato purée
2½ pints (1.5 litres) hot chicken or other poultry broth (see page 289)
2 stale white bread rolls, cubed
oil for deep-frying

Clean and cube the cardoon or other vegetable(s), being sure to strip off any stringy parts. Wash carefully and place in a basin. Cover with fresh cold water and add the lemon juice and a large pinch of salt. Soak for about 15 minutes, then drain, transfer to a saucepan and cover with fresh water. Boil for about 15 minutes or until tender.

Mix the veal, half the Parmesan, 2 of the eggs and a little salt and pepper together and shape them into hazelnut-sized balls. Heat half the sunflower or olive oil and butter and fry the meatballs quickly. Drain on kitchen paper and set aside.

Fry the giblets in the remaining oil and butter for 4 minutes. Pour the wine over the giblets and allow the fumes to evaporate, then add the tomato purée and the cooked cardoon or other vegetable(s). Pour the hot broth over this mixture, stir and cook for 2 minutes, then add the meatballs and simmer, covered, for 15 minutes.

Soak the bread cubes in the remaining egg for about 10 minutes, then deep-fry in hot oil until golden and crisp. Drain on kitchen paper.

Transfer the soup to a warmed tureen, mix in the hot fried bread and cover with grated Parmesan. Serve at once.

ZUPPA di PESCE LUCANA
Lucanian Fish Soup

This recipe for a very simple fish soup comes from the fishing port of Maratea in Basilicata. Like all recipes from this poverty-stricken area, it is almost completely devoid of any fancy ingredients and is made with what is easily available. You can recognise its origin almost at once, thanks to the presence of the diavolicchio *(little devil) or chilli pepper among the ingredients. Most recipes from Basilicata use large quantities of chilli. As it is more like a fish stew than a smooth soup, the dish can be served as a main or first course. The bread layer underneath serves a useful purpose, absorbing flavour and liquid from the soup itself.*

SERVES 6

2¼ lb (1.2 kg) assorted fresh white and rock fish (such as cod, coley, red mullet, eel, huss, monkfish)

2 large cloves garlic, peeled and crushed

2 fl oz (50 ml) olive oil

salt

1 handful parsley, finely chopped

about ½ teaspoon chilli powder

½ dried red chilli pepper, left intact

10 fl oz (300 ml) cold water

4 slices coarse bread *or* 8 slices cut diagonally from a French stick, lightly toasted

Wash and dry the fish, then cut it all into equal-sized chunks.

In a large pan fry the garlic in the olive oil until it is soft and transparent, then add the fish and seal it on all sides. Sprinkle with salt to taste. Scatter in the parsley, then add chilli powder to taste and the ½ chilli. Cover with the water, place a lid on the pan and simmer for about 30 minutes or until the fish is just falling apart. Remove the ½ chilli and discard it. Lay the bread in the bottom of a warmed soup tureen, pour the fish soup on top and serve at once.

CIUPPIN

Fish Soup with Garlic and Wine

This is a combination of various kinds of fish blended into a creamy soup with vegetables, a hint of garlic and wine. It makes a wonderfully satisfying soup, with a layer of coarse toasted bread lining each plate. If you like, you can allow it to cool and thicken, then use it as a sauce to dress pasta. It is a very traditional recipe from Liguria and an excellent way of using cheap fish that you might not bother buying for anything else.

SERVES 6

3 lb (1.5 kg) assorted fish (such as coley, red mullet, mackerel, cod, hake)

1 onion, peeled and chopped

1 stick celery, chopped

1 carrot, scraped and chopped

2 cloves garlic, peeled and chopped

1 handful parsley, chopped

½ wine glass best-quality olive oil

1 glass dry white wine

4 canned tomatoes, de-seeded and chopped

½ dried red chilli pepper (optional)

2½ pints (1.5 litres) boiling water

salt and pepper

12 small or 6 large slices coarse white bread *or* baguette

Gut and clean the fish, then divide it into groups according to how long each type of fish will take to cook. (The fleshier the fish, the longer it will take.)

In a large deep pan, fry the onion, celery, carrot, garlic and parsley in the olive oil for about 6 minutes over a very low heat so that the onion does not brown. Then pour in the wine, stir and raise the heat. Stir until you can no longer smell wine, then lower the heat.

Add the tomatoes and the chilli (if using). Stir and simmer for 2–3 minutes, then add the water, season, cover and simmer for 20 minutes. Add the fish, starting with the kinds that take longest to cook. Check the seasoning and cover.

Simmer for about 10 minutes – the fish should be just starting to fall apart. To test if it is done, insert a knife into the centre: the flesh should flake. Remove from the heat and cool slightly. Remove the chilli, if using, and discard. Push all the fish and the liquid through a sieve or mouli, reducing everything to a smooth purée. (For a thicker consistency, do not sieve all the liquid but leave some in the pan.) Discard what is left in the sieve, return the smooth soup to the pan and bring to a slow boil. Toast the bread and lay one or two slices in the bottom of each of 6 warmed soup plates.

Pour the soup on top of the bread and serve.

Il CACCIUCCO del CINQUALE
Cinquale Fish Soup

Ever since I can remember, the largest and undoubtedly the best portion of my summer holidays has been spent on the beach at Cinquale, a tiny seaside resort near my family home in Tuscany on the Versilia coast. My family has been going to the same stabilimento *(privately run beach, of which there are literally hundreds up and down the Italian coast) since my brothers were babies, and there is some comfort in spending one's holiday time surrounded by familiar faces. Although the area has changed enormously, and the beach at Cinquale has expanded in terms of deck chairs and beach umbrellas and the more exotic refreshments available at the bar, the spirit has not altered at all. Giovanna is one of the women who run the beach and here is her recipe for the delicious chunky fish soup, originally from the port city of Livorno.*

SERVES 6

equal amounts of
  cuttlefish, shrimps and
  prawns, mussels, huss,
  red mullet, octopus, cod,
  hake or any other white
  fish, giving a total weight
  of approximately 6 lb
  (2.75 kg)
7 cloves garlic, peeled
8 tablespoons olive oil
½ red chilli pepper, de-
  seeded and chopped
12 tablespoons passata *or*
  equivalent whole canned
  tomatoes
2 glasses dry white wine
salt
12 slices coarse white bread
  or slices from a French
  stick

Prepare and clean all the fish. Divide it up into 2 piles, one of white fish and one of all the other varieties.

Crush 4 of the garlic cloves and fry them in the oil with the chilli for about 5 minutes, then add the non-white fish, stir and cook for a few minutes. Add the passata or whole tomatoes and the wine and season with salt, cover and leave to simmer very slowly for about 30 minutes.

In a separate pan, boil all the white fish in enough water to cover it, with a little salt. When cooked, push the white fish through a sieve to make a thin soup. Stir this into the rest of the fish. Toast the bread lightly, rub it with the remaining garlic and lay it at the bottom of a large warmed soup tureen or bowl. Pour the soup over it and serve at once.

PASTA, RICE, GNOCCHI

Le LASAGNE DI ALESSANDRA
Alessandra's Lasagne

The Delle Fratte family live on top of a hill just outside the lovely little town of Zagarolo in the province of Rome. All of us who were there will remember the genuine hospitality and warmth that we were given that day. The luncheon we were invited to was to celebrate the birth of my nephew, Lytton Scott, whose mother is a very close friend of the Delle Frattes. So this Lasagne, cooked by Alessandra Delle Fratte, the eldest daughter, was really in his honour. Maybe it should be re-named Lytton's Lasagne!

SERVES 6

For the pasta

1¼ lb (500 g) plain white
    flour
6 large brown eggs
pinch salt
1 teaspoon olive oil
or 1¼ lb (500 g) dried
    lasagne

For the filling

1 onion, peeled and finely
    chopped
14 oz (400 g) lean minced
    beef
2 tablespoons olive oil
18 fl oz (500 ml) passata *or*
    sieved canned tomatoes
salt and pepper

Pre-heat the oven to gas mark 6, 400°F (200°C).

Make the pasta as usual (see page 298), roll it out and cut it into strips about as wide as the palm of your hand. Boil these 3 at a time in plenty of salted water (a spoonful of oil in the water will prevent them sticking) and lay them on a damp tablecloth until required. (I recommend that you do this once the meat filling is simmering.) If you are using dried pasta, follow the instructions on the packet.

To make the filling fry the onion and beef in the oil until the meat is well browned and the onion is soft. Stir in the passata, add salt and pepper, cover and simmer for about 30 minutes.

To make the Besciamella melt the butter in a second saucepan, add the flour and stir vigorously to make a roux. Add the milk and stir thoroughly. Simmer gently for about 25 minutes, or until you can no longer taste flour. Season to taste with salt and nutmeg.

Minestrone con la Zucca (page 87)

Top: The brilliant purples of the beans
on sale at a Trento market.
Bottom: Edible flowers from the
courgette plant.

For the Besciamella

3 oz (75 g) butter

4 level tablespoons plain white flour

18 fl oz (500 ml) milk

salt

grated nutmeg

4 oz (100 g) mozzarella cheese, cubed

3 oz (75 g) Parmesan cheese, grated

Cover the bottom of a 9 inch (23 cm) baking dish with a layer of Besciamella. Arrange a layer of pasta on top, cover with a layer of meat sauce and another of Besciamella. Scatter cubes of mozzarella and grated Parmesan on top. Continue in this way until you have filled the dish. The last layer should be of Besciamella, over which you should sprinkle any leftover mozzarella or Parmesan.

Bake for 20 minutes. Remove from the oven, leave for 5 minutes to allow it to set so you can cut it easily, then serve.

SPAGHETTI alla CARBONARA
Spaghetti Carbonara

This is my own version of this classic dish. There are two stories about its origins. Some say it was created by the carbonari *(the charcoal makers). As it requires very little cooking and all the ingredients are transportable, they were able to make it on an open fire. Others say that it was invented to satisfy the American allies who became fed up with spaghetti and tomato sauce and demanded 'ham and eggs'. With typical Italian flair, local cooks created a dish using ham and eggs, without leaving out the spaghetti!*

SERVES 4

14 oz (400 g) spaghetti

salt and plenty of freshly ground black pepper

4 large eggs, beaten

4 heaped tablespoons grated Parmesan cheese

about 1 tablespoon softened butter

6-8 rashers streaky bacon, cut into small squares

Bring a large pan of salted water to a rolling boil. Add the spaghetti, stir and cook for the required time. (Check the instructions on the packet, as brands vary.)

Meanwhile, beat the eggs, cheese and butter together and grill the bacon until crisp, reserving the fat. When the pasta is *al dente* (firm to the bite) drain it and return to the pan. Pour over the egg mixture, the bacon and its fat, and freshly ground black pepper. When the eggs are lightly scrambled, transfer to a serving dish. Add more butter for a richer finish.

97

LASAGNE VERDE
alla BOLOGNESE
Green Lasagne Bolognese

This is the most original and most traditional version of the quintessential Bolognese dish which has become so popular (and has been so bastardised) all over the world. Starting from this basic recipe, many other traditional versions of the dish have since evolved. If lasagne verde (green lasagne) is not your favourite, the white, plain variety works equally well.

Because of its lengthy preparation, this dish is reserved for special occasions.

SERVES 6

For the meat sauce

4 oz (100 g) pork loin, boned

4 oz (100 g) beef steak, boned

4 oz (100 g) prosciutto crudo

4 oz (100 g) unsalted butter

1 carrot, finely chopped

1 stick celery, finely chopped

1 onion, finely chopped

2 oz (50 g) pancetta *or* bacon, finely chopped

1 heaped tablespoon tomato purée diluted with 1 glass hot water

salt and pepper

1½ ladles hot broth *or* water

4 oz (100 g) chicken livers, washed, trimmed and finely chopped

6 tablespoons double or single cream

1 small truffle, cleaned and thinly sliced (optional)

Pre-heat the oven to gas mark 4, 350°F (180°C).

Have ready a suitable ovenproof dish which is attractive enough to carry to the table – 9 × 12 × 3 inches (23 × 30 × 7.5 cm) is approximately the right size for the quantity of lasagne made in this recipe. A square or oblong dish is easier to use than a round or oval one.

Make the meat sauce first. Mince or process the pork, beef and prosciutto crudo together. Melt half the butter and fry the carrot, celery, onion and pancetta or bacon for 5–6 minutes. Then add the minced meats, pour in the diluted tomato purée, season and stir. Cover and leave to simmer for about 1 hour. During this time never let it dry out, but keep adding a little hot broth or water and stir it frequently.

Meanwhile, prepare the pasta. Squeeze the spinach completely dry in your hands, and push it through a sieve or process to a pulp. Put about 11 oz (300 g) of the flour in a mound on a work-surface, plunge your fist in the centre to make a hollow and put the spinach purée into this hollow. Break the eggs on top of the spinach and add a large pinch of salt. Knead all this together with your hands, adding a little more flour as necessary as you will need a fairly stiff dough. Roll it and fold it over as normal several times until you hear it 'pop' (see page

For the pasta

11 oz (300 g) cooked
  spinach
12 oz (350 g) plain white
  flour
2 large eggs
salt

1 quantity Besciamella (see
  page 291)
4 oz (100 g) Parmesan
  cheese, grated

298), and then roll it out to a thickness of ¼ inch (5 mm). Cut it up into strips about 4½ inches (11 cm) wide and long enough to fit the dish you are using to bake the lasagne in.

Make the Besciamella (see page 291). Season and brush the top with a little butter to prevent a skin forming. Set it aside in a warm place.

Bring a very large pan of salted water to the boil and cook the pasta strips in it 1 or 2 at a time for about 2 minutes. Remove them with a fish slice, rinse in cold water and lay out on a wet tablecloth without letting them overlap or touch each other. Continue until all the pasta strips are cooked and laid out on the tablecloth.

By this time the meat sauce should be ready. Stir in the chicken livers and cook for 5 minutes, then pour in the cream and add the truffle (if using). Stir and taste, adjusting the seasoning if necessary, heat through for 2 minutes and remove from the heat.

At this point you must clear the decks as much as possible to give yourself room to assemble the dish. You will need your ovenproof dish, the Besciamella, the pasta strips, the meat sauce, the remaining butter and the Parmesan. Everything else can be washed up and put away.

Butter the dish, then arrange a layer of pasta strips on the bottom. Cover with a layer of meat sauce, then a layer of Besciamella, then some Parmesan. Continue in this way until you have used up all your ingredients. The last layer should be pasta covered with a thin coating of Besciamella with the last scraps of butter dotted over it and a final dusting of Parmesan. Now the dish is ready for the oven. Bake it for 30 minutes, remove and rest for 5 minutes and serve it directly from the dish. Resting it in this way makes it much easier to cut and serve.

VINCISGRASSI

Layered Pasta Baked with Mushrooms and Chicken

Vincisgrassi is probably the most typical of the many layered pasta dishes of the Marche. It follows the tradition of richly stuffed and filling food, and is full of flavour and very rich in texture. The story goes that it was first prepared by the cook of the Austrian General Windisch-Graetz, who held a very powerful position in this area during the Napoleonic Wars. The Italian title of the recipe is a local version of his name.

To allow the flavours to develop, it is best made the day before you eat it. If you don't want to make the pasta yourself, you can use bought, fresh pasta squares suitable for making lasagne-type dishes. This dish is a lot of hard work, but well worth the effort if you can manage the time. My mother used always to make it for special family occasions like birthdays.

SERVES 6

For the pasta

11 oz (300 g) plain white flour

5 oz (150 g) semolina

1 oz (25 g) unsalted butter

2–3 tablespoons Marsala wine

3 large eggs

or 1 lb (450 g) ready-made fresh lasagne

For the rest of the dish

2 oz (50 g) dried porcini mushrooms *or* 4 oz (100 g) fresh mushrooms, thinly sliced

3 oz (75 g) unsalted butter

1 onion, peeled and chopped

1 fresh or canned black truffle, thinly sliced (optional)

Make the pasta as usual, using the flour, semolina, unsalted butter, Marsala and eggs. Proceed as you would for normal egg and flour pasta (see page 298). Roll it out as thinly as possible, and cut it into oblong strips about 4 × 6 inches (10 × 15 cm). Alternatively you can use bought fresh pasta. Cook in plenty of boiling salted water, 4 or 5 pieces at a time, for about 3 minutes each. Remove them from the water with a fish slice, then lay them all out on a wet tablecloth without overlapping, until you need them.

If using dried porcini mushrooms, soak them in tepid water for 15 minutes. Drain and chop coarsely.

Melt about 2 oz (50 g) of the butter in a large saucepan, then add the onion. Fry very gently for about 5 minutes. Add the mushrooms and the truffle, if using. Cook for about 5 minutes, stirring. Then add the stock, stir and simmer very gently for a further 10 minutes.

Add the strips of chicken breast and cook for about 3 minutes on each side. Add the chicken

4 tablespoons very rich
   chicken stock (see page
   292)
3 plump chicken breasts,
   weighing in total about
   2 lb (1 kg), skinned,
   boned and sliced into
   finger-sized strips
11 oz (300 g) chicken livers,
   trimmed, washed and
   chopped
4 tablespoons Madeira
   wine
5 tablespoons boiling water
salt and pepper
1 quantity thick
   Besciamella (see page
   291)
3 oz (75 g) Parmesan
   cheese, grated

To finish
½ quantity Besciamella
   (see page 291), made
   with 14 fl oz (400 ml)
   milk to give a runny
   sauce

livers, and fry them quickly until they are no longer dark red. Add the Madeira, bring the heat up to evaporate the alcohol for 1 minute, then add the boiling water, cover and simmer for about 25 minutes over a very low heat. Season with salt and pepper, then stir in the thick Besciamella.

Butter an ovenproof dish thoroughly, cover the bottom with a layer of pasta, and sprinkle a little Parmesan on top. Then pour some of the chicken filling over the pasta, spread it out evenly and sprinkle with more Parmesan. Cover with another layer of pasta and continue in this way until you end up with a final top layer of pasta. Dot the top with all the remaining butter. Leave the dish to rest for 6 hours, preferably overnight.

The next day, pre-heat the oven to gas mark 7, 425°F (220°C). Cover the rested dish with the runny Besciamella and put it into the oven to bake for 30 minutes. Leave for 5 minutes before serving, as it will be easier to slice if it is not bubbling hot.

PASTA alla NORMA come la fa ELEONORA

Eleonora's Pasta alla Norma

Eleonora Consoli made this for me and the Count and Countess Notabartolo di Salandra at their country estate of Lentini, in southern Sicily. The Lentini estate functions as an Agriturismo organisation – in other words, you can go there for lunch (and soon it will be possible to stay overnight as well) and enjoy genuine Sicilian country food in a lovely simple setting.

Eleonora Consoli is a great expert on Sicilian food and has written a huge two-volume book on her subject. She also presents a RAI television programme devoted to the superb cuisine of Sicily. As an old family friend of the Notabartolo family, it was she who introduced me to Lentini. I can definitely recommend it as a lovely place to eat or spend a leisurely holiday, and the wine is wonderful too!

SERVES 4–6

1 large aubergine
salt and pepper
10 canned tomatoes, de-
    seeded and chopped
1 clove garlic, peeled
1 teaspoon granulated
    sugar
2 tablespoons olive oil
oil for deep-frying
14 oz (400 g) maccheroni
4 oz (100 g) salted ricotta
    or Parmesan cheese,
    grated
1 very generous handful
    fresh basil leaves, torn up
    with your fingers

Peel the aubergine and slice it into rounds, lay them out in a colander and sprinkle them generously with salt. Put a plate on top and put the colander in the sink for 1 hour to allow the bitter juices of the aubergine to drain out.

Meanwhile, put the tomatoes in a pan and cook them gently over a moderate heat for 10 minutes. Then add a pinch of salt, the whole garlic clove, a little pepper, the sugar and olive oil. Stir thoroughly and continue to cook for another 15 minutes, or until the sauce has reduced and thickened, stirring occasionally.

Wash the aubergine and dry it carefully. Heat the oil until sizzling hot, then deep-fry the aubergine slices until golden brown on both sides. Remove them from the oil, drain them very thoroughly on kitchen paper and cut them into cubes.

Bring a large pan of salted water to the boil, toss in the pasta and cook until *al dente* or firm to the bite. (See the instructions on the packet for cooking times, as brands vary.)

Drain the pasta very thoroughly, return it to the pan and add half the tomato sauce. Mix the pasta and tomato sauce together and transfer it to a warmed serving dish or large bowl. Sprinkle the pasta with a thick layer of grated cheese and all the cubed aubergine. Cover with the other half of the tomato sauce, then more cheese and finally the basil. Serve at once.

SPAGHETTI AGLIO, OLIO e PEPERONCINO

Spaghetti with Garlic, Oil and Chilli Pepper

This dish, of spaghetti with garlic- and chilli-flavoured olive oil, is one of the simplest and most delicious ways of preparing pasta. You must use good-quality olive oil, preferably one that has a strong flavour. The amount of chilli and garlic you use depends on your personal taste.

This dish is a very good cure for a hangover, especially if you eat it just before you retire for the night. In Rome, it is sometimes served at the end of the meal, after the dessert, to help you digest and ward off the effects of alcohol. I can remember creeping home after late-night disco sessions, giggling furiously, and making great bowlfuls of it with seventeen people helping! My parents must have been woken up by the smell, if nothing else!

A plea from the heart: please wash your hands very carefully after rubbing the chilli, just in case you accidentally rub your eyes.

SERVES 4
salt and pepper
14 oz (400 g) spaghetti or spaghettini
4 fl oz (120 ml) good-quality, strong olive oil
2-5 cloves garlic, peeled and lightly crushed
½-3 dried red chilli peppers, rubbed between your hands to release maximum flavour

Bring a large pot of salted water to a rolling boil, toss in the pasta and stir. Cook until *al dente* – firm to the bite. (Check the instructions on the packet for timing, as brands vary.) While the spaghetti is cooking, heat the oil without burning it in a separate pan with the garlic and chillies. Drain the spaghetti and transfer to a warm bowl. Remove the garlic and chillies from the oil and discard them, then pour the oil over the spaghetti and toss together. Add pepper to taste and serve, without cheese.

PISAREI e FASÒ
Pisarei with Beans

This is a very nourishing dish of hand-made pasta mixed with beans.

If tagliatelle are the glorious representation of Bologna's culinary heritage, then these shell-shaped pasta are Piacenza's greatest pride and glory.

In days gone by, before a girl married, her prospective in-laws would subject her right thumb to close scrutiny. If it revealed a collection of small calluses then it was obvious that the girl was used to making pisarei and it therefore logically followed that she would make a good wife and mother! Perhaps this is just legend, but what is certain is that to make this intricate pasta shape requires great practice and expertise – it is indeed an art!

Pisarei were once much more widely available than they are nowadays. These days they are considered more of a gastronomic speciality reserved for festive occasions. Like many other things, they have fallen victim to the high speed of current living.

SERVES 4

For the pasta

1 lb (450 g) plain white
  flour
1½ oz (40 g) stale white
  bread, grated
about 5–7 tablespoons very
  hot water

For the sauce

8 oz (225 g) dried borlotti
  or cannelini beans,
  soaked overnight, *or*
  equivalent canned
1 onion, peeled
1 tablespoon olive oil
2 oz (50 g) unsalted butter
1½ oz (40 g) lard
1 clove garlic, peeled and
  crushed
2 tablespoons chopped
  parsley

Three hours before you wish to eat, drain and wash the beans. Place in a pan and cover with fresh cold water. Cut the onion in half and add one half to the beans (set aside the remaining half). Add the olive oil and cover with a tight-fitting lid. Cook over a moderate heat for 1 hour or until the beans are just tender. Do not add salt at this stage as it hardens the skin of the beans. Drain the beans, reserving the cooking water.

Meanwhile, make the pasta. Tip almost all the flour on to a work-surface, mix in the bread and add enough hot water to make a pliable dough. Work at it, kneading and rolling, for about 15 minutes. Then break off a piece and roll it out to the size of a pencil. Keep the rest of the dough under a cloth. Break a piece off the end of the 'pencil' and press it down with your thumb to make it concave. You should end up with a shell shape the size of a very large butter bean.

Continue in this way with all the dough,

9 canned tomatoes, de-
   seeded and chopped
6–7 leaves fresh basil
pinch ground white pepper
salt
5 oz (150 g) Parmesan
   cheese, grated

using the leftover flour to help you as you work. Keep the surface and your hands lightly floured. Lay the shells out as soon as they are ready on a lightly floured cloth.

Then continue with the sauce. Finely chop the reserved onion half and fry in a deep, heavy-bottomed pan with the butter. Mash the lard with the garlic and parsley and add it to the butter and onion. Mix together and cook for 5–6 minutes. Add the tomatoes, stir and continue to cook. Pour about 1 glassful of the reserved cooking water from the beans into the pan, add the beans, basil and pepper, but no salt yet! Stir and cover. Simmer for a further hour, or until the beans are very tender. The mixture should be quite wet; if it seems to be drying out, add more of the reserved bean water. Then add salt to taste.

Bring a big pan of salted water to the boil, toss in the pisarei and cook them for 15 minutes. As they come up to the surface, remove them with a large slotted spoon and transfer to a warm bowl with the beans and their sauce. Toss very thoroughly. When all the pisarei are in the bowl, add the Parmesan, toss once more and serve at once.

NOTE
Pisarei can also be served with other dressings, e.g. Tomato (see page 284) or Ragu (see page 282).

MALTAGLIATI con SALSA al POMODORO
Rough-cut Pasta with Tomato Sauce

Maltagliati *translates literally as 'badly cut', which makes this the easiest pasta shape to make by hand – perfect for beginners and children! The tomato sauce is also simplicity itself. The recipe is from Tuscany.*

SERVES 6

For the pasta

1¼ lb (500 g) plain white flour

6 large eggs

pinch salt

or 1 lb (450 g) ready-made fresh pasta

For the sauce

1 carrot, finely chopped

1 onion, finely chopped

1 stick celery, finely chopped

2 tablespoons chopped mixed fresh herbs or
2 tablespoons parsley or
½ teaspoon dried mixed herbs

3 tablespoons cooking oil or margarine or butter or olive oil or lard

1 × 14 oz (400 g) can tomatoes, drained and puréed

salt and pepper

grated Parmesan cheese to serve

Tip the flour on to a work-surface and plunge your fist into the centre. Break the eggs into the hole and add a pinch of salt. Knead together and continue to make the pasta dough in the usual way (see page 298). Leave it to rest while you prepare the sauce.

Fry the carrot, onion, celery and herbs in the oil or fat for about 6 minutes or until the onion is translucent and soft. Stir in the tomatoes thoroughly, season with salt and pepper and cover. Simmer for about 30 minutes.

Roll out the pasta dough and divide it into 3 sheets. Fold each sheet into 3 and cut across to the centre, on a slant from left to right, then do it again in the other direction from right to left. Cut straight across to create a straight edge. Repeat, until you have cut all your dough into irregular, vaguely triangular shapes. Scatter them, opened out, on a floured work-surface and leave them to dry out a little for about 10–20 minutes. Bring a large pan of salted water to the boil, toss in the pasta and cook for 2–3 minutes, drain and return to the pan.

Pour over the tomato sauce, toss together thoroughly and arrange in a warmed dish. Serve immediately, with plenty of grated Parmesan handed separately.

MACCHERONI di FUOCO
Fiery Macaroni

This is not a dish for people who dislike hot, spicy food! In Basilicata, which is where the recipe comes from, chilli pepper features very strongly in all the local dishes. The pasta is turned a brilliant, fiery red, but do please warn your guests that the redness comes from the chillies and not tomatoes!

Chilli was once believed to be a sure cure for everything from malaria to worms and other health problems which have ravaged this region so badly over the centuries of neglect. In an area with such poor soil, it was the one thing which seemed to grow happily and vigorously.

Again, please wash your hands very carefully after handling chilli just in case you rub your eyes or lips accidentally.

SERVES 4

14 oz (400 g) bucatini *or* other hollow dried durum wheat pasta
1 wine glass olive oil
4 cloves garlic, peeled
6 dried red chilli peppers, left whole
salt

Bring a large pan of salted water to the boil. Toss in the pasta, stir and cook for 10–12 minutes or until the pasta is *al dente* – firm to the bite. (Check the instructions on the packet, as cooking times vary according to brand.)

Pour half the oil into a frying-pan and add 3 of the garlic cloves and the chillies. Stir over a medium heat until the chillies have swollen up and become shiny. Don't let the garlic or the chillies burn. Remove from the heat, pour into a food processor or liquidiser and reduce to a creamy consistency. (Alternatively, remove the chillies and garlic from the oil, pound them to a pulp with a pestle in a mortar, then stir the pulp back into the oil.)

Wipe the pan, then put the rest of the oil into the pan with the last clove of garlic and fry over a medium heat until the garlic is golden brown. Stir in the chilli and garlic sauce. Stir and simmer for about 5 minutes. Remove the whole garlic clove and add salt to taste. Drain the pasta and transfer to a warmed bowl, pour over the sauce, toss together very thoroughly and serve at once.

I TAJARIN di GIORGIO ROCCA
Giorgio Rocca's Tajarin

Tajarin are a Piedmontese form of tagliatelle, but slightly narrower.

This delectable recipe from the Alba province of Piedmont was cooked for me by Giorgio Rocca, who is the authority on Piedmontese food, at his restaurant Al Giardino da Felicin in Monforte d'Alba, a tiny village deep in the Langhe hills of Piedmont.

To use truffles you really need a truffle shaver, but a cheese grater will do equally well. The important thing is to get fine flakes rather than chunks.

The size of the truffle used in the dish depends entirely on what you can afford! But in my opinion there is nothing better to splash out on than this marvellous bit of luxury; you can keep all your Beluga caviar and smoked salmon and champagne – I'll just have a truffle, thank you! Nothing in the world can beat this as a special occasion treat.

SERVES 4

For the pasta

1 lb (450 g) plain white
   flour
4 egg yolks
or 1 lb (450 g) ready-made
   fresh or dried tagliatelle

For the sauce

1 white truffle
3½ oz (90 g) unsalted
   butter
8 tablespons freshly grated
   Parmesan cheese
large pinch white pepper
large pinch nutmeg
1 tablespoon hot chicken
   broth (see page 289)
salt

Make the pasta first. Pile the flour on to a work-surface. Make a hole in the centre with your fist. Put the egg yolks into the hollow and blend them into the flour with your fingertips. Knead the dough until it is smooth and elastic. Roll and fold it over several times, until you hear a 'pop' as the pin rolls over the fold and the air is forced out (see page 298). Roll it out thinly for the last time, then cut it evenly into strips ¼ inch (5 mm) wide. Lay out on a floured cloth until needed.

Brush the truffle carefully to remove every trace of earth and grit. Melt the butter over a low heat, stir in the cheese, pepper and nutmeg, then stir in the hot broth. Keep this mixture warm. Bring a large pan of salted water to the boil. Slide the pasta into the boiling water and cook for just 1 minute, then drain and return to the saucepan. (If using dried pasta, cook according to the instructions on the packet.) Dress with the butter mixture and toss thoroughly. Arrange the pasta on a warmed platter, shave the truffle all over it and serve at once.

VARIATIONS

Instead of truffles, dress the pasta with butter, a few chopped sage leaves and grated Parmesan cheese to taste; chopped ripe tomatoes with chopped basil, garlic and olive oil; or Bolognese sauce (page 282) in which you have lightly cooked some chopped chicken livers.

FUSILLI alla VESUVIANA
Fusilli with Tomato and Mozzarella Sauce

In the Naples area, all plain tomato sauces are cooked for the least possible time, to keep the colour and fragrance intact. Naturally, to do the dish justice, you should be using fresh, red, soft tomatoes such as those which grow in such profusion all over the volcanic-rich fields of Campania; but even with canned tomatoes, this sauce remains one of my most beloved.

SERVES 4

14 oz (400 g) fusilli or other dried durum wheat pasta
salt and pepper
3½ fl oz (100 ml) olive oil
14 oz (400 g) fresh, ripe tomatoes or 1 × 14 oz (400 g) can tomatoes, chopped
4 oz (100 g) mozzarella cheese, thinly sliced
2 oz (50 g) pecorino cheese, grated
generous pinch dried oregano

Pre-heat the oven to gas mark 8, 450°F (230°C).

Bring a big pan of salted water to the boil. Toss in the pasta, stir it and cook it until *al dente* – firm to the bite. (Check the instructions on the packet for timing, as brands vary.)

While the pasta is cooking, put the olive oil in a smaller saucepan with the tomatoes, mozzarella, grated pecorino, oregano and salt and pepper to taste. Mix and cook fast on a high heat for the same amount of time as it takes for the pasta to cook (approximately 9–12 minutes). Drain the pasta and return it to the pan, pour over the sauce and mix well together. Transfer to an ovenproof dish and pop it in the oven for about 5 minutes before serving.

LASAGNE AI SEMI di PAPAVERO
Pasta Ribbons with Brown Butter and Poppy Seeds

Contrary to what many people might think when they read this recipe, it is served as a starter, just like any other pasta dish. At the beginning of this century it was all the rage in the lovely and very fashion-conscious city of Trieste. It is obviously a dish that has filtered into the local traditions from the long period of Austro-Hungarian rule over this area. The original name of the dish is Möhnnudeln (poppy noodles). It has a very traditional and typical sweet flavour which is much loved in the area.

If you are making the pasta yourself, you must prepare this dish well in advance, as the pasta dough has to be left for 24 hours before it is cooked.

SERVES 6

For the pasta

1¼ lb (500 g) plain white flour

6 large eggs

pinch salt

or 1 lb (450 g) ready-made fresh pappardelle or similar wide ribbons of pasta

1 oz (25 g) poppy seeds

½ oz (15 g) rock salt

5 oz (150 g) butter

1½ oz (40 g) caster sugar

Make the pasta dough as usual with the flour, eggs and salt (see page 298). When you have a nice soft dough, cover it with a slightly damp cloth and leave it to rest for 24 hours. Next day, roll it out and cut it into long strips about 1 inch (2.5 cm) wide. (This is known as lasagne in the area around Trieste.)

Crush the poppy seeds with the salt with a pestle and mortar, or alternatively use a food processor.

Bring a large pan of salted water to a rolling boil. Toss the pasta into the boiling water, stir and cook for about 4 minutes. Drain and transfer to a warmed bowl.

In a second pan, heat the butter until it is hazelnut brown. Cover the pasta with the brown butter and toss, then sprinkle with the poppy seeds and sugar and toss once more before serving.

PASTA 'CHI VRUOCCOLI ARRIMINATA'

Pasta Sautéed with Cauliflower

The verb arriminare *is Sicilian dialect for sautéeing food, or moving it about quickly over heat.* Vruoccoli *refers to all members of the cauliflower family. In this quintessentially Sicilian dish, short, stubby pasta tubes are combined with cauliflower florets, then sautéed with garlic, sardines, raisins and other ingredients to make a splendidly exotic concoction, bursting at the seams with treasures from the East and looking not unlike a curry when it is finished!*

SERVES 4

8 fl oz (250 ml) olive oil

3 cloves garlic, peeled and finely sliced

2 sardines preserved in salt, cleaned, *or* 2 sardines canned in oil, drained

2 tablespoons tomato purée diluted with about 3 tablespoons boiling water

salt and pepper

1 medium cauliflower, divided into small florets

1 heaped tablespoon seedless raisins

1 heaped tablespoon pine kernels

¼ teaspoon powdered saffron

14 oz (400 g) short macaroni

3 oz (75 g) pecorino *or* Parmesan cheese, grated, to serve

Heat the oil in a very large pan and add the garlic and the sardines. Allow the sardines to break up, mixing with a fork, then stir in the diluted tomato purée and a little pepper and salt. Cover and simmer slowly for 10 minutes.

Meanwhile, cook the cauliflower in salted water for 8–10 minutes or until half cooked. Drain and reserve the water.

Add the drained cauliflower to the sardine mixture. Stir and simmer, covered, until the cauliflower is completely cooked and soft. Then stir in the raisins, pine kernels and saffron. Remove the pan from direct heat but keep it warm.

Bring the reserved cauliflower water back to the boil, toss in the pasta and stir. Cook until *al dente* or firm to the bite (check the instructions on the packet for timing, as brands vary). Drain and transfer to the pan containing the cauliflower. Sauté all the ingredients together over a low to medium heat, then cover and leave to rest off the heat for about 4 minutes. Transfer to a warmed serving dish and serve with the cheese handed separately.

TAGLIATELLE al PROSCIUTTO di PARMA

Tagliatelle with Parma Ham

In this recipe the delicious tagliatelle are combined with another speciality from the same region – best-quality Parma ham. Tagliatelle are reputed to have been created in honour of Lucrezia Borgia's beautiful golden hair.

SERVES 6

For the pasta

1¼ lb (500 g) plain white
  flour
6 large eggs
salt
or 1 lb (450 g) ready-made
  fresh or dried tagliatelle

5 oz (150 g) prosciutto
  crudo
5 oz (150 g) unsalted butter
¼ large onion, finely
  chopped
freshly ground black pepper
grated Parmesan cheese to
  serve

If you are making your own pasta, prepare the dough with the flour, eggs and salt (see page 298). Let the dough rest under a cloth for 10 minutes, then roll it out as thinly as you can. Fold it into 3 and cut straight across so you have strips ¼ inch (5 mm) thick. Open out the strips as you cut them and let them dry out slightly on a floured work-surface. Alternatively, a hand-turned or electric machine will give you a very even and tidy finish.

Divide the prosciutto into fat and lean parts. Cut each part up finely into small cubes, keeping the fat and lean separate. Put half the butter in a small saucepan over a very low heat and fry the onion for 3 minutes, then add all the fat prosciutto. Cook until the fat has almost melted, then add all the lean prosciutto and cook for another 2–3 minutes. Season with plenty of fresh ground black pepper. Remove from the heat but keep it warm.

Bring a pan of salted water to the boil, toss in the tagliatelle and cook for about 2 minutes. If using dried pasta, cook according to the instructions on the packet. Meanwhile melt the remaining butter. Drain the pasta and transfer to a warmed bowl, pour over the melted butter, and toss together. Add half the prosciutto and toss together again. Make a hollow in the centre of the tagliatelle and put the remaining prosciutto in the hollow before serving. Serve freshly grated Parmesan separately.

Bucatini all'Amatriciana (page 117)

Top: A backstreet in Bari, where ladies spend hours making orecchiette for their families. *Bottom:* Tortellini in Brodo, the very best soup that Emilia Romagna has to offer.

VARIATION

A typically simple, very quick, but wickedly rich dish from Emilia Romagna using fresh cream and cooked peas.

Toss the cooked tagliatelle with 8 oz (225 g) cooked, buttered, warm peas and 10 fl oz (300 ml) warmed double cream. Add freshly grated Parmesan, salt and pepper to taste.

SPAGHETTI alla TARANTINA
Spaghetti with Mussels and Garlic

This is another of Signor Balducci's superb seafood recipes from the Riva del Sole hotel near Bari. Unlike him, I don't know how to shuck mussels open with a graceful flick of my wrist. He opens them first and then cooks them, but I like to cook mussels first because it is the greatest test for their freshness and edibility. So here is the recipe, very slightly adapted, for the most marvellous spaghetti dish that is simplicity itself to prepare.

SERVES 4

30 fresh mussels
salt
12 oz (350 g) spaghetti
4 tablespoons olive oil
3 cloves garlic, peeled and
  finely chopped
freshly ground black
  pepper to taste
1 tablespoon parsley,
  chopped

Steam the mussels in a large pan for about 5–8 minutes. Discard any that have not opened after this time and take the rest out of their shells. Leave to cool. (Save some of the prettier shells for decorating the finished dish.) Strain the liquid and reserve.

Bring a large pan of salted water to a rolling boil, then toss in the spaghetti and cook according to the instructions on the packet.

In a wide, deep pan, heat the oil and fry the garlic for about 5 minutes, then add pepper and parsley.

As soon as the pasta is cooked, strain it and add it to the pan with the cooked mussels and their liquid, strained. Toss to mix all the ingredients. Heat for 1–2 minutes, then serve.

NOTE
Cheese is *never* served with fish pasta dishes!

SPAGHETTI alle VONGOLE
Spaghetti with Baby Clam Sauce

There are two versions of this dish: one is 'red' (with tomato) and one is 'white' (without tomato). The 'red' sauce has the advantage that canned clams can be used, whereas the 'white' version needs live, fresh clams for the sauce to be a success. Here are both versions of this originally Neapolitan dish. As clams bought in the UK are often quite gritty, I recommend you leave them in a basin of cold salty water for about 14 hours before you use them. Change the water frequently and wash them with care. If using fresh clams, some people prefer to remove them from the shells before adding them to the sauce, but I love the musical crashing which the clams make on the sides of the bowl as you serve the finished dish!

'Red' Sauce

SERVES 4

1½ lb (750 g) fresh small clams in their shells *or* canned clams in brine
juice of ½ small lemon
4 tablespoons olive oil
2 cloves garlic, peeled and finely chopped
1 lb (450 g) passata *or* canned tomatoes, sieved
salt and freshly ground black pepper
3 heaped tablespoons chopped parsley
14 oz (400 g) spaghetti *or* vermicelli

If you are using fresh clams, scrub them very thoroughly, then place them in a very large pan with the lemon juice. Put the pan over a medium heat and cover. Shake the pan energetically over the heat for about 8 minutes to help the clams open. Any that have not opened after this time should be thrown away. If using canned clams, drain them thoroughly, rinse briefly and drain again.

Heat the oil in a wide pan and fry the garlic gently for about 5 minutes. Add the passata and stir together. Season, cover and simmer for about 20 minutes. Add plenty of freshly ground black pepper, then the clams, and stir together gently until heated through. Mix in the parsley and remove from the heat.

Bring a big pan of salted water to the boil, toss in the pasta, stir and cook until *al dente* – firm to the bite. (Check the instructions on the packet for timing, as brands vary.) Drain and return to the pan, pour in the warm sauce and toss together quickly. Arrange on a warmed platter or in a bowl and serve at once.

'White' Sauce

SERVES 4

3½ lb (1.5 kg) fresh small
  clams
6 tablespoons olive oil
3 cloves garlic, peeled and
  chopped
salt and freshly ground
  black pepper
14 oz (400 g) spaghetti or
  vermicelli
3 heaped tablespoons
  chopped parsley

Scrub the clams very thoroughly. Place them in a wide pan with 2 tablespoons of the olive oil and cover with a tight-fitting lid. Shake over a medium heat to open up the clams. This should take 8 minutes or less – discard any that have not opened up after this time. Drain the clams, reserving their liquid; strain this and set it aside.

Heat the remaining oil, add the garlic and fry for about 5 minutes. Add the clams and mix together very quickly. Then add the reserved liquid, bring back to the boil and remove from heat. Cover with a lid and keep just warm.

Bring a big pan of salted water to the boil, toss in the pasta and stir. Return to the boil and cook until al dente – firm to the bite. (Check the instructions on the packet for timing, as brands vary.) Drain the pasta and return it to the pan, tip in the clams and toss together, then add the parsley and plenty of freshly ground black pepper. Toss again, arrange on a warm platter or in a bowl and serve.

SPAGHETTI al RAGÙ di TOTANO
Spaghetti with Cuttlefish Sauce

This is one of my all-time favourites, a delightful dish from Calabria using cuttlefish blended with garlic, tomatoes, olive oil and basil. You could use squid (which is widely available frozen from supermarkets) or octopus instead of cuttlefish; and I have also used cubed monkfish, adding it into the pan with the oil, when none of the above were available.

SERVES 4

1 lb 11 oz (750 g) fresh *or* frozen cuttlefish, cleaned and cut into rings or small chunks (see page 177)

salt

3½ fl oz (100 ml) olive oil

1 onion, peeled and finely chopped

2-3 cloves garlic, peeled

1 large tablespoon tomato purée

3 leaves fresh basil *or* ½ teaspoon dried basil *or* 1 tablespoon chopped fresh parsley

pinch granulated sugar

3-4 tablespoons hot water

14 oz (400 g) spaghetti

Wash the fish and put it into a heavy saucepan with a couple of pinches of salt. Place over a lowish heat. The fish will release natural liquid into the saucepan and then re-absorb it. When this liquid is completely re-absorbed (in about 10–15 minutes), pour the oil over the fish, then add the onion and the whole cloves of garlic. Stir and continue to cook until the onion is soft and the fish lightly browned. Add the tomato purée, basil or parsley and the sugar, stir and continue to cook for about 10 minutes or until the tomato begins to separate from the oil. When this happens, add the hot water, stir and remove from the heat and keep hot.

Bring a large pan of salted water to the boil, toss in the spaghetti and stir. Cook until *al dente* – firm to the bite. (Check the instructions on the packet for timing, as brands vary.) Then drain and return to the pan. Pour over the sauce, toss together and transfer to a warm platter to serve.

BUCATINI all'AMATRICIANA
Bucatini with Bacon and Tomato Sauce

*Once exclusively a dish of the Abruzzi, this delicious bacon and tomato sauce
has been adopted by Rome and the whole region. Traditionally it is eaten
with bucatini (thick, hollow spaghetti), but you can use any kind of dried
durum wheat pasta. You will never get two locals to agree upon the correct
ingredients for this sauce: countless kitchens have resounded with arguments
over whether garlic should be included or not, or how much chilli matters to
the flavour . . .*

*Originally the dish comes from the town of Amatrice, where they happen
to be very good at raising and butchering pigs – hence the most vital
ingredient for the authenticity of the dish, a special kind of bacon called
guanciale. If you cannot find guanciale, use ordinary, good-quality streaky
bacon instead – although most good Italian delicatessens will order
guanciale for you, if you give them enough notice.*

SERVES 4

6 oz (175 g) guanciale *or*
   thick-cut streaky bacon,
   cubed
2 tablespoons olive oil
1 small onion, peeled and
   chopped
½ dried red chilli pepper,
   de-seeded and chopped
1 × 14 oz (400 g) can
   tomatoes, drained, de-
   seeded and chopped
salt
14 oz (400 g) bucatini *or*
   other dried durum wheat
   pasta with a chunky
   shape
3 oz (75 g) pecorino or
   Parmesan cheese, grated

Fry the cubed guanciale or bacon in the olive
oil until the fat is translucent and running.
Scoop out the bacon and keep warm on one
side. Add the onion and chilli to the pan and
fry for 6 minutes or so. Add the tomatoes and
cook for a further 20 minutes, stirring
frequently.

Bring a large pan of salted water to the boil,
add the pasta and cook until *al dente* – firm to
the bite. (Check the packet for cooking times, as
brands vary.)

Add the bacon cubes to the tomato sauce, stir
and adjust the seasoning. Drain the pasta and
return it to the pan. Pour on the sauce, add the
cheese, mix and toss together very thoroughly.
Arrange on a warmed platter and serve at once.

ORECCHIETTE con BRACIOLETTE
Little Ears with Beef Rolls

From Puglia comes this very typical one-pot meal, in which the meat is cooked in a rich sauce. The sauce is used to dress the pasta and becomes the first course; then the meat is served as a second course with vegetables. Alternatively, you can eat it all together and serve cheese and salad to follow. In Puglia horsemeat is quite likely to be used for this dish. Orecchiette is the most widely used pasta form in Puglia. Very heavy and thick, and slightly spongy when cooked, it is made by hand and is supposed to resemble little animal ears. It takes a longer time to cook than other dried durum wheat pastas.

SERVES 4

4 oz (100 g) pancetta *or* fat bacon

4 oz (100 g) pecorino *or* Lancashire cheese

1¼ lb (500 g) beef steak (rump or sirloin), in 4 slices

4 sprigs parsley

1 large clove garlic, peeled and cut into 4 pieces

salt and pepper

5 tablespoons olive oil

1 onion, peeled and sliced

1 glass red wine

¼ teaspoon beef extract

1 × 14 oz (400 g) can tomatoes, sieved

14 oz (400 g) orecchiette *or* other small stubby pasta shape

Cut the pancetta or bacon and the cheese into slices roughly the same size as the slices of beef. The pancetta and cheese must sit comfortably on top of the meat. Trim the meat of gristle and fat, then flatten it out with a meat mallet. Put the pancetta, cheese, a few leaves of parsley and a piece of garlic on top of each slice of meat and season generously. Roll the meat up around the filling and tie it securely with cook's string.

Heat the oil in a pan and fry the onion until it is softened. Lay the beef rolls in the onion and brown the meat thoroughly all over. Pour the wine over the beef, raise the heat and cook for about 2 minutes to evaporate the alcohol. (When you can no longer smell wine, this operation is complete.) Add the beef extract and the tomatoes, stir carefully and simmer, covered, for about 45 minutes.

Bring a large pan of salted water to the boil, toss in the orecchiette and stir. Cook for about 15–20 minutes or until tender, then drain and return to the pan. Remove the beef rolls from their sauce and set them aside to keep warm until required. Pour the sauce all over the orecchiette and toss together thoroughly.

Transfer to a warm platter. If you are going to serve everything together, arrange the beef rolls on top. Alternatively, serve the pasta and the sauce first and have the meat afterwards.

Variation: Natalizia's Orecchiette

When we visited my friend Natalizia in Puglia recently, she made orecchiette for us by hand with wholemeal flour and served them with this basic household sugo or sauce. This sauce varies from household to household and from day to day. It is a simplified version of a Bolognese sauce, i.e. a tomato and meat sauce for which any cut of meat can be used.

SERVES 4

4 tablespoons olive oil

1 carrot, scraped and finely chopped

1 stick celery, finely chopped

1 onion, peeled and finely chopped

2 cloves garlic, peeled and finely chopped

3 tablespoons chopped parsley and any other herb of your choice

8 oz (225 g) minced beef *or* veal *or* pork *or* chicken *or* cubed stewing meat *or* any other meat you have in the house

1 × 14 oz (400 g) can tomatoes, de-seeded if you wish

salt and pepper

a few leaves fresh basil (optional)

cooked orecchiette or other pasta and grated Parmesan or pecorino cheese to serve

Heat the oil and fry all the vegetables for about 8 minutes or until soft and, in the case of the onion, transparent. Add the herbs and the meat. Brown the meat thoroughly, then add the tomatoes. Season generously and add the fresh basil if using. Stir thoroughly, then cover and simmer for a minimum of 1 hour or until the meat is tender. Stir frequently and add a little water if the sauce appears to be drying out. Serve hot over pasta, toss together thoroughly and serve with grated Parmesan or pecorino to taste.

N O T E

The longer and slower the sauce cooks, the better it tastes.

MACCHERONI alla CHITARRA
Abruzzese Macaroni

The chitarra *('guitar') used to make this kind of pasta is unique to the Abruzzi. It is actually a rectangular frame with metal strings stretched across the hollow of the box, just like a musical instrument. The pasta is laid on top of the strings and a rolling pin is rolled on top of the pasta, pushing it through the gaps between the strings to fall underneath. You end up with square-sided spaghetti which are known locally as* maccheroni alla chitarra. *You can buy a* chitarra *in any of the local shops of the Abruzzi.*

Marisa Lazzarro made this delicious dish for us in her lovely kitchen in L'Aquila. You could use the sauce with any type of pasta.

SERVES 4 (generously)

For the maccheroni

1¼ lb (500 g) plain white flour

3 eggs and 1 egg yolk, mixed together

or 14 oz (400 g) ready-made maccheroni

For the sauce

2 tablespoons olive oil

1 onion, chopped

4½ oz (120 g) guanciale *or* pancetta *or* bacon, cubed

1 dried red chilli pepper, chopped, or to taste

1¼ lb (500 g) canned tomatoes, de-seeded and coarsely chopped

salt

Make a pasta dough with the flour and eggs (see page 298) and roll it out into sheets about 6 inches (15 cm) wide. If you have a *chitarra*, cut these sheets into maccheroni. Alternatively cut the dough into any shape you like.

Heat the oil and fry the onion with the guanciale or pancetta or bacon until the onion is soft and the fat is running. Add the chilli and fry for a further 5–10 minutes. Add the canned tomatoes and their juice and a little salt and cover. Simmer for about 30–40 minutes.

Toss the pasta into boiling salted water and cook until just tender. Drain carefully, transfer to a warm bowl and toss thoroughly with the sauce before serving.

CULIGIONIS
Sardinian Ravioli

In order for these ravioli to merit the title 'Sardinian', the filling should include genuine Sardinian pecorino cheese, which is only available in the very best delicatessens. If you cannot get hold of Sardinian pecorino, use ordinary pecorino or good-quality, fresh Parmesan.

SERVES 4

For the filling
1½ lb (750 g) fresh *or* frozen spinach
1 oz (25 g) butter
3 eggs
11 oz (300 g) softest possible Sardinian pecorino *or* fresh pecorino *or* Parmesan cheese, finely chopped
pinch grated nutmeg
salt and pepper
1-2 tablespoons flour

For the pasta
11 oz (300 g) fine semolina
3 eggs
salt

To serve
1 quantity basic tomato sauce (see page 284), kept warm
2 oz (50 g) mature pecorino or Parmesan cheese, grated

If using fresh spinach, wash it well, put the spinach in a heavy-bottomed pan with no water and cook over a low heat for about 5 minutes until the leaves wilt.

Toss the spinach with the butter in a pan over a low heat for 5-6 minutes. Then put it in a bowl and stir in the 3 eggs, cheese, pinch nutmeg and salt and pepper to taste. Mix together with your hands, adding just enough flour to prevent stickiness. Set it to one side.

Make the pasta dough as usual (see page 298), using semolina instead of flour. Roll out the dough as thinly as possible, then cut it into 2 × 2 inch (5 × 5 cm) squares. Lay one spoonful of filling on half the squares, lay the other squares over the filling and press down firmly all around to seal the squares. Press round the edges again with the prongs of a fork to create grooves. Knead and re-roll any scraps of dough and cut again. You will end up with rather big, chunky ravioli, but don't worry: this is what you want.

Place the ravioli on a tray, not overlapping. Cover with a clean cloth and leave to rest for 15 minutes. Bring a large pan of salted water to the boil, slide in the ravioli and boil for about 4 minutes, or until they are floating near the surface. Drain them with care so as not to break them and transfer to a warm bowl. Pour over the tomato sauce and toss them gently, then scatter over the cheese, toss again and serve.

RAVIOLI ABRUZZESI
Spicy Ravioli with a Ricotta Filling

There is a delicious combination of flavours in this recipe. The cloves used in the sauce marry very well with the cinnamon used in the filling. It makes a fabulous dish for special occasions such as weddings which, in the Abruzzi villages, are of prime importance! I can recall weddings in these parts where the feasting began at noon and ended at 8 p.m. at the earliest!

SERVES 6

For the sauce

3 oz (75 g) unsalted butter

1 large onion, peeled and coarsely chopped

8 oz (250 g) minced beef *or* pork *or* veal *or* rabbit

1 clove garlic, peeled and finely chopped

2 cloves

5 tablespoons dry red or white wine

10 oz (275 g) canned tomatoes, drained, de-seeded and chopped or sieved

salt and pepper

For the filling

12 oz (350 g) ricotta cheese

2 teaspoons granulated sugar

½ teaspoon ground cinnamon

1 large egg, beaten

For the pasta

12 oz (350 g) plain white flour

5 large eggs

salt

First make the sauce. Melt the butter and fry the onion and the meat together until the onion is soft and the meat well browned, then add the garlic and the cloves, cover and simmer for about 10 minutes. Pour in the wine, raise the heat and evaporate the alcohol for 2–3 minutes, then add the tomatoes. Stir thoroughly together, then season with salt and pepper to taste. Cover and simmer for about 1 hour.

Now make the filling. Mash the ricotta to a smooth consistency. Beat the sugar and cinnamon into the egg, then stir in the ricotta to make a creamy mixture. Set this to one side while you prepare the pasta.

Make the pasta dough as usual with the flour, 4 of the eggs and the salt (see page 298). Roll the dough out into 2 very thin sheets of approximately equal size. Beat the remaining egg with 4 tablespoons water and brush 1 pasta sheet with this mixture. Place small lumps of the filling in neat, regular lines on this sheet of pasta, leaving equal spaces between each lump. Lay the second sheet of pasta on top and press down with the side of your hand in between each row of filling, in both directions. Then cut around each lump of filling with a 1½ inch (4 cm) pastry cutter or upturned wine glass. Press round the edges of each filled pasta pocket with the prongs of a fork to seal it carefully. Lay the ravioli on a tray, without overlapping, until

To serve

4¾ oz (135 g) Parmesan cheese *or* a mixture of Parmesan and pecorino, grated

required. Leave them to rest for 30 minutes.

Bring a large pan of salted water to the boil. Slide in the ravioli and cook them for about 6–7 minutes, or until they return to the surface. Scoop them out with a slotted spoon and arrange them on individual warm plates. Spoon a little of the meat and tomato sauce over each portion and hand the grated cheese separately.

CAPPELLETTI ROMAGNOLI di MAGRO

Stuffed Pasta Hats

This recipe is for little hat-shaped pasta parcels with a non-meat filling. On holy days, such as Christmas Eve and Good Friday, meat is traditionally not eaten in Italian Catholic households. This is generally what is meant by magro – a meat-free recipe which is eaten on such occasions. The dough uses one less egg than usual, to make the dish less rich. The Cappelletti are cooked in broth, then strained and coated in melted butter and grated Parmesan.

SERVES 6

For the filling
1 lb (450 g) fresh *or* frozen spinach
5 oz (150 g) ricotta *or* whipped cream cheese
4 oz (100 g) soft cheese (such as stracchino or mozzarella), cut into tiny cubes
pinch salt
¼ teaspoon grated nutmeg

For the pasta
1¼ lb (500 g) plain white flour

If using fresh spinach, wash it carefully. Place the spinach in a heavy-bottomed pan and cook for about 5 minutes until the leaves wilt. When cool, mince or chop finely.

Mix the spinach, ricotta or whipped cream cheese, soft cheese, salt and nutmeg together very thoroughly. Set aside until required.

Make the pasta dough as usual (see page 298). Roll it out and cut it into 2½-inch (6 cm) squares. Place 1 teaspoon of the spinach and cheese mixture in the middle of each square and fold over the dough to make a neat triangle. Be sure that all the triangles are well sealed around the edges so that none of the mixture escapes during cooking. Wrap each triangle around your index finger so that two of

5 large eggs
salt

2½ pints (1.5 litres) meat
or vegetable broth (see
page 289)
4 oz (100 g) unsalted butter
4 oz (100 g) Parmesan
cheese, grated

the points overlap and the third point stands upright. Press the two overlapping points together, fold back the third point and push the 'hat' off the end of your finger.

Bring the broth to the boil, slip in the cappelletti and cook for about 3–4 minutes. (They will rise to the surface when cooked.) Scoop them out with a large slotted spoon and arrange them in a wide, warm dish. Heat the butter without browning it, then pour it all over the cooked cappelletti. Scatter the Parmesan over the top and serve.

TORTELLINI
Venus' Belly Buttons

The legend of tortellini goes like this: the lovely Venus, having been denied access to Heaven because of her unchristian status, was left to wander lonely and abandoned in Limbo. In the course of her meandering, she ended up in Bologna, at an inn. (Don't question the logic of this, it's only a legend!) She was dutifully shown to her room by the innkeeper, who was inflamed with passion for the beautiful and sad young woman. Once she was inside the room, Venus locked the door and undressed, not realising that the innkeeper was peeping through the keyhole. But all he could see was her belly button and so, in a fit of outrageous lust, he tore down to his kitchen and created the famous tortellini as a eulogy to her beauty. So when you next make or eat these delicious filled pasta shapes, do remember that they are supposed to look like Venus' belly button. They can be served in a variety of ways: with warmed cream, butter and grated Parmesan, or floating in broth, or with sage-flavoured melted butter, or even with a basic tomato sauce.

SERVES 4–6
For the filling
2 oz (50 g) unsalted butter
4 oz (100 g) pork loin,
cubed

First make the filling. Melt the butter and fry the pork and turkey for 10 minutes. Mince them three times, or process them once in a food processor, together with the prosciutto and mortadella. Stir in the eggs, salt and

2 oz (50 g) turkey breast,
  cubed
4 oz (100 g) prosciutto
  crudo
4 oz (100 g) mortadella
2 eggs, beaten
salt and pepper
6 oz (175 g) Parmesan
  cheese, grated
large pinch nutmeg

For the pasta
11 oz (300 g) plain white
  flour
3 large eggs
salt

3½ pints (2 litres) best-
  quality meat *or* chicken
  broth (see page 289)
grated Parmesan cheese to
  serve

pepper, Parmesan and nutmeg. Mix together
very thoroughly – you can do it in a liquidiser
or food processor if you like – and set aside
until required.

To prepare the pasta, tip the flour out on to a
work-surface, plunge your fist into the centre
and break the eggs into the resulting hollow.
Add a pinch of salt and knead together to make
a pasta dough as usual (see page 298). Roll it
out and cut it into 1½ inch (4 cm) circles using
a pastry cutter or upturned egg cup. Put a tiny
amount of the filling into the middle of each
one, fold the circle in half and press the open
edges tightly closed with your fingertips. Now
wrap the half circle around your index finger
and cross over the two ends, curling the rest of
the dough backwards to make a belly button
shape. Push it off the end of your finger and lay
on a floured tray until required. It should not
overlap or touch any of the other tortellini. If
you find it difficult to fold such tiny circles,
make bigger circles and try again. I would
advise you roll out a small amount of dough,
cut it and fill it, then try to see if you can make
it into a tortellino before you use up all the rest
of the dough. The important thing is that you
should be happy with the finished effect; size is
of secondary importance. When all the
tortellini are made, they can be left to rest
overnight under a lightly floured cloth if you
prefer, or used immediately.

Bring the broth to a rolling boil, slide in all
the tortellini and cook them for 3 minutes, then
pour everything carefully into a warmed soup
tureen or ladle out into individual soup plates.
Serve with grated Parmesan, handed separately,
and *always* with a bottle of the best Lambrusco.

GNOCCHI di RICOTTA
Spinach and Ricotta Gnocchi

This recipe, from the Casentino area of Tuscany, is pure nostalgia! I can remember, as a small child, watching these gnocchi being made when my chin rested on the marble table top very comfortably. The secret is to work the mixture very lightly with your fingertips so it stays light and fluffy. Green bullets are not what you are trying to achieve! Keep your fingers stiff, use a minimum of flour on your hands as you shape, and work as fast as you possibly can.

SERVES 4

2 lb (1 kg) fresh *or* 12 oz (350 g) frozen spinach
12 oz (350 g) ricotta cheese
4 tablespoons plus 4 oz (100 g) grated Parmesan cheese
3 large eggs, beaten
salt and pepper
¼ teaspoon grated nutmeg
3–4 tablespoons plain white flour
4½ oz (120 g) unsalted butter

If using fresh spinach, wash it thoroughly. Place the spinach in a heavy-bottomed pan and cook for about 5 minutes or until the leaves wilt. Cool.

Squeeze the spinach dry in your hands, then process or sieve it finely. Put it into a bowl with the ricotta, 4 tablespoons Parmesan and eggs. Mix lightly but thoroughly together, then season with the salt, pepper and nutmeg. Using your hands, add enough flour to thicken the mixture so that you can handle it easily without too much stickiness. The better you have dried your steamed spinach and the less flour you use at this point, the better your finished dish will be. Shape quickly into 3 inch (7.5 cm) croquette shapes, dust very lightly with flour and set aside.

Bring a large pan of salted water to the boil. Gently slip in the gnocchi and cook for 1–2 minutes or until they are floating on the surface. Scoop them out with a slotted spoon and lay them on a warm platter. Melt the butter without browning and pour over the gnocchi. Sprinkle 4 oz (100 g) Parmesan all over the top and serve at once.

GNOCCHI di SEMOLELLA
Semolina Gnocchi

This is a lunchtime dish, served as a first course and followed by a light dish such as poached fish with salad. Also known as Gnocchi alla Romana, this is a very old and traditional recipe from Rome and the Lazio. Sometimes two egg yolks are blended into the semolina when you have removed it from the heat – this makes for a much richer dish. Although it is now considered very much a part of the Roman food scene, many gastronomical experts claim that it originally came from Piedmont.

SERVES 4

1¼ pints (750 ml) milk
pinch salt
1 tablespoon plus 4 oz (100 g) unsalted butter
8 oz (225 g) semolina, sifted once
3 oz (75 g) Parmesan cheese, grated
1 heaped tablespoon grated Gruyère *or* Emmenthal cheese

Pre-heat the oven to gas mark 7, 425°F (220°C).

Bring the milk to the boil, then stir in the salt and 1 tablespoon butter. Let the semolina rain lightly into the boiling milk, stirring constantly to prevent lumps. Cook over a low heat for 20 minutes, stirring all the time. Remove from the heat and stir in 1 tablespoon grated Parmesan.

Pour the hot semolina out onto 2 flat platters or trays, or straight on to a work-surface. Smooth it all out with a knife to a thickness of ¼ inch (5 mm), and cut into equal-sized circles with an upturned wine glass or pastry cutter.

Butter an ovenproof dish thoroughly and lay across the bottom the rough bits left over from cutting out the circles. Melt the remaining 4 oz (100 g) butter without browning. Trickle a little melted butter on the semolina in the bottom of the dish and sprinkle with Parmesan. Cover with a layer of overlapping semolina circles, then more butter and Parmesan. Continue in this way until you have used up all the ingredients in layers. Sprinkle the top with the grated Gruyère or Emmenthal and bake for about 20 minutes, or until the top is well browned but not burnt. Serve at once, directly from the dish.

GNOCCHI di PATATE di ALESSANDRA

Alessandra's Potato Gnocchi

Alessandra Delle Fratte and her mother made this very traditional Lazio speciality for us all when we visited them. The only 'trick' is learning how to make the gnocchi concave on one side and with grooves on the other. You can serve them with any basic sauce – for example, the one used for the lasagne filling (see page 96) – and grated Parmesan.

SERVES 6 *(generously)*
2 lb (1 kg) potatoes, well
  scrubbed
up to 1¼ lb (500 g) plain
  white flour
salt
meat or tomato sauce of
  your choice and grated
  Parmesan cheese to serve

Boil the potatoes, unpeeled, until just soft but not coming apart. Peel and mash them quickly before they cool down. (And before you scald yourself!) Blend the flour and potatoes together until you have a smooth and elastic mixture. (Don't over-knead or the result will be very heavy.)

Roll the mixture out into 'snake' shapes about the width of your thumb, then cut it into dice-sized cubes. Press each cube against the prongs of a fork with your index finger to make a deep dent in one side and grooves on the other. Lay them out on a floured surface as you prepare them.

Bring a large pan of salted water to a rolling boil. Toss in the gnocchi and cook them for about 3–4 minutes or until they rise to the surface. Scoop them out with a slotted spoon and place them in a warm bowl. Dress with hot meat or tomato sauce of your choice and toss together thoroughly. Sprinkle with freshly grated Parmesan and serve.

CANEDERLI
Bread Dumplings

Olmi is a chocolate-box-picture village, just over the border from Trentino in Alto Adige. We discovered it quite by chance, following our instincts and the sound of rushing water as melted snow gushed its way through the dense, ferny ground cover. The little houses are all built in traditional Tirolean style, with carved wooden shutters and bright window boxes in summer. The village slopes gracefully down on either side of the valley, with sparkling streams on either side, crisscrossed by tiny wooden bridges. In the heart of the village is the Gasthaus Bernard, where the Bernard family provide just the sort of food required for skiing or hiking in the clean crisp air, like these wonderfully filling Canederli.

This kind of poached dumpling, a culinary legacy from neighbouring Austria, is tremendously popular all over the Alto Adige area. There are many versions: this is my own personal favourite. Serve, floated in bowls of hot broth, as a starter or instead of pasta or as a side dish with a rich stew.

MAKES 9 DUMPLINGS

1 lb (450 g) unsliced white bread, crusts removed

2 tablespoons chopped parsley

7 oz (200 g) speck *or* prosciutto crudo *or* smoked back bacon

4 eggs, beaten

pinch salt

½ onion, peeled and finely chopped

1 tablespoon butter

5 tablespoons sunflower oil

3 wine glasses milk

4 tablespoons plain white flour

Chop the bread, parsley and speck (or prosciutto or bacon) finely and mix together. Beat the eggs thoroughly with the salt. Fry the onion in the butter until the onion is soft. Combine the bread mixture with the onion and oil. Add the milk and eggs, cover and rest for about 30 minutes.

Mix in the flour and shape the mixture into balls about the size of tennis balls. Slip into boiling salted water and cook for 10–15 minutes. Scoop them out with a slotted spoon and serve as described above.

NOTE

Speck is a kind of ham which is cured in Alto Adige. It is rather like smoked prosciutto crudo and is not all that easy to find in the UK. Ordinary prosciutto crudo or smoked back bacon make very good alternatives.

RISI e BISI
Rice and Peas – Venice Style!

This delicately flavoured combination of rice and fresh peas is probably one of the oldest and most traditional specialities of the Veneto. Some very old recipes I have come across include fennel seeds amongst the ingredients, stirred in as the rice cooks. In times gone by, cooks used peas so fresh and tender in this recipe that their pods would be cooked and puréed, then added to the dish. This was intended to give the dish more flavour and a brilliant green colour. If you use canned or frozen peas, you will only have a vague semblance of the true nature of this dish. I suggest you double the quantity of grated Parmesan to improve it a little! The consistency of this dish should be much wetter than that of a Risotto, but not runny like soup.

SERVES 4

2 lb (1 kg) fresh peas in their pods *or* 1 lb (450 g) frozen peas

2 pints (1.2 litres) meat *or* chicken stock (see pages 292–3)

2½ oz (65 g) unsalted butter

2 tablespoons olive oil

2 oz (50 g) pancetta *or* prosciutto crudo, chopped

1 shallot, finely chopped

8 oz (225 g) long-grain or Vialone rice

salt and pepper

2 oz (50 g) parsley, chopped

3 heaped tablespoons grated Parmesan cheese

Shell the peas (if using fresh) and wash them with care. Heat the stock slowly to boiling point. Heat half the butter and the olive oil and fry the pancetta or prosciutto with the shallot for about 6 minutes, stirring constantly. Add the peas, either fresh or frozen, and a little stock and stew gently for about 6–7 minutes, then add the rice and stir. Pour in the rest of the stock, check the seasoning and adjust as necessary. Simmer, uncovered, for 20 minutes, stirring occasionally. When the rice is tender, stir in the remaining butter, the parsley and the Parmesan and serve at once.

RISO e PORRI degli ORTOLANI d'ASTI

Rice and Leeks Cooked in the Asti Style

The origins of this dish go right back to the Middle Ages, to a time when the flourishing fields around Asti were mainly given over to the cultivation of garlic and leeks. Some elderly local peasants gave me this recipe, telling me that leeks purify the blood and improve the eyesight. Whether or not this is true, the soup is cleansing and refreshing to eat and can be very economical if you use up any odd bits of cheese you might have in the fridge. The soup has a very thick texture indeed as it is supposed to represent a whole meal in one dish. Peasants used to eat soups like this on a daily basis to nourish and warm themselves.

SERVES 4

8 oz (225 g) leeks, cut into
   thickish rounds
2½ oz (65 g) unsalted
   butter
1 bay leaf
½ clove garlic, peeled
1 oz (25 g) belly pork,
   finely cubed
4 oz (100 g) potatoes,
   peeled and cut in half
2 pints (1.2 litres) cold
   water
salt and pepper
8 oz (225 g) short-grain rice
large pinch grated nutmeg
2 oz (50 g) fontina *or*
   mature Cheddar cheese,
   cubed
2 oz (50 g) Gruyère *or*
   mature Emmenthal
   cheese, cubed
2 oz (50 g) Parmesan
   cheese, grated

Wash the leeks carefully and fry half of them lightly in half the butter with the bay leaf, garlic and belly pork for 20 minutes over a low heat and under a lid. Stir occasionally.

Remove the garlic and add the rest of the leeks and the potatoes. Stir and cook for 5 minutes. Then add the water, salt and pepper and bring to the boil. Simmer for 15 minutes, then add the rice. Stir and season with the nutmeg.

Continue to simmer for 15–20 minutes or until the rice is tender, stirring occasionally. Just before you remove it from the heat, mash the potatoes with a fork. Stir the three cheeses thoroughly into the mixture and remove from the heat. Mix in the remaining butter and let the soup rest for 3 minutes under a lid to allow the flavour to develop fully before serving.

RISOTTO alla MILANESE
Milanese Risotto

This is one of those incredibly controversial recipes. I know that if any of my gourmet Italian relatives read this, there will be much discussion!! So let me prepare myself for the verbal onslaught by saying that many Milanese families use wine, either red or white, adding it after the rice has been toasted. If you do this you must wait until the wine has been completely absorbed before continuing the cooking. Many people maintain that for the risotto to be really Milanese, it has to be cooked with the juices of a veal roast – a joint of veal cooked with butter, sage and rosemary. Some people cover the finished risotto with a few spoonfuls of these roasting juices. When a Milanese risotto is cooked like this, it is dark amber in colour. The original recipe also calls for Lodigiano cheese and beef bone marrow, both of which I have omitted in my recipe. All those considerations apart, let me tell you my favourite story about the origins of this delicious dish.

Several centuries ago, the master stained-glass window painter of Milan was busy colouring one of the windows of the cathedral. His apprentice had the job of mixing the yellow colour and painting the folds of the dress of a saint. So engrossed did he become in his job that his master nicknamed him Zafferano (saffron), for this was the spice used to obtain the rich golden colour they needed. 'Ah, you,' the master would laugh, 'you're so keen on using saffron, you will end up putting it in your risotto!'

A couple of months later, the daughter of the boss was married and Zafferano was duly invited to the banquet. Suddenly, in the middle of the festivities, the guests were surprised to hear a loud fanfare, which was immediately followed by the entry of four small page boys – each one carrying a big tureen, covered with a lid. When the children were standing in the centre of the banqueting hall and had the undivided attention of all the wedding guests, they raised the lids on their tureens to reveal golden yellow saffron-scented risotto. It was Zafferano's wedding gift to the bride and groom – he had finally put saffron in his risotto, just as his master had predicted!

Conceived, as it was, for a very special occasion, the original dish was extremely rich. It was also representative of a type of cooking which uses butter and grated cheese in generous amounts. I've adapted it slightly, cutting down on the animal fats. The colour of the dish is not really relevant – all that matters is that you should be able to taste the saffron.

SERVES 4

2 generous pinches saffron
    threads *or* ½ teaspoon
    powdered saffron
2¾ pints (1.6 litres) hot
    chicken *or* beef broth or
    stock (see page 292)
1 small onion, peeled and
    chopped as finely as
    possible
3 oz (75 g) unsalted butter
14 oz (400 g) risotto rice
2-4 oz (50-100 g)
    Parmesan *or* Grana
    Padano cheese, grated

Put the saffron threads (if using) into a teacup and cover with about 3 or 4 tablespoons of boiling hot broth or stock. Leave to infuse until required.

In a pan fry the onion in half the butter until soft but not coloured. Add the rice and raise the heat to toast it lightly all over – it should look shiny and translucent. Lower the heat.

Begin to add the broth or stock, 1 ladleful at a time. Stir each ladleful into the rice and wait for it to become completely absorbed by the rice before you add the next one. Continue in this way until the rice is cooked but still firm to the bite – this will take about 20 minutes from the moment you add the first ladleful of broth or stock.

Don't worry if the rice sticks to the bottom as you stir and add liquid: all the experts agree it should have the unmistakable flavour of *de tacaa gio* (stuck to the bottom)! Keep tasting the rice as you reach the point where you think it is ready. When it is at the right texture, remove it from the heat.

Strain the saffron threads and pour the liquid into the rice mixture, or add the saffron powder. Stir very thoroughly. Add the remaining butter and the grated cheese. Stir again and cover with a lid. Rest for about 3–5 minutes off the heat, then arrange on a platter and serve at once.

NOTE

The risotto must not be dry so don't be afraid to add more broth or stock rather than less. Aim for a creamy, wetter texture.

RISO ASCIUTTO con POMODORI e FUNGHI

Boiled Rice with Tomato and Mushroom Sauce

This delicious rice dish from Liguria uses freshly picked porcini mushrooms (Boletus edulis), *but any sort of wild mushroom can be used instead. Dried porcini are not suitable. I have even used giant puffballs, which grow in profusion near my home in Norfolk, with marvellous results. Unusually for an Italian rice dish, it isn't a Risotto but a dish of dressed boiled rice. I have often used brown rice as it complements the flavour of the mushrooms very well. The dish is normally served as a starter but it can also be a main course.*

SERVES 4

12 oz (350 g) ripe, soft tomatoes

2–3 tablespoons tomato purée

3½ oz (90 g) unsalted butter

½ clove garlic, peeled and crushed

1 small onion, peeled and finely sliced

3 tablespoons olive oil

3 fresh basil leaves

salt and pepper

7 oz (200 g) fresh wild mushrooms, cleaned and thinly sliced

1 handful parsley, finely chopped

12 oz (350 g) long-grain white *or* brown rice

4 heaped tablespoons grated Parmesan cheese

Scald the tomatoes in boiling water for 1 minute, then peel, de-seed and chop coarsely. Stir the tomatoes and the tomato purée together in a bowl. Melt just less than half the butter in a pan, add the garlic, onion and olive oil, and fry gently for 5–6 minutes. Add the tomato mixture and the basil and season to taste. Stir and cover. Simmer slowly for about 20 minutes. Then add the mushrooms and the parsley, stir and continue to simmer for 30 minutes.

Boil the rice in plenty of salted water until tender – about 20 minutes for white rice and 40 for brown. Drain and return to the saucepan. Dress with half the sauce, the remaining butter and the Parmesan. Toss and mix together carefully, then arrange the rice on a warm platter in a ring shape. Pour the other half of the sauce all over the ring of dressed rice and serve at once.

RISOTTO con i CARCIOFI
Artichoke Risotto

This is a delightful recipe from the lovely city of Siena. The combination of rice with artichokes is quite unusual, but really excellent. This has always been a family favourite, especially as risotto is a very convenient dish to cook for large numbers of people and we were never less than twenty around our table. The creaminess of the rice sets off the slightly bitter taste of the artichoke perfectly. The younger and more tender your artichokes, the better it will taste. This would normally be served as a starter, though it can be a main course dish if you prefer.

SERVES 4

6 young globe artichokes

juice of 1 lemon

approximately 1¾ pints (1 litre) chicken *or* beef broth (see page 289)

2 oz (50 g) unsalted butter *or* margarine

2 oz (50 g) prosciutto crudo, finely chopped

1 small handful parsley, finely chopped

12 oz (350 g) risotto rice

salt and pepper

2 oz (50 g) Parmesan cheese, grated

Prepare the artichokes as explained on page 231. Cut them into quarters and put them in a basin of cold water with the lemon juice for about 30 minutes.

Heat the broth. Meanwhile, in a separate pan, melt the butter or margarine and fry the prosciutto and half the parsley for about 5 minutes over a low heat.

Drain the artichokes, dry them carefully and slice them finely. Add the artichokes to the frying prosciutto, stir together and cook gently for about 10 minutes, adding a little broth if necessary to prevent sticking.

Add the rice to this mixture, stirring to coat it with fat and toast it all over. Add the boiling hot broth, 1 ladleful at a time, stirring constantly. Always wait for the broth to be absorbed before adding any more. Cook for about 20 minutes or until the rice is done. Take it off the heat, season with salt and pepper, and stir in the rest of the parsley and the Parmesan. Stir thoroughly, arrange on a warmed platter and serve.

RISOTTO di FINOCCHI
Fennel Risotto

If fennel is not your vegetable, this delicious Venetian risotto can also be made with the same quantity of courgettes or asparagus tips following the same procedure. The beauty of risotto is that there is absolutely no limit to the combination of ingredients. The strangest risotto I have ever eaten was made with sour cherries!

SERVES 4

11 oz (300 g) small, tender
  fennel bulbs, trimmed
2 oz (50 g) pancetta *or*
  unsmoked bacon,
  chopped
1 onion, peeled and finely
  chopped
½ clove garlic, peeled and
  chopped
2 tablespoons olive oil
salt and pepper
12 oz (350 g) risotto rice
2½ pints (1.5 litres) hot
  chicken *or* vegetable *or*
  beef stock (see page 292)
1 handful parsley, chopped
1 oz (25 g) unsalted butter
3 heaped tablespoons
  grated Parmesan cheese

Slice the fennel into quarters with a sharp knife, then slice again into thin strips. Fry the pancetta or bacon, onion and garlic in the olive oil until the onion is softened. Add the fennel, cover and stew together slowly for about 10 minutes. Now put in the rice and season with salt and pepper. Add the stock, 1 ladleful at a time, always waiting for the first lot to be absorbed before you add any more and stirring constantly. The rice will take 20 minutes to cook, during which time you must keep adding ladlefuls of hot stock. As soon as the rice is tender, stir in the parsley and the butter. Let it rest for 3 minutes under a lid, then stir in the cheese. Mix it all together, arrange it on a warm platter and serve at once.

RISOTTO al RADICCHIO
Radicchio Risotto

This is one of two radicchio recipes contributed to this book by Silvia Rossi. She and her farmer husband run a little restaurant called Al Sile. They live near Treviso where the best radicchio grows in perfect climatic conditions.

SERVES 8

4 tablespoons sunflower oil

1 onion, finely chopped

4 heads radicchio, washed and shredded

2 glasses dry white *or* red wine (preferably Tocai or Prosecco, Cabernet or Merlot)

11 oz (300 g) risotto rice

8 tablespoons double cream

1¼ pints (750 ml) hot vegetable *or* meat stock (see page 292)

2 tablespoons butter

salt and pepper

5 tablespoons grated Parmesan *or* Grana Padano cheese

3 tablespoons brandy

Heat the oil and fry the onion for about 5 minutes or until soft. Add the radicchio and stir thoroughly. Cook slowly for about 10–15 minutes, then add 1 glass of wine. Add the rice and cream and stir, adding a little stock as soon as the previous amount of liquid has been absorbed. Continue to add stock 1 ladleful at a time, stirring constantly and always waiting for each lot of stock to be absorbed before you add the next. You will probably not need to use all the stock.

After about 18 minutes, add the second glass of wine, stir in the butter, season with salt and finish cooking the rice. All of this should take about 2–3 minutes. Remove from the heat and add the cheese. Stir in the brandy, cover with a lid and leave to stand for about 3 minutes, then turn out on to a platter and serve.

RISOTTO RICE

This type of Italian rice is sold in all good supermarkets and comes in a box which is clearly marked 'Italian Risotto Rice' or 'Risotto Rice'. You must use this type of rice as opposed to using long-grain rice for making risotto, to achieve the correct texture. If you cannot get hold of risotto rice, it is preferable to use pudding rice rather than long-grain. Long-grain rice tends to separate too well for risotto: you need to achieve a creamier, more tacky consistency when the rice is cooked. Arborio rice is the top of the range, and tends to be more expensive than ordinary risotto rice, but there are other varieties.

RISOTTO NERO
Black Ink Risotto

This is the original recipe for risotto made with the ink taken from squid. If you cannot get hold of squid with their ink sac, you will have to abandon the idea of making this dish until your next self-catering holiday in Italy!

Although the most off-putting thing about this dish is undoubtedly its colour – we are simply not used to eating black food! – it's a delight for those amongst us who love really strong fishy tastes.

SERVES 4

2¼ lb (1 kg) fresh *or* frozen squid, with ink sacs
8 tablespoons olive oil
¼ onion, peeled and finely chopped
1 large clove garlic, peeled and finely chopped
1 handful parsley, chopped
1 glass dry white wine
11 oz (300 g) risotto rice
2 tablespoons tomato purée, diluted with 5 tablespoons warm water
1¾ pints (1 litre) hot vegetable *or* fish stock (see page 293)
salt and pepper

Peel each squid carefully as explained on page 177 and then slip out the black ink sac intact and reserve. Cut the squid open and remove and discard the yellow sac and the bone. Slice the fish into neat strips or squares, wash it carefully and set aside until required.

Heat the oil in a deep, heavy-bottomed pan and fry the onion and garlic until the onion is transparent. Then add the parsley and fry for a further 4 minutes. Add the squid and stir thoroughly, then add the wine and allow the alcohol to evaporate for about 2 minutes. Split open the ink sacs and pour the ink over the squid. Stir and lower the heat. Simmer gently for about 15 minutes.

Then add the rice and stir. Add the tomato purée and begin to cook the risotto, putting in 1 ladleful hot stock at a time and waiting for the rice to absorb it before adding the next ladleful, stirring constantly. The rice will take 20 minutes to cook, at which point add the seasoning to taste. Serve at once, arranged on a platter.

RISOTTO de PESCE
Fish Risotto

Chioggia is a tiny little fishing port town near Venice. At 5 o'clock in the morning the famous wholesale fish market leaps into action with restaurateurs from as far away as Milan buying for that day's menu. All kinds of fish are available, even live sturgeons from a nearby breeding farm. (How does one breed sturgeon, I wonder?) Later in the day, the public fish market begins trading on a wide quayside by one of the more picturesque canals. One of the fishermen, Renato Renier, invited us back for a meal, and his wife Giovanna cooked a delicious mussel and shrimp risotto.

SERVES 4

4–5 tablespoons sunflower oil

1 large onion, peeled and very finely chopped

1–3 cloves garlic, peeled and finely chopped

7 oz (200 g) risotto rice

about 2½ pints (1.5 litres) very hot fish stock (see page 293)

4 oz (100 g) cooked prawns

7 oz (200 g) cooked mussels

1 glass dry white wine

salt and pepper

2 tablespoons chopped parsley

Heat the oil and fry the onion and garlic until soft but not browned. Add the rice and stir together for about 30 seconds, then add the first ladleful of fish stock. Allow the liquid to become absorbed before you add the next ladleful. Stir constantly while you continue to add stock in this way and cook the rice. After about 10 minutes, the rice should be half cooked.

Setting aside a few cooked prawns and mussels to garnish the finished dish if you feel so inclined, shell the rest and cut them into ¾ inch (2 cm) pieces. Stir them into the rice, add the wine and cook for about 2–3 minutes to evaporate the alcohol. Season with salt and pepper to taste, and continue to add fish stock and stir until the rice is cooked. It should be tender but still firm to the bite.

Remove the saucepan from the heat, stir in the parsley and arrange the risotto on a warmed platter to serve. You can garnish the platter with cooked mussels in the shell and unpeeled cooked prawns if you have reserved some for this purpose.

POLENTA di PATATE
Potato Polenta

Polenta is a thick, wettish dough that provides a starchy base for a meal in exactly the same way as rice, bread or potatoes. In this recipe it is made with potatoes, though usually it would be just cornmeal and water.

The local white potatoes of Trentino are famous throughout Italy for their excellent flavour and quality. In this recipe they are combined with polenta flour and mashed to smooth texture, using a local tool called a trisa, *which is very similar to a classic Irish potato masher. (An ordinary potato masher and heavy duty wooden spoon will be quite suitable for the job.)*

The traditional accompaniments are cold boiled beans dressed with a very sharp vinaigrette, bowls of very vinegary pickles and sometimes sliced raw onion. It is really very delicious, and filling. Any leftovers taste even better the second time around, toasted under the grill until slightly blackened and crispy.

SERVES 8

7 lb (3 kg) best-quality
  white potatoes, peeled
salt and pepper
9 tablespoons yellow
  polenta flour
1 oz (25 g) unsalted butter
1 fl oz (25 ml) olive oil
1 onion, peeled and finely
  chopped
11 oz (300 g) pancetta *or*
  bacon, finely diced
11 oz (300 g) Cioncada *or*
  Taleggio *or* mature
  Gouda cheese, cubed

Boil the potatoes until soft, then drain and place them in a large pan (preferably copper, but this is not essential) over a very low heat. Begin to mash and stir them with a sturdy potato masher. Add salt and pepper and then trickle in the polenta flour like a soft rainfall, mixing and mashing all the time. After approximately 20 minutes, the polenta should start to come away from the sides of the pan.

Melt the butter and oil together, and fry the onion and pancetta or bacon until they are well browned and almost crispy.

When the polenta comes away from the sides of the pan effortlessly as you mix, stir in the cubed cheese and the sizzling hot, fried ingredients. Mix vigorously to combine all the flavours and textures, then tip the mixture out on to a board – it will have the texture of very stiff mashed potato. Shape it into a cake using a spatula, and serve it in thick slices with sharp pickles and bean salads as described above.

POLENTA e SPEZZATINO di CONIGLIO

Polenta with Rabbit Stew

Polenta used to be the staple diet of Italian peasants all over central and northern Italy, from Emilia Romagna upwards.

If you are one of the many who recoil from cooking or eating rabbit, this dish works equally well with chicken or stewing veal, pork or beef.

SERVES 4

- 1 × 4½ lb (2 kg) rabbit, jointed
- 1 large glass white wine
- 5 tablespoons olive oil
- 2 cloves garlic, peeled and finely chopped
- 1 small carrot, scraped and chopped
- 1 stick celery, chopped
- 1 sprig fresh rosemary
- 2 tablespoons tomato purée, diluted with 4 tablespoons warm water
- 3 oz (75 g) black olives, stoned
- salt and pepper
- 2 pints (1.2 litres) cold water
- 12 oz (350 g) polenta flour (preferably yellow and fairly coarse in texture)

Wash the rabbit and dry it carefully, put it in a bowl and cover with the white wine. Heat the oil and fry the garlic for about 5 minutes, then add the carrot, celery and rosemary. Stir and cook for about 8 minutes, then add the diluted tomato purée and stir carefully.

Drain the rabbit pieces, reserving the wine. Put the pieces of rabbit in the pan with the carrot and celery and raise the heat to seal them quickly all over. Then add the wine and cook quickly for about 2 minutes to evaporate the alcohol. Lower the heat, add the olives, season and cover. Simmer for about 45 minutes or until the rabbit is tender, adding water if it appears to be drying out.

In the meantime, cook the polenta. Bring the water to the boil, then trickle in the polenta flour like a fine rain, stirring constantly. This is much easier if you get somebody to help you. Boil the polenta slowly for about 50 minutes, stirring continuously. Make sure you scrape well round the edges of the pan to prevent lumps forming. You need a good strong arm and a heavy duty wooden spoon or whisk to achieve a smooth and lump-free texture.

When the polenta is cooked, tip it out on to a large serving dish and shape it like a cake with a spatula. Make a deep trough in the top with a big spoon and tip in the rabbit stew. Serve at once, with plenty of full bodied red wine.

POLENTA con FUNGHI
Polenta with Wild Mushrooms

Vitti Gabrielli and her husband have spent a great deal of time and effort restoring an old mountain cottage in the tiny village of Vattaro, near Trento, as their holiday retreat. It was here that we went to spend the day with them and several friends to eat mountains of steaming polenta with a deliciously rich sauce of wild woodland mushrooms. Gathering mushrooms is a local obsession. Everyone does it, either for pleasure or profit, and the baskets of bounty are then taken to Trento's tiny central market to be checked by the mushroom policemen. The mushroom policemen are ordinary vigili urbani, *who have been trained to recognise and select wild mushrooms. To stand and watch these serious, uniformed gentlemen, gravely checking basketfuls of mushrooms at eight o' clock of a weekday morning, is one of the highlights of a visit to Trento. Here is the recipe for the polenta and mushrooms that Vitti made for us (with carefully checked mushrooms!).*

SERVES 6

For the sauce
4½ lb (2 kg) wild
   mushrooms (*Boletus
   edulis*, puffball or field)
½ wine glass olive oil
1 handful of parsley,
   chopped
3 cloves garlic, peeled and
   chopped
½ onion, peeled and
   chopped
salt and pepper

For the polenta
4.5 pints (2.5 litres) water
1 small fistful of coarse sea
   salt
1 lb (450 g) polenta flour

Clean all the mushrooms very carefully and cut them up into even-sized pieces. Put them in a saucepan with all the other sauce ingredients. Stir everything together, cover and simmer for a generous hour, or until the mushrooms are cooked through and have re-absorbed their juices.

To make the polenta, pour the water into a large deep saucepan, preferably made of copper, and bring it to the boil with the salt. When the water boils, trickle in the polenta flour like fine rain, whisking constantly with a balloon whisk to prevent lumps from forming. When the mixture is smooth, cover with a lid and boil slowly, whisking very frequently. Cook for a total of 40 minutes, making sure it is boiling constantly.

Tip the cooked polenta out on to a wooden board, shape it into a cake using a spatula and let it set slightly. Cut it into slabs and serve 1 slab per person with the mushroom sauce.

PIZZA, PIES

TORTA VERDE
Piedmontese Easter Pie

This delicious savoury pie is served in honour of the Easter festivities in Piedmont, especially on Easter Monday, when all over Italy it is traditional to go on picnics in the countryside. Like most of the savoury pies in this section of the book, it is ideal picnic fare. Serve it warm, in generous slices.

SERVES 4–6

3 tablespoons olive oil
3½ oz (90 g) butter
1 large leek, finely chopped
2 oz (50 g) bacon fat, finely chopped
1 large clove garlic, peeled and chopped
2¼ lb (1 kg) fresh *or* frozen spinach, coarsely chopped
salt
5 oz (150 g) pudding rice
1¾ pints (1 litre) hot chicken *or* vegetable stock (see page 292)
4 eggs, beaten
6 tablespoons grated Parmesan cheese
2 pinches ground mixed spice
3 tablespoons stale breadcrumbs

Pre-heat the oven to gas mark 4, 350°F (180°C).

Put the oil and approximately 1½ oz (40 g) of the butter into a large, heavy-bottomed pan over a medium heat. Add the leek and stir gently, cooking until the leek begins to colour. Add the bacon fat and the garlic and continue to stir to make sure the garlic doesn't burn. When the leek and garlic are soft and pale golden, add the spinach and stir together. Add 2 pinches of salt and cover with a lid. When the spinach is cooked through – it will take about 8 minutes – add the rice and stir.

Cook like a normal risotto, adding 1 ladleful hot stock, stirring and waiting for it to be absorbed before adding any more. After 20 minutes the rice should be tender and cooked through. Remove from the heat and add the eggs, Parmesan, spice and another pinch of salt. Mix together thoroughly.

Generously butter an 11 inch (28 cm) cake tin, sprinkle with the breadcrumbs and turn it upside down to remove any excess. Reserve the excess breadcrumbs. Tip the mixture into the tin, smooth it flat and dot with the remaining butter.

Scatter with the reserved breadcrumbs. Bake for about 1 hour or until golden and set.

TORTA di SPINACI
Genoese Spinach Pie

Pies and savoury cakes are very popular in Ligurian cuisine, as they are very convenient foods to take on sea voyages and suit the life style of the region perfectly. I especially like this one as I love spinach, and I serve it as part of a cold buffet lunch or warm as a supper dish. Serve it with lots of salads if it's to be eaten cold, and with simple boiled vegetables dressed with just a gleam of olive oil if you are going to have it warm. To make things much easier, I have adapted this recipe to prepare it with sheets of frozen puff pastry, available from all good supermarkets.

SERVES 6

1 lb (450 g) fresh *or* frozen
  spinach
3 large eggs
1½ oz (40 g) Parmesan
  cheese, grated
4 oz (100 g) ricotta *or*
  whipped cream cheese
salt and pepper
generous pinch grated
  nutmeg
1 teaspoon butter, melted
4 × 8 inch (20 cm) square
  sheets of frozen puff
  pastry, thawed, *or* home-
  made puff pastry
2 tablespoons milk

Pre-heat the oven to gas mark 4, 350°F (180°C).

If you are using fresh spinach, remove all the stalks from the leaves and wash the leaves very thoroughly. Cook them without water in a heavy saucepan for 10 minutes after they first start to wilt. Alternatively, cook and drain the frozen spinach and proceed as follows.

Tip the spinach into a colander and cool until you can touch it with your hands. Squeeze it dry in your fists, then put it on to a chopping board and chop it coarsely with a sharp knife or *mezzaluna*. Put the spinach into a bowl. Beat the eggs and Parmesan together and stir them into the spinach. Mix in the ricotta or cream cheese, plenty of salt and pepper and the nutmeg. Make sure this mixture is well blended.

Lightly butter a deep 10 inch (25 cm) cake tin (preferably spring-loaded to ease removal of the pie). Lay the first square of pastry in the cake tin – it should cover the bottom and go up the sides a little. Lay the second sheet of pastry on top, so that the 4 corners of the pastry square cover the areas on the sides of the cake tin that were not covered by the first square. Press the 4 corners together as much as possible to make a fairly even finish around the sides of the tin.

Risotto di Finocchi (page 136)

Polenta e Spezzatino di Coniglio
(page 141)

Spoon all the spinach mixture into the lined cake tin. Arrange one square of pastry on top, then the second over it, but with the 4 corners at different angles. Fold all 8 corners inwards to form a deep crust around the edges. Brush the finished pie all over with the milk. Bake in the oven for approximately 45 minutes, or until crisp and golden brown. Take it out of the oven and rest it for 5 minutes. Remove it from the cake tin and put the pie on a platter to serve.

TORTA di PATATE
Potato Pie

This recipe comes from the Val Taro in Emilia Romagna, where they are almost as keen on savoury pies and cakes as in neighbouring Liguria. The idea behind them is that they are eaten out of doors as part of a harvest feast, or on picnics and similar occasions. This one contains a delicious potato filling, combined with onion, leek and cheese. It makes an excellent supper dish served with a mixed salad, and is equally good hot or warm.

SERVES 8

2 lb (1 kg) unpeeled potatoes, suitable for boiling and mashing

salt

2 oz (50 g) belly pork, finely chopped

6–8 tablespoons olive oil

1 oz (25 g) unsalted butter

1 large leek, finely chopped

1 large onion, peeled and finely chopped

1 tablespoon tomato purée, mixed with ¼ teaspoon beef extract and 2 tablespoons hot water

Pre-heat the oven to gas mark 4, 350°F (180°C).

Scrub the potatoes, put them into a pan and cover them with cold water. Add a pinch of salt, place a lid on the pan and boil until soft. This will take about 18 minutes.

Put the belly pork rashers, 1 tablespoon of the olive oil and the butter in a pan and cook over a medium heat until the pork fat is completely melted, stirring frequently to prevent burning. Add the leek and onion, stir well, lower the heat and simmer slowly until the leek and onion are mushy. Then stir in the diluted tomato purée and beef extract.

Drain the potatoes and peel them quickly. Push them through a mouli into a large bowl, or put them in the bowl and mash them with a

4¾ oz (135 g) Parmesan
  cheese, grated
2 fl oz (50 ml) milk
9 oz (250 g) plain white
  flour
2¾ fl oz (70 ml) warm
  water
4 tablespoons stale
  breadcrumbs

large fork. Stir the fried ingredients into the mashed potatoes, then stir in the Parmesan and season to taste with a little salt. Finally, mix in the milk.

Then prepare the pastry. Put 8 oz (225 g) of the flour in a mound on a work-surface (keep the rest for flouring surfaces and your hands while you work). Plunge your fist into the flour, pour the warm water into the hole and add a large pinch of salt and about 1 tablespoon of the oil. Knead together very quickly to make an elastic dough, flouring your hands frequently. Divide the dough into 2 pieces.

Oil a 10 inch (25 cm) cake tin thoroughly and scatter with breadcrumbs all over the bottom. Roll the dough out as thinly as possible and line the cake tin completely with it. Cut off all the dough hanging over the edges. Spread the potato mixture inside the lined cake tin and make sure it is even. Roll out the second piece of dough and lay it on the top.

Press all around the edges tightly with your fingers, brush the surface with oil and pierce the top in about 10 places with the prongs of a fork. Bake in the oven for 1 hour. Remove from the oven and rest for 10 minutes before serving.

CALCIONI di RICOTTA RUSTICI
Rustic Ricotta Pasties

This is a speciality from the rather remote and poor region of Molise, where they have for many centuries produced excellent, top quality ricotta. Traditionally, these pasties are served with a dish of batter-coated, deep-fried foods such as cauliflower, artichokes, mozzarella. They can be served as an antipasto or as a main course with salad – although my children have them for tea!

MAKES 6–8 PASTIES

For the filling

11 oz (300 g) ricotta *or* whipped cream cheese

4 oz (100 g) prosciutto crudo, finely cubed

4 oz (100 g) provolone *or* very mature Cheddar cheese, finely cubed

2 eggs, beaten

2 oz (50 g) parsley, finely chopped

salt and pepper

For the pastry

14 oz (400 g) plain white flour plus about 1 oz (25 g) for dusting

pinch salt

4 oz (100 g) lard *or* margarine

juice of 1 lemon

2 eggs

oil for deep-frying

Mash the ricotta thoroughly to soften it (if using whipped cream cheese, you do not need to do this), then stir in the prosciutto, cheese, eggs, parsley and salt and pepper to taste. Blend them all together carefully.

Put the flour in a bowl with a pinch of salt, add the fat and rub it into the flour until the mixture resembles fine breadcrumbs, then add the lemon juice and the eggs. Knead thoroughly but lightly to achieve a soft dough.

Roll it out as thinly as possible on a floured work-surface and cut into 12 or 16 circles with a 3 inch (7.5 cm) pastry cutter. Place a mound of the filling in the centre of half of the circles, cover with another circle and press the edges together very carefully to seal them securely.

Heat the oil until a piece of bread dropped into the pan sizzles instantly. Fry all the Calcioni for 6–7 minutes or until crisp and golden brown, turning them over when one side is well coloured. Drain on kitchen paper and serve.

PIZZA di MAIYU
Calabrian Pizza

This type of pizza is from the province of Reggio Calabria, in particular from the town of Ardore. The sun-dried tomatoes give it an absolutely unmistakable southern flavour and texture. You can buy sun-dried tomatoes in delicatessens and 'foodie' shops. However, if you don't have any, use a yellow and a red pepper, sliced into strips and sautéed in a pan with a little oil and garlic. Like all Calabrian dishes it is full of body and strong-flavoured with a substantial texture. As it was originally a poor man's dish, the pizza is very thick and doughy so as to be as filling as possible.

SERVES 6

14 oz (400 g) plus about
    4 oz (100 g) strong white
    bread flour
½ oz (15 g) fresh yeast,
    blended in about 2 fl oz
    (50 ml) warm water, *or*
    1½ teaspoons dried
    yeast, diluted in about
    2 fl oz (50 ml) water with
    a large pinch sugar, and
    allowed to stand in a
    warm place until frothy
2½ fl oz (65 ml) plus
    1 tablespoon olive oil
1 fl oz (25 ml) warm water,
    mixed with ½ teaspoon
    salt, plus up to 10 fl oz
    (300 ml) extra warm
    water to mix
5 eggs
salt and pepper
4 oz (100 g) ricotta cheese,
    sliced
4½ oz (120 g) sun-dried
    tomatoes *or* yellow and
    red peppers, sliced and

Make the bread dough first, allowing at least 4 hours for rising and proving. Tip 14 oz (400 g) of the flour out on to a work-surface and plunge your fist into the centre to make a hole. Put the diluted yeast, 1 tablespoon oil and the salty water into the hollow and knead together very thoroughly for about 15 or 20 minutes. Add extra warm water as necessary. When it is all properly kneaded, put the dough in an oiled bowl, cover with a cloth and set in a warm place to rise for 2½ hours or until doubled in bulk. Remove it from the bowl, knock it back and replace it in the bowl, covered, for another hour.

Hardboil 3 of the eggs, cool them under running water, shell them and slice thinly.

Put the dough on a work-surface, make a hollow in the middle and break the 2 remaining eggs into the hollow. Knead the eggs thoroughly into the dough, then add about two thirds of the remaining oil and mix that in also. You will need to use about 3 oz (75 g) of the extra flour now to prevent it from becoming too sticky. When it is all well blended, divide it in half and roll each half out on a floured surface.

Oil a 12 inch (30 cm) square cake tin with the

sautéed in olive oil with
1 clove garlic until soft
5 oz (150 g) mozzarella
cheese, sliced
5 oz (150 g) salame, rind
removed, *or* prosciutto
crudo, cubed
3 tablespoons milk

remaining oil, spread one semi-rolled half of
dough in the bottom and use your hands to
press and stretch it out, using the back of a
spoon dipped in cold water to help you if
necessary. Sprinkle with a little salt and pepper.

Arrange the filling ingredients on the top: the
ricotta, sun-dried tomatoes or sautéed peppers,
hard-boiled eggs, mozzarella and salame or
prosciutto. Cover them with the other half of
the dough, rolled out to fit over the top. Press
the edges carefully together all the way around
to seal it thoroughly. Put it in a warm place to
rise once more for 1 hour.

Pre-heat the oven to gas mark 2, 300°F
(150°C). Brush the surface of the risen dough
lightly with milk and pierce the top in about 10
places with the prongs of a fork. Bake in the
oven for about 1 hour. Serve hot or cold.

NOTE
The original version of this dish would have
had strips of pork fat in the filling to make it
more nourishing. You can add olives and
capers, herbs or different kinds of cheese to
make it more varied.

PIZZA RUSTICA
Rustic Pizza

Many variations of this classic Campanian dish are cooked and enjoyed all over the country. It is a very distant cousin to the original Pizza with its tomato topping, and should not be confused with it in any way. Pizza rustica is very much a dish in its own right and the filling can vary according to who makes it. Although the original recipe calls for basic pastry (see page 299), nowadays it is often made with bread dough (see page 294), using 4 fl oz (120 ml) of olive oil to every 1 lb (450 g) of flour. This savoury pie should be eaten as part of a picnic or buffet, as informally as possible!

SERVES 6–8

Savoury pasta frolla made with 14 oz (400 g) plain white flour (see page 299) *or* 1 lb (450 g) bread dough (see page 294)

2 oz (50 g) salame, in thickish slices

2 oz (50 g) prosciutto crudo, sliced

4 oz (100 g) mozzarella cheese

4 oz (100 g) smoked provolone *or* mature Cheddar cheese

11 oz (300 g) fresh ricotta *or* whipped cream cheese

4 eggs, separated

2 tablespoons grated Parmesan cheese

salt and pepper

1½ oz (40 g) butter

Pre-heat the oven to gas mark 4, 350°F (180°C).

Prepare the pastry or dough and set aside until required.

Chop the salame, prosciutto, mozzarella and provolone or Cheddar into even-sized cubes. Push the ricotta or whipped cream cheese through a sieve.

Remove ½ egg yolk from the 4 egg yolks and set it aside until later (you will use it to brush the surface of the finished pie). Beat the rest of the egg yolks until pale yellow and foaming. Whisk the egg whites until stiff. Fold the egg whites into the egg yolks. Add all the other ingredients except the butter, blending very slowly and carefully so that the egg mixture does not flop and go flat.

Butter a deep 11 inch (28 cm) spring-loaded cake tin generously. Divide the pastry or dough into 2 pieces, 1 larger than the other. Roll out the larger piece and use it to line the tin. Pour the filling into the lined tin and smooth it flat with the back of a spoon. Roll out the second piece of pastry or dough and arrange it on the top, making sure the edges overlap and form a thick crust. Press it all around the edges with the tips of your fingers. Brush the surface all over with the remaining ½ egg yolk. Bake for

40 minutes in the centre of the oven. Remove from the oven and take out of the tin. Leave for 10 minutes before serving, to make it easier to slice.

FIVE BASIC TOPPINGS *for* PIZZA

Basing all these recipes on a 4-person pizza (see page 295), here are five traditional ways to dress your pizza.

1. The Original Pizza: La Marinara (The Marinara)

The original pizza was invented by a backstreet Neapolitan baker, though sadly his name has gone unrecorded and has been forgotten. One shivers to think of what he could have become had he patented his invention – pizza is the fastest selling fast food in the world, even beating hamburgers – but such is life! The first pizza ever baked had a topping of tomato, garlic and dried oregano, plus salt and pepper. Some people claim that fresh basil was added too, but I somehow doubt it. This was, and still is, Pizza Marinara. Despite its name it has nothing whatsoever to do with seashores or marine life!

about 8 tablespoons passata
2 large pinches dried oregano
2–4 cloves garlic, peeled and chopped
1 tablespoon finely chopped fresh basil (optional)
2 tablespoons olive oil
salt and pepper

Pre-heat the oven to gas mark 9, 475°F (240°C).

Spread the passata all over the pizza, leaving a 1 inch (2.5 cm) space around the edges.

Scatter the dried oregano, garlic and basil (if using) all over the tomato. Sprinkle with the olive oil, salt and pepper.

Bake for about 10 minutes or until the crust around the edge of the pizza is crisp and cooked through.

2. La Margherita (The Margherita)

This pizza, the first variation on the classic Pizza Marinara, was created in honour of Queen Margherita of Savoy when she and her husband were on holiday in Naples at the end of the plague epidemic. The queen had heard tell of this wonderful new speciality called pizza and was very keen to try it out. Raffaelle Esposito, the best local pizza maker, was called to the court. He created a pizza with a topping of tomato, basil and mozzarella and named it Margherita. The queen was delighted with such an honour and enjoyed the pizza so much that soon all of Naples was eating it too. It wasn't long before somebody noticed that the three colours of the pizza (red, white and green) were also the colours of the Italian flag, although Signor Esposito always claimed this was purely coincidental!

about 8 tablespoons
  passata
about 4 oz (100 g)
  mozzarella cheese,
  chopped
large pinch dried oregano
8 leaves fresh basil, torn
  into pieces
salt and pepper
2 tablespoons olive oil

Pre-heat the oven to gas mark 9, 475°F (240°C).
  Spread the passata all over the pizza, leaving a 1 inch (2.5 cm) space around the edges.
  Scatter the mozzarella, oregano and basil over the tomato. Sprinkle with the salt, pepper and oil.
  Bake for about 10 minutes or until the pizza is crisp and the cheese melted.

3. La Napoletana (The Napoletana)

This is the only pizza which traditionally uses anchovy.

about 8 tablespoons
  passata
3 oz (75 g) mozzarella
  cheese, chopped
1½ oz (40 g) canned
  anchovy fillets, drained
  and chopped, *or* 1½ oz
  (40 g) anchovy paste
2 tablespoons olive oil
salt and pepper

Pre-heat the oven to gas mark 9, 475°F (240°C).
    Spread the passata all over the pizza, leaving
a 1 inch (2.5 cm) space around the edge.
    Scatter the mozzarella all over the tomato.
Dot evenly with pieces of anchovy fillet or
small squeezes of anchovy paste.
    Sprinkle with olive oil and salt and pepper.
    Bake for about 10 minutes, or until the pizza
is crisp and the cheese has melted.

4. Pizza ai Funghi (Mushroom Pizza)

about 8 tablespoons
  passata
about 3 oz (75 g)
  mushrooms, peeled and
  thinly sliced
about 3 oz (75 g)
  mozzarella cheese,
  chopped
2 tablespoons olive oil
salt and pepper
pinch dried oregano
  (optional)

Pre-heat the oven to gas mark 9, 475°F (240°C).
    Spread the passata all over the prepared pizza
base, leaving a 1 inch (2.5 cm) space round the
edge.
    Scatter the mushrooms and mozzarella
evenly all over the tomato.
    Sprinkle with olive oil, salt and pepper and
oregano, if using.
    Bake for about 10 minutes or until the crust
around the edge of the pizza is cooked through
and the cheese has melted.

5. Pizza alle 4 Stagioni (4-Season Pizza)

This is one pizza recipe where you really can use your imagination. The idea is to divide the pizza into quarters and put something different on each quarter. Here is the way I like to do it:

1st QUARTER
2 oz (50 g) mozzarella
   cheese, chopped
2 thin slices prosciutto
   crudo
1 tablespoon olive oil

Pre-heat the oven to gas mark 9, 475°F (240°C).
   Sprinkle the cheese on the 1st quarter, cover it with prosciutto and drizzle the oil on top.

2nd QUARTER
3 tablespoons passata
1 clove garlic, finely
   chopped
large pinch oregano
salt and pepper
1 tablespoon olive oil

Cover this quarter with the passata, sprinkle with garlic, oregano and salt and pepper, then sprinkle with olive oil.

3rd QUARTER
3 tablespoons passata
2 tablespoons assorted
   cooked shellfish (such as
   mussels, clams, prawns)
1 tablespoon olive oil
1 tablespoon chopped
   parsley
salt and pepper

Cover this quarter with passata, then scatter the shellfish on top. Sprinkle with olive oil, chopped parsley and salt and pepper.

4th QUARTER
2 tablespoons passata
2 oz (50 g) mushrooms,
   sliced
1 tablespoon olive oil
2 oz (50 g) mozzarella
   cheese, chopped
salt and pepper

Cover this quarter with passata, then scatter the mushrooms on top. Sprinkle with olive oil, then cover with mozzarella and season with salt and pepper.
   Bake the pizza for 10 minutes, or until cooked through.

FOCACCIA al FORMAGGIO
Flat Ligurian Cheese Bread

This is a very simple and delicious kind of flat bread with a wonderful gooey cheese filling. It is another recipe from lovely Liguria where, as I have already mentioned, they adore this sort of food! I have always eaten this as an antipasto, with cheeses and cured meats, olives and pickles, or else served it as a supper dish with a salad. However, you can eat it at any time of day, even as an afternoon snack or with wine as a pre-prandial delight!

Stracchino and pecorino cheese are both readily available from good Italian delicatessens. If you prefer a milder flavour, use very mature Cheddar or Bel Paese.

SERVES 4
14 oz (400 g) strong plain flour
about 8 tablespoons water
salt
4 tablespoons olive oil
11 oz (300 g) stracchino *or* pecorino cheese, cubed

Pre-heat the oven to gas mark 8, 450°F (230°C).

Knead the flour together with as much water as you need to make a smooth elastic dough, adding a pinch of salt as you go along. Work the dough carefully and vigorously. Cover it with a cloth and let it rest for at least 30 minutes.

Oil an 8 inch (20 cm) cake tin thoroughly. Roll out half of the dough and use it to cover the base of the cake tin. Arrange the cheese all over it evenly and cover with the second piece of dough. Cut a few slits in the top with a pair of scissors to prevent it rising. Sprinkle generously with salt, brush with the remaining oil and put in the oven to bake for 10 minutes. Serve piping hot so that the cheese is runny.

La FOCACCIA e i SUOI RIPIENI
Focaccia and Some Fillings

In my home town of Forte dei Marmi is Pietro's, a small, back-street osteria where they make the best Focaccia I have ever tasted. The huge, round, thick and oily shapes are taken out of the oven and cooled, and you choose a filling from one of the many terracotta pots lining the counter. You can literally go wild – everything is available, from braised onions to mozzarella and tomatoes to seafood and roasted peppers. The choice is absolutely up to you, but because this is an incredibly fashion-conscious and trendy resort, every season has its 'in' filling. Last time I was there, in 1986, the filling of the summer was soft cheese and braised peas! Anyway, whatever you choose goes into the opened-out envelope of Focaccia that has been cut for you, and then slid back into the oven to heat through. When you get it back, take it outside and sit down with a cool glass of wine or walk with it, wandering past Gianni Versace's boutique as you go, and take a glance at Gucci and Emporio Armani too! As you bite through the golden, crisp yet soft Focaccia, imbued with the flavour of your filling, you'll really know you are on holiday, and in Tuscany.

SERVES 4

1 lb (450 g) strong white
   bread flour
1 oz (25 g) fresh yeast
   or ¼ oz (10 g) Easyblend
   yeast *or* ½ oz (15 g) dried
   yeast
about 4 tablespoons warm
   water
salt
about 8 tablespoons olive
   oil

If using fresh or dried yeast, blend it with the warm water and leave until frothy. If using Easyblend yeast, mix it into the flour – no water is necessary.

Tip the flour out into a mound on a work-surface. Make a hollow in the centre with your fist. Put the yeast mixture into the hole and begin to blend it together with your fingers. Add as much liquid as you need to make a pliable dough. Add a pinch of salt and about 2 tablespoons olive oil. Knead it energetically and firmly until it is elastic and workable. Keep kneading for about 10 minutes. Roll the dough up into a ball, place it in a bowl and cover it with a clean cloth. Put it in a warm place to rise for about 2–2½ hours or until doubled in volume.

Pre-heat the oven to gas mark 7, 425°F (220°C).

Take the risen dough out and knead it again. Oil a shallow 11 inch (28 cm) tin with half the remaining oil. Put the dough in the middle and flatten it out as much as possible with your fingertips, pushing it towards the edges. Pour the remaining oil on top and spread it all over the surface with your fingers. Sprinkle with salt and put aside to rest for about 10 minutes.

Bake until brown and crisp on top, but still fairly soft in the middle: this should take about 12–16 minutes. Remove from the oven and slide out of the tin. Cool until required on a rack. When you want to serve it, either cut it into small wedges and serve as bread, or cut into bigger wedges and slit open horizontally like a sandwich so that you can fill it with any of the following:

Fillings

All these fillings are for 1 whole Focaccia – i.e. 4 servings.

BRAISED ONIONS

6 tablespoons olive oil

2 large onions, peeled and thinly sliced

salt and pepper

Heat the oil and fry the onions over a low heat until soft and golden brown. Season with salt and pepper and cool until required. Pile the onions on one half of the open Focaccia, sandwich the wedge back together and heat through in the oven at gas mark 5, 375°F (190°C), for about 6 minutes.

PROSCIUTTO AND MOZZARELLA

about 10 slices prosciutto crudo

5 oz (150 g) mozzarella cheese, thinly sliced

salt and pepper

Line the inside of the wedge of Focaccia with as many slices of prosciutto as you like. Cover with thin slices of mozzarella and sandwich the Focaccia back together. Heat through in the oven at gas mark 5, 375°F (190°C), for about 6 minutes.

MOZZARELLA AND TOMATOES

2 large marmande or
  beefsteak tomatoes,
  thinly sliced
5 oz (150 g) mozzarella
  cheese, thinly sliced
salt and pepper

Line the Focaccia wedge with as much tomato
and mozzarella as you like. Season and close
the wedge up. Heat through in the oven at gas
mark 5, 375°F (190°C), for about 6 minutes.

BRAISED PEPPERS

1 green, 1 yellow and 1 red
  pepper
6 tablespoons olive oil
2 cloves garlic, peeled and
  chopped
salt and pepper

Slice open the peppers, remove the seeds and
membranes and slice them thickly. Heat the oil
in a large pan and fry the garlic for about 5
minutes or until soft and golden. Add the
peppers and mix together. Season and continue
to cook for about 15 minutes or until the
peppers are completely soft. Spoon as much of
the pepper mixture as you like into a Focaccia
wedge, then heat through in the oven at gas
mark 5, 375°F (190°C), for about 6 minutes.

FOCACCIA con la CIPOLLA alla ROMANA
Roman Onion Bread

*You can buy slabs of this delicious, flat, oiled bread, coated in sliced onions
and rosemary, all over the country; but nowhere do they make it quite so
tingling and tasty as in the Pizzerie a Taglio of Rome. Usually this sort of
thing is a between-meals snack, best eaten from its brown paper wrapping
as you walk along. If you make it at home, as I do sometimes, serve it as
delicious party food, or for a buffet, or with a dish of thinly sliced prosciutto
as an antipasto.*

SERVES 6

1 lb (450 g) strong white
  bread flour
pinch salt
5 tablespoons olive oil

Put the flour in a mound on a work-surface and
make a hole in the centre with your fist. Put a
pinch of salt, 1 tablespoon olive oil and the
diluted fresh or dried yeast into the hole. Knead
very vigorously together for about 15 minutes,

1 oz (25 g) fresh yeast *or*
  2 teaspoons dried yeast,
  blended in about 2 fl oz
  (50 ml) warm water
2 large onions, peeled and
  finely sliced, covered in
  cold water and left to
  soak for about 15
  minutes
1 large sprig fresh rosemary,
  leaves removed and
  finely chopped *or* 1
  tablespoon dried
  rosemary
salt and pepper

adding more water as required. Leave in an oiled bowl covered with a cloth to rise in a warm place for 1 hour.

Take the dough out of the bowl, knock it back and replace it to rise for another hour.

Pre-heat the oven to gas mark 8, 450°F (230°C).

Oil a wide, shallow, preferably metal ovenproof dish. The bigger it is, the thinner your Focaccia will be. I use an incredibly battered old tin, about 12 × 15 inches (30 × 38 cm).

Knead the dough again very briefly. Flatten it and spread it out over the base of the tin with your hands, pulling it in every direction. Press the surface over and over again to make sure it is spread out as evenly as possible, and also to force it to stick to the edges. Rub oil all over the flattened dough.

Drain and dry the onions, then lay them on top of the dough in a thick layer, leaving a 1 inch (2.5 cm) space round the edges. Drizzle oil all over the onion, scatter with rosemary and season with plenty of salt and pepper. Place in the oven and bake for 15 minutes – the onions should be just soft and the rest of the Focaccia fairly pale in colour. Allow to cool for about 3 minutes, then slice and serve.

FISH AND SEAFOOD

PESCE SPADA alla GRIGLIA
Grilled Swordfish Steaks

The noble swordfish is fished off the coasts of Sicily and Calabria and cooked in lots of different ways. One of the most simple and certainly my favourite is to marinate steaks and grill them either on a barbecue or under an ordinary grill. It's best to marinate them as the fish is not naturally juicy and can dry out. Shark steaks can also be cooked in this way. I like to serve the finished dish with Aulivi Cunsati (page 285) for a very Sicilian effect. You can also cook them with Salmoriglio (page 281) to brush over them as they cook.

SERVES 4

4 thick fresh or frozen
   swordfish *or* shark steaks
juice of ½ lemon
6 tablespoons extra virgin
   olive oil
salt and pepper
large pinch dried mixed
   herbs

Trim and clean the fish as required. Lay the steaks in a shallow dish, side by side but not overlapping. Mix together the lemon juice, oil, salt and pepper and herbs. Pour this over the fish and cover with foil. Put the dish in the fridge for about 4 hours. Heat the barbecue or grill to an even maximum heat. Remove the fish from the marinade and cook for about 5 minutes on each side or until tender and flaking, basting with the marinade as it cooks. Serve piping hot.

Pizza Margherita (page 151)

Top: Dino Lazzaro, the L'Aquila
representative of L'Accademia della
Cucina Italiana, enjoying his lunch of
Maccheroni alla Chitarra. *Bottom:* The
basic simplicity of Sardinian bread:
Carta da Musica.

FILETTI di MERLUZZO all'ISTRIANA

Cod Fillets with Chilli, Garlic and Capers

This recipe from Friuli Venezia Giulia uses very unusual ingredients for the area. It is not usual to find ingredients that are so typical of the south so far north and so close to the Austrian and Yugoslavian borders. But the main thing about it is that it tastes so good!

SERVES 4

1 lb (500 g) cod fillets, trimmed, washed and patted dry

1 onion, peeled and finely sliced

1 clove garlic, peeled and crushed

1 handful parsley, chopped

4 tablespoons olive oil

salt and pepper

1 tablespoon capers, drained, washed and dried

2 sardines canned in oil

1 small potato, peeled and grated

4 tablespoons fish stock (see page 293)

½ dried red chilli pepper, rubbed lightly between your palms to release the oils (remember to wash your hands afterwards)

juice of 1 lemon, strained

Place the cod in a heavy-bottomed saucepan and cover with the onion, garlic, parsley and oil. Season with salt and pepper and cook gently over a low heat for about 12 minutes. Remove from the saucepan with a fish slice and arrange on a warmed platter; keep warm.

Chop the capers very finely, add them to the oil remaining in the saucepan and stir. Trim and chop the sardines and add them to the capers. Stir in the potato, stock and chilli. Stir and simmer for about 5 minutes or until the potato is cooked. Lay the cod carefully in this sauce and heat through for about 3 minutes. Remove the chilli, put the cod back on the platter and sprinkle with the lemon juice before serving.

BURIDDA
Ligurian Fish Casserole

Also called Pesce in Tocchetto, *this is a lovely, simple fish casserole which can be made extra special with the addition of porcini mushrooms if you can get them. The fish must be in thick chunks no larger than 3–4 inches (8–10 cm) square, or you can use whole small fish. What is important is to have a good variety of fish, for a mixture of tastes and textures. Don't be afraid to use whole small fish with their heads on – it all adds to the flavour!*

SERVES 4

3 cloves garlic, peeled
1 small onion, peeled and
  chopped
1 small carrot, scraped and
  chopped
1 stick celery, chopped
4 sprigs parsley, chopped
6 tablespoons olive oil
3 canned tomatoes,
  drained, de-seeded and
  chopped
2 anchovy fillets, boned
  and washed
1 oz (25 g) dried porcini
  mushrooms, soaked in
  tepid water for 15
  minutes (optional)
1 oz (25 g) pine kernels
1 tablespoon plain white
  flour mixed with 3
  tablespoons warm water
salt and pepper
2¼ lb (1 kg) mixed fish
  from the following list:
  hake, bass, swordfish,
  monkfish, squid,
  mackerel, whiting, John
  Dory, witch, plaice, grey

Chop 2 of the garlic cloves and put with the onion, carrot, celery and parsley into a heavy-bottomed flameproof casserole with the olive oil. Fry gently, stirring, for about 8 minutes. Add the tomatoes and stir for 2–3 minutes, then add the anchovy fillets and stir again. Drain the mushrooms (if using) and reserve the water. Strain it carefully and add to the casserole. Chop the mushrooms finely. Chop the pine kernels very finely and mix them with the mushrooms. Alternatively whizz them together for 30 seconds in a food processor using the blade attachment. Mix the mushrooms and pine kernels with the flour and water and pour this mixture over the ingredients in the casserole. Stir and season generously with salt and pepper.

Now lay all the pieces of fish (or small whole fish) in the casserole, beginning with the larger ones. Cook for about 6 minutes on one side, then carefully turn the fish over and cook it on the other side. Pour in the wine and let the alcohol evaporate. Stir carefully, making sure that you do not break up the fish, and cook, covered, over a low heat for about 20 minutes.

Rub the toasted bread with the remaining garlic clove, lay the bread at the bottom of a warmed tureen, pour the fish casserole all over it and serve at once.

mullet and red mullet,
gutted, washed and cut
into equal-sized chunks
if over 4 inches (10 cm)
long
1 glass dry white wine
4 thick slices coarse, white
bread, toasted
4–5 tablespoons olive oil

SEDANI e BACCALÀ
Celery and Salt Cod Casserole

This recipe from the Abruzzi town of L'Aquila shows off the celery for which the town is famous. Combined with dried salt cod, sultanas and olives, pine kernels and tomatoes, celery makes a really superb dish. You can, of course, use any kind of fish suitable for stewing, such as huss, chunks of mackerel, monkfish or squid.

SERVES 4

1 lb (500 g) fresh, crisp
celery
1½ oz (40 g) sultanas
1 large onion, peeled and
chopped
2 fl oz (50 ml) olive oil
5 canned tomatoes,
drained, de-seeded and
coarsely chopped
1¾ lb (800 g) salt cod,
soaked overnight, rinsed,
dried and cut into
chunks
1½ oz (40 g) pine kernels
10 black olives, stoned
salt and pepper

Wash and trim the celery and slice it into little finger-sized sticks. Cover the sultanas in tepid water and leave them to swell for 15 minutes, then drain. Fry the onion in the oil for about 7 minutes or until soft. Stir in the tomatoes and cook for 10 minutes more. Add the fish and heat through thoroughly, turning it over after about 5 minutes, then add the celery, pine kernels, the drained sultanas and the olives. Season with salt and pepper and stir. Cover and cook for about 30 minutes. Arrange on a warmed dish and serve.

FRITELLE di BACCALÀ alla SPEZZINA
Salt Cod Fritters

Salt cod is one of those foods which unfortunately looks extremely unattractive, but which, when treated right, tastes delicious. It originated in times well before the refrigerator age, when more ingenious ways of preserving food had to be found. When you buy the fish, remember that it is supposed to look like a dirty floorcloth, but it won't actually taste like one! In this recipe from the port of La Spezia in Liguria, the fish is soaked for 2 days, coated in a water-and-flour paste and deep-fried until golden and crisp.

SERVES 4

1 lb (450 g) dried salt cod
5 oz (150 g) plain white
   flour
2 tablespoons olive oil
oil for deep-frying
salt
lemon wedges

Cover the cod in about 3½ pints (2 litres) cold water and soak it for 48 hours, changing the water frequently. When the fish is soaked through, take it out of the water and scrape all the scales off with a knife, trim it and cut it into chunks about 1½ × 3 inches (4 × 7.5 cm).

Work the flour, olive oil and about 1½ pints (900 ml) tepid water together with a heavy-duty whisk to make a very smooth-textured batter.

When you are ready to cook, pour about 5 inches (13 cm) oil into a 12 inch (30 cm) lidded deep-fryer and heat until sizzling – it should sizzle instantly when you drop in a small piece of bread. Dip the chunks of fish into the batter and deep-fry for about 8 minutes or until crisp and a rich golden-brown all over. The cooking time will vary according to the size of the fish pieces and the temperature of the oil. Drain the fritters on kitchen paper, sprinkle with salt and serve with lemon wedges.

PESCE RAGNO all'ASTIGIANA
Bass in Asti Wine

For this recipe you need a decent bottle of dry white wine, which is certainly not hard to find in Asti – surely everybody must have drunk Asti Spumante at least once? The dish is also an excellent way of cooking pike, if you can cope with all the bones with which, unfortunately, this fish is blessed. The traditional accompaniment is small, boiled potatoes.

SERVES 4

1 bass, weighing about 1¾–
   2¼ lb (800 g–1 kg),
   scaled, gutted, washed
   and patted dry
1 bottle dry white wine
   (preferably from Asti)
½ teaspoon salt
1½ tablespoons unsalted
   butter
lemon wedges and parsley
   sprigs to garnish

Pre-heat the oven to gas mark 5, 375°F (190°C).

Make sure that the fish is properly cleaned and that the larger scales have been scraped off. Lay it in a fish kettle or other large, ovenproof container and pour the wine over it. Add the salt and butter and cover tightly. Bake in the oven for about 35 minutes. When cooked, the eyes of the fish will have turned completely white and opaque and will pop out slightly; the juices in the kettle should also be thick and glutinous.

Remove the fish from the kettle and place it on a warmed platter. Garnish with lemon wedges and parsley. Slice across the skin horizontally several times, bring the juices in the fish kettle to simmering point and pour all over the fish.

SPIGOLA ARROSTO alla BRACE
Roast Sea Bass

*I got this simple recipe from Alessandro Manconi who, with his father,
uncles and brothers, runs the delightful seashore restaurant called Lo Scoglio,
just outside Cagliari in Sardinia. The fresh flavour of the fish remains
completely unadulterated when you prepare it so simply.*

SERVES 4

1 sea bass, weighing about
3¼ lb (1.5 kg), gutted,
washed and patted dry *or*
2 sea bass, weighing
about 1½–2 lb (750–
900 g) each

5 tablespoons cold water

½ tablespoon sea salt

1 clove garlic, peeled and
finely chopped

1 bay leaf

1 sprig rosemary

2 tablespons olive oil

Ideally, cook the bass on a barbecue, over an
even and quite gentle heat. Failing this, grill it
under a medium grill for about 8 minutes on
either side, depending upon how thick the fish
is.

While the fish is cooking, prepare the
dressing. Mix the water and salt together. Crush
the chopped garlic and stir this into the salted
water. Add the bay leaf, rosemary and oil and
stir carefully, pressing the rosemary and bay leaf
hard with a spoon to release their flavour into
the water. When the fish is cooked, arrange it
carefully on a warmed platter and pour the
dressing all over it before serving.

SOGLIOLA in GRATELLA
Grilled Stuffed Lemon Sole

*This is another of those stuffed-to-bursting-point dishes from the Marche. It
is important that the fish be unskinned in order for the method to work.*

SERVES 4

4 lemon soles, weighing
about 2¼ lb (1 kg)
altogether

1½ oz (40 g) parsley,
chopped

2 cloves garlic, peeled and

Wash the soles carefully and gut them without
tearing, or get your fishmonger to do this for
you. Open them up on the gut side and stretch
the opening so that the stuffing will fit. Wash
them again and leave them to drain. Mix the
parsley, garlic, breadcrumbs, salt, pepper and
about 4 tablespoons of the olive oil to a smooth

finely chopped
2 tablespoons fresh
  breadcrumbs
salt and pepper
about 7 tablespoons olive
  oil
lemon wedges

paste. Fill each drained sole with this mixture and carefully press them closed. Grill them under a medium heat for about 5–6 minutes on each side or until cooked through (the eyes should be white and opaque). Serve with the remaining oil and lemon wedges handed separately.

TRIGLIE alla VERNACCIA
Red Mullet in Vernaccia Wine

I love the way the Sardinians cook fish. This recipe in particular reflects the island's Catalan history. It is unquestionably the best recipe for red mullet I have ever come across.

SERVES 4
1 oz (25 g) parsley, chopped
2 cloves garlic, peeled and
  finely chopped
1 wine glass olive oil
1 lb (450 g) canned
  tomatoes, drained, de-
  seeded and chopped
1¾ lb (800 g) red mullet *or*
  red snapper
1 lemon, sliced very thinly
  in rounds
pepper
7 fl oz (200 ml) Vernaccia
  wine

Fry the parsley and garlic in the oil in a wide, fairly deep pan for about 2 minutes, then stir in the tomatoes and simmer slowly for about 20 minutes.

Meanwhile, clean and gut the fish, removing the very big scales with a sharp knife. Wash them repeatedly, then add them to the tomato mixture together with the lemon slices. Season with pepper, cover and cook for about 10 minutes, then turn the fish over and cook for about 6 minutes longer. Take the mullet or snapper out of the saucepan and lay them on a warmed platter. Pour the wine into the saucepan, stir and raise the heat. Boil quickly for 1 minute, then pour over the fish and serve at once.

PALOMBO con i PISELLI
Huss and Fresh Pea Casserole

As there are many recipes which include peas in the cuisine of Lazio and Rome, you get the impression that this is the favourite vegetable of the inhabitants! In this dish, slices or chunks of huss are cooked in a rich tomato sauce with tender, fresh peas. If fresh peas are not available, frozen will do. Other fish can be cooked in the same way provided that they stand up well to long, slow stewing. Squid, for example, works very well.

SERVES 4

1½ lb (750 g) huss *or* monkfish

1½ fl oz (30 ml) olive oil

3 cloves garlic, peeled and finely chopped

1 handful parsley, finely chopped

1½ lb (750 g) fresh peas (shelled weight) *or* frozen peas

7 fl oz (200 ml) passata

1 teaspoon tomato purée

salt and pepper

Trim the fish and cut it into steaks or chunks depending on its width. A larger, older fish will slice into thick steaks, whereas a smaller, younger fish must be cut into chunks. Wash the fish, pat it dry and set it aside.

Put the oil, garlic and parsley into a shallow saucepan wide enough to take all the fish in one layer. Fry for about 6 minutes, then add the peas and stir. Cook for about 3–4 minutes, add the passata and tomato purée, stir very carefully and cover. Simmer very slowly for about 10 minutes. Make sure that the peas are completely tender, especially if you are using fresh ones, then arrange the fish in the saucepan in one layer with the peas and tomato. Season generously with salt and pepper, cover and simmer for about 5 minutes. Turn the fish over and simmer for 5–7 minutes on the other side. Take the fish out of the pan and arrange it on a warmed dish, cover with the peas and tomato and serve at once.

TEGAME alla VERNAZZANA
Vernazza Fish Bake

_____

Vernazza is one of the five villages that make up the Cinque Terre, little fishing ports along the Ligurian coast between La Spezia and Genoa. Apart from being incredibly pretty, the villages are famous for producing some of the very best of Liguria's wines, white and pure, clean-tasting wines that are heady and delightful. I make a point of visiting Vernazza whenever I am near the area. At the Ristorante Belforte, built into the top of the stone fortress in the tiny village, Mirella Basso made this delicious traditional dish for me. I ate it on the terrace overlooking the lovely little bay whilst admiring the view along the coast line.

_____

SERVES 8-10

2 tablespoons olive oil

2¼ lb (1 kg) potatoes, peeled and sliced into thick rounds

3 cloves garlic, peeled and finely chopped

1 handful parsley, finely chopped

4 lb (1.75 kg) fresh anchovies *or* sardines, cleaned, boned, washed and patted dry

9 oz (250 g) fresh *or* canned tomatoes, drained, de-seeded and coarsely chopped

1 teaspoon dried *or* 2 teaspoons fresh oregano

1 teaspoon fresh rosemary leaves

salt and pepper

1 large glass dry white wine (preferably from the Cinque Terre)

Pre-heat the oven to gas mark 4, 350°F (180°C).

Heat the oil in a large frying-pan and cook the potatoes for about 5 minutes or until slightly browned.

Oil the bottom of an 11 inch (28 cm) shallow baking tin or ovenproof dish. Cover with the chopped garlic and parsley and then lay all the potato slices on top in a single layer, slightly overlapping. Put the anchovies or sardines on the top to make a compact covering with no gaps. Cover with the tomatoes, sprinkle with the herbs and season generously. Pour the wine over the top and bake in the oven for about 30 minutes. Check the dish occasionally and add water if it appears to be drying out.

SARDE FRESCHE in TORTIERA
Baked Fresh Sardines

This is a deliciously simple, wonderful dish from Puglia, in which sardines are layered and baked, coated with a savoury custard.

SERVES 4

1¾ lb (800 g) fresh *or* frozen sardines, scaled, gutted, washed and patted dry

6 tablespoons water mixed with ½ teaspoon salt

5 oz (150 g) fresh breadcrumbs

4 oz (100 g) pecorino *or* Parmesan cheese, grated

1 handful parsley, chopped

salt and pepper

1 small wine glass olive oil

2 large eggs, beaten with a pinch salt

Pre-heat the oven to gas mark 4, 350°F (180°C).

Prepare the fish with care, open them out flat and remove the heads and the central bones. Put the salted water in the bottom of an ovenproof dish large enough to take all the fish in 2 layers and put 1 layer of fish on the bottom. Mix together the breadcrumbs, grated cheese and parsley and season generously with salt and pepper. Cover the fish with half this mixture. Lay the remaining fish on top and cover with the remains of the bread, parsley and cheese mixture. Pour the oil all over, then pour the beaten eggs over that. Cook in the oven for about 25 minutes, or until the eggs are solidified and well coloured. Serve from the dish.

ANGUILLA alla COMACCHIESE
Eel and Onion Casserole

Comacchio is the centre of the eel-fishing industry, and here is one of the most traditional and simple recipes for cooking this surprisingly delicious fish. The local method for removing the scales from the fish is to rub the whole length of it with handfuls of wood ash, placed on sheets of robust paper. You can substitute dogfish, huss or rock salmon for the eel. Whatever type of fish you are using, you could ask your fishmonger to prepare it for you and cut it into 2 inch (5 cm) pieces. Serve with slabs of polenta (see page 140) or potatoes and vegetables.

SERVES 4

3–4 onions, peeled and sliced

1 large clove garlic, peeled and sliced

4 tablespoons olive oil

3 tablespoons red wine vinegar

3 tablespoons tomato purée, diluted with 1 glass warm water

about 2 lb (1 kg) medium-sized eels *or* dogfish *or* huss *or* rock salmon, scaled, gutted, washed and patted dry

salt and pepper

Place the onions and garlic in a wide, shallow saucepan with the oil and fry for about 6 minutes. Sprinkle with the vinegar, pour in the diluted tomato purée and leave to simmer gently while you prepare the eel or fish.

Cut each eel or fish into 2 inch (5 cm) chunks, lay these in the saucepan and simmer gently for about 45 minutes. Do not stir but just shake the pan gently from time to time and spoon the sauce over the chunks as they cook.

TROTA alla CERTOSINA
Trout with Mushrooms and Red Wine

The marriage of trout and red wine is one of my favourite flavour combinations. As a member of a family of extremely keen trout fishermen, with countless Irish fishing holidays to my credit, I find that the preparation and eating of this noble fish is something that is very close to my heart. For this recipe you need one of those big, fat fish with a hearty flavour and firm texture. The recipe is from Lombardy.

SERVES 4

1 large trout, weighing about 2¼ lb (1 kg)
2 small onions, peeled
1 handful parsley, finely chopped
2 shallots, peeled and finely chopped *or* 1 large clove garlic, peeled and chopped
3 large flat mushrooms, finely chopped
pinch salt
1 teaspoon black peppercorns, crushed
3½ oz (90 g) unsalted butter
1 carrot, scraped
1 stick celery
about ½ bottle dry red wine
1 tablespoon plain white flour

Scrape the larger scales off the fish and wash it carefully. Gut it and wash it on the inside. Let it drain in the sink until required. Chop one of the onions finely and mix with the parsley, shallots or garlic and mushrooms. Stir in the salt and the peppercorns and then mash in half the butter to make a paste. Dry the inside of the trout and fill with this mixture. Lay the trout in a fish kettle or large, lidded frying-pan and add the carrot, celery and remaining whole onion. Pour in the wine, which should only just cover the fish – don't drown it. Put the lid on the kettle or pan, place it over a medium heat and bring to the boil. Simmer gently for about 20 minutes or until the eyes of the trout have turned white and popped out slightly. Take great care not to let it bubble too quickly or you risk breaking the fish up. Slide a knife through the back of the fish to make sure that it is flaky and cooked, not sticky and raw.

When you are satisfied that the fish is cooked, remove it from the fish kettle or pan and lay it on a warmed platter. Skin it very carefully and discard the skin. Strain the liquid remaining in the fish kettle and return it to the heat. You should have about 1 wine glass of liquid: if there is more, raise the heat to evaporate the excess; if you have the right amount of liquid, just keep it bubbling gently.

Mash the remaining butter and the flour together until smooth, then drop it into the gently boiling liquid. Whisk until smooth and thick, pour all over the skinned trout and serve at once. As the trout will have been cooling during the skinning and sauce preparation, it is a good idea to serve it on to piping-hot plates.

TROTA in BLU
Trout Poached in Wine

This recipe for poached trout comes from the Alto Adige. If possible, use fish that has only just come out of the river – there is nothing like the flavour of freshly caught trout. However, if you cannot get hold of really fresh trout, even the most dull frozen type can be perked up with this recipe.

SERVES 1

1 very fresh trout, weighing about 10 oz (275 g)

1 wine glass best-quality white wine vinegar

2 glasses dry red or white wine

1 carrot, scraped and cut in half

4 sprigs parsley

rind of 1 lemon

3 bay leaves

2 cloves

1 teaspoon black peppercorns

salt

To serve

1 lemon, cut into wedges

parsley

2 oz (65 g) unsalted butter, melted and hot

Gut, wash and trim the fish, then lay it in a bowl. Put the vinegar in a pan and slowly bring it to the boil. When it boils, pour it slowly over the fish and leave it to soak for 15 minutes.

Pour the wine into another pan, add half the same volume of water, the carrot, parsley, lemon rind, bay leaves, cloves and peppercorns. Add a pinch of salt and bring this to the boil very slowly.

Drain the trout, discarding the vinegar, and lay it in a fish kettle or lidded frying-pan. Strain the boiling liquid over the fish (it may not cover it completely) and cover tightly with a lid. Cook the trout over a gentle heat for 15 minutes, then remove it from the fish kettle or pan and place it on a warmed dish. Decorate with lemon wedges and parsley and serve with the melted butter handed separately.

CAPESANTE alla VENEZIANA
Venetian Scallops

In Italy the scallop enjoys several different names: it is known as ventaglio, pettine maggiore *or* conchiglia del pellegrino. *In this recipe from Venice scallops are cooked very simply with garlic, parsley, olive oil and lemon juice. You can serve this either as a starter or as a main course.*

SERVES 4

12–14 large scallops, opened by your fishmonger

1 wine glass best-quality olive oil

1 clove garlic, peeled and finely chopped

1 handful parsley, chopped

salt and pepper

juice of 1 lemon, strained

Remove the molluscs from their shells and clean them carefully, discarding the yellow outer skirt but not the orange corals. Put them into a heavy-bottomed pan with the oil, garlic and parsley and season to taste with salt and pepper. Cover and cook slowly for 5–6 minutes. Sprinkle with the lemon juice and return the scallops to their shells before serving.

COOKING SHELLFISH

Having experienced being in Italy during a cholera epidemic, and been badly caught out with not-quite-perfect seafood once or twice, I always feel happier using cooked instead of raw shellfish in my recipes. I have therefore adapted recipes in this collection by using steamed shellfish in place of raw in all cases. To steam shellfish, simply place the cleaned, washed mussels, or whatever you are using, in a large, deep pan. Cover with a lid and place the pan over a high heat. Shake the pan constantly to help the shellfish to open up. Once they have opened, remove them from the pan. Any shellfish which do not open after 8 minutes should be discarded. I know that many people are worried about the health risks in eating shellfish, but nowadays most of them are purified in water treated with ultra-violet light, and the above method will successfully sort out any that are no good.

SOFFIATO di GAMBERI
Shrimp Soufflé

This sort of delicately flavoured dish is a legacy of Caterina de'Medici's Renaissance cuisine. It was probably transported to France, along with many other superb recipes, when she left Florence as a child bride with her retinue of cooks, in order to teach the French about cooking! In Tuscany you would most probably find this dish featured as a first course.

SERVES 8

1¾ lb (800 g) cooked brown or pink shrimps
1¾ pints (1 litre) milk
3 oz (75 g) unsalted butter
4½ oz (120 g) plain white flour
1 tablespoon tomato purée
5 tablespoons grated Parmesan cheese
pinch salt
¼ teaspoon white pepper
¼ teaspoon grated nutmeg
8 egg yolks, not mixed together
10 egg whites

Pre-heat the oven to gas mark 4, 350°F (180°C).

Peel the shrimps carefully, put the flesh to one side and pound the heads and shells in a pestle and mortar to a smooth paste. Alternatively whizz the heads and shells in a food processor for about 2 minutes. Push the paste through a sieve.

Heat the milk until just boiling. Meanwhile, melt about three quarters of the butter in a heavy-bottomed 2¾ pint (1.6 litre) saucepan and add the flour. Stir together very thoroughly, then gradually pour in the boiling milk. Mix well and cook for about 6 minutes or until thickened, stirring constantly. Pour the resulting white sauce into a bowl to cool it completely, then stir in the shrimp shell paste, the shrimp flesh, the tomato purée and the Parmesan, salt, pepper and nutmeg. Stir all this together very carefully, then stir in the egg yolks one at a time. Beat the egg whites into stiff peaks and fold very carefully into the shrimp mixture. Butter an 8-portion soufflé dish with the remaining butter, carefully pour in the well-blended mixture and place immediately in the oven to bake for 30–45 minutes or until golden on top. Serve straight away, otherwise the soufflé will flop and sink dramatically!

ZUPPA di COZZE
Mussel Casserole

All the flavours and colours of Naples are brought together in this delightful dish of mussels.

SERVES 4

about 50 fresh, live mussels
5 cloves garlic, peeled
6 tablespoons olive oil
2 handfuls parsley, chopped
1–2 dried red chilli peppers
  (optional)
10 fl oz (300 ml) passata
salt and pepper
15 fl oz (450 ml) fish stock
  (see page 293)
4 or more large slices coarse
  white bread, lightly
  toasted

Scrub and de-beard all the mussels with great care. Wash them very carefully in several changes of water, then put them into a deep saucepan over a medium heat and steam them open. Shake the pan to encourage them, and remove them as they open up. (Discard any that do not open after 8 minutes.) Put them into a bowl, strain the juices from the saucepan into a second bowl and leave to settle: the aim is to end up with very little sand and sediment.

Chop 3 of the garlic cloves and fry them in the olive oil in a heavy, flameproof casserole with 1 handful of the chopped parsley for about 5 minutes. If you are using the chillies, add them, then add the passata, season with salt and pepper and stir. Strain the mussel liquor and fish stock into the pan and simmer to reduce the liquid by about half. Tip in the open mussels and raise the heat. You are not cooking the mussels, simply heating everything through – it will take 3–4 minutes.

Cut the remaining 2 garlic cloves in half and rub the bread with them. Lay the bread at the bottom of a warmed tureen or wide bowl and pour all the mussels and their liquid over it. Scatter with the remaining chopped parsley and serve.

Sarde Fresche in Tortiera (page 170)

Above: The colourful boats of a tiny
Ligurian harbour. *Below:* Crayfish –
bounty from the Sardinian sea.

CLEANING CUTTLEFISH, SQUID OR OCTOPUS

Unless you buy these ready-cleaned, you will have to prepare them yourself. It is a very messy job, so do it on a wooden board by the sink or on the draining board – you need to be near running water to wash your hands and the fish constantly. First of all, peel off as much as possible of the fine outer skin, using your fingers. Separate the body from the head and tentacles (1). (The head is the bit with the eyes and the body is sac-shaped.) Slide the flat, oval bone out of the body, taking care not to split the sac (2). Discard the bone.

Remove the sac of black liquid and put it aside in case you need it for the recipe. Remove the yellow sac if there is one and keep this also to add to the recipe, though many people do throw it away because its flavour is so very strong. Cut out the eyes and small round cartilage at the base of the tentacles (3). Peel off the reddish membrane which covers the body sac (4) and rinse thoroughly. The fish is now ready to cut up into strips or leave intact, according to the recipe.

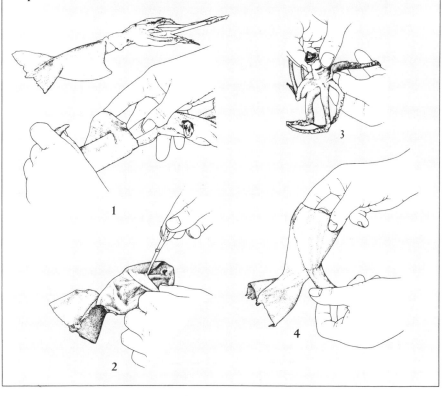

SEPPIOLINE alla CETRULLO
Stuffed Baby Squid

Although it is difficult to get baby squid in the UK, larger squid is now very widely available and you can substitute this, sliced into small, even shapes. The recipe, from Pescara, has more than a hint of fiery chilli about it. The flavours of this cuisine are characterised by their strength – the intense, vivacious flavours of capers, anchovies preserved in salt, very strong garlic and chilli peppers. The fish dishes of Pescara have a long-standing and jealously preserved tradition, and recipes are handed down from generation to generation with few alterations.

Serve with sautéed potatoes and courgettes stewed with tomatoes.

SERVES 4

about 2¼ lb (1.2 kg) squid (preferably weighing about 4½ oz (120 g) each), gutted, washed and patted dry
3 cloves garlic
1 whole chilli
1 handful parsley, chopped
1 tablespoon capers preserved in salt or brine
4 anchovies preserved in salt, cleaned and boned or 8 canned anchovy fillets, drained
3 tablespoons fresh breadcrumbs
about 4 tablespoons plus ½ wine glass olive oil
salt and pepper
1 glass dry white wine
10 fl oz (300 ml) hot fish stock (see page 293)

Prepare the squid, but be careful to leave the body sacs intact. If they are very large, remove the tentacles and keep the sacs separate, otherwise try to keep the whole fish in one piece. Set them aside.

Peel 1 of the garlic cloves. Chop the parsley again with it, the capers and the anchovies until everything is very fine. Mix the chopped ingredients with the breadcrumbs and enough oil (about 4 tablespoons) to make a smooth paste. Season with salt and pepper. Push this stuffing into the sacs of the squid and tie or sew them closed with cook's string.

Put the remaining oil in a shallow pan wide enough to take all the squid in one layer. Fry the remaining 2 unpeeled garlic cloves and chilli in the oil until brown, then remove them and lay the squid in the pan. Brown on both sides, then pour the wine over them and sprinkle with salt and pepper. Cover with fish stock and simmer for about 30 minutes. Remove the chilli. Remove the squid from the pan and take off the string. Arrange the squid on a warmed serving dish with all their juices and serve.

SEPPIE in UMIDO
Squid Casserole

If you cannot bear the thought of the crowds in Venice during the warmer months, opt for a visit to nearby Chioggia. This very pretty little fishing port has its own network of canals and bridges, dark alleys and front doorways graced by jetties, but with fewer crowds and no San Marco. Fish is eaten a great deal all along the Veneto coast, but especially among the fishermen and their families. Here is an excellent recipe for squid given to me by Giovanna Renier, the wife of one of the local fishermen. Polenta is recommended as an accompaniment to this dish, though it is also excellent served on a bed of mashed potatoes or rice.

SERVES 6

4 tablespoons sunflower oil

1 large onion, peeled and chopped

2 cloves garlic, peeled and chopped

1 × 3½ inch (9 cm) sprig fresh rosemary, leaves removed and chopped finely

2 lb (1 kg) fresh or frozen squid, cleaned and sliced into ½–1 inch (1-2.5 cm) strips (see page 177)

about 18 fl oz (500 ml) cold water

1 small can tomatoes, drained, de-seeded and chopped

1 teaspoon tomato purée

salt and pepper

pinch cinnamon

pinch nutmeg

Heat the oil and fry the onion and garlic until soft but not coloured. Add the rosemary and then the squid. Mix together, then cover with the water. Bring to the boil and simmer gently for 45 minutes.

Add the tomatoes, tomato purée, the salt and pepper and spices. Cover and simmer slowly for a further 45 minutes or until the squid is tender and the liquid has thickened into a rich sauce. Serve piping hot.

EGG & CHEESE DISHES

FRITTATA alla TRENTINA
Plain Trentino Omelette

It is definitely true that the plainest dishes are often the most difficult to make because there are no lavish sauces to cover up the basic ingredients. This is certainly the case with this very simple omelette from the Trentino Alto Adige region.

SERVES 4

6 large eggs, separated

9 oz (250 g) plain white flour

5 tablespoons milk

salt and pepper

3½ oz (90 g) unsalted butter

Beat the egg yolks very thoroughly, adding the flour a little at a time. Dilute this mixture with the milk and add salt and pepper. Beat the egg whites into stiff peaks and fold them carefully into the egg yolk mixture. Melt the butter in an omelette pan until sizzling, pour in the egg mixture and cook it until golden on the underside. (This should take about 6 minutes.) Then turn it over on to a lid or plate, slide it back into the pan and cook it for the same length of time on the other side. Fold it into 3, tip it on to a warmed plate and serve.

NOTE

If your omelette pan is small, you can do the frying in 2 or more batches.

FRITTATA CALABRESE di POMODORI

Flat Calabrian Omelette with Tomatoes

In Italy it is rare to find a folded-over omelette with the filling inside such as you would have in France. The technique in this recipe from Calabria is to mix the vegetable flavouring into the egg mixture and then fry it flat, using a lid or large plate to turn it over so you end up with something like a cake shape.

SERVES 4

4 large beefsteak tomatoes, sliced
4 tablespoons olive oil
6 large eggs
salt and pepper

Wash the tomatoes carefully and cut them into thin slices. Put them with half the oil in a frying-pan over a medium heat and stew them slowly, adding a little water as necessary, for about 10 minutes or until tender. Beat the eggs in a bowl with salt and pepper and add the cooked tomatoes to the egg mixture. Stir together thoroughly. Put the remaining oil in the pan and, when it is sizzling hot, tip in the egg mixture. Flatten the omelette with a palette knife and shake the pan to prevent sticking. Cook over a medium heat for about 8 minutes or until the underside is well browned. Slide the omelette on to a large lid or plate, then turn it the other way up back into the pan, being careful not to break it up. Press down with a palette knife and cook for a further 5 minutes. Slide on to a platter and serve either hot or cold.

NOTE
The same procedure is followed with all Frittatas, and you can use vegetables such as peas, French beans, onions, globe artichokes, courgettes, peppers, spinach or chard. If you prefer you can use lard, butter or vegetable oil instead of olive oil.

FRITTATA di PREZZEMOLO e BASILICO
Parsley and Basil Omelette

This is another recipe from Puglia, typically simple and delicious. I love to take slices of these omelettes on picnics, to be eaten cold with crusty bread and fresh tomatoes.

SERVES 2

4 large free-range eggs
1 handful fresh mint
1 handful fresh basil
salt and pepper
2 tablespoons milk
4 tablespoons olive oil

Beat the eggs lightly. Remove the leaves from the herbs, wash them and dry them, then tear them up with your fingers. Mix the leaves into the eggs and add salt, pepper and milk.

Heat the olive oil in a heavy-bottomed omelette pan until just beginning to smoke, then tip in the egg mixture. Smooth it out flat with the back of a spoon and cook it on one side for about 5 minutes or until golden. Turn it over on to a lid or large platter, then slide it back into the pan. Cook for a further 3 minutes, transfer to a serving dish and serve hot or cold.

UOVA alla PIEMONTESE
Piedmontese Truffle Omelette

To my mind, one of the simplest and most delicious ways in which to enjoy the superb white truffles of the Alba province of Piedmont is in an omelette made with fresh, free-range eggs – the sort with a glowing, orange yolk. If you prefer, a teaspoon of truffle purée, from a tube, can be used instead, blended into the beaten eggs.

SERVES 4

5 large eggs
salt and pepper
4 tablespoons grated
  Parmesan cheese

Beat the eggs in a bowl with salt and pepper to taste, and stir in the Parmesan cheese and the truffle. Melt the butter and oil in an omelette pan until sizzling hot but not brown. Pour in the omelette mixture and spread it out, pressing

2 tablespoons shavings
   from a cleaned fresh
   white truffle
walnut-sized lump of butter
1 tablespoon olive oil

it down with a spatula to make a flat cake shape.

After about 5 minutes, when the underneath is golden brown, turn the pan upside down on to a large plate or lid and slide the omelette back into the pan the other way up. Cook the second side for a further 5 minutes, then slide on to a platter to serve. This omelette can be served warm or cold.

UOVA in TRIPPA
Layered Baked Omelette

This Lazio dish is cooked in the same way in Lombardy, only there it is called Busecca Matta. The eggs are cooked in a similar way to tripe – the poorer people would have been more likely to be able to get eggs than fresh tripe. In the Lazio they cook the dish as follows, with herbs such as mint and parsley. It is delicious as an antipasto or with a salad as a simple lunch dish.

SERVES 4
1 handful parsley
6 large eggs
salt and pepper
about 12 tablespoons olive
   oil
about 12 leaves fresh mint,
   chopped
about 12 tablespoons
   grated pecorino *or*
   Parmesan cheese, or a
   mixture of the two
10 fl oz (300 ml) passata

Pre-heat the oven to gas mark 4, 350°F (180°C).

Chop the parsley finely and mix it well into the eggs. Season generously and beat until frothy.

Heat a little oil in an 8 inch (20 cm) frying-pan, and fry the mixture in small batches to make little pancake-thin omelettes. Cook them for about 2 minutes on each side, roll them up and slice them into strips.

Arrange the strips in layers in an ovenproof dish, scattering chopped mint, grated cheese and passata in between each layer. Place the dish in the oven for about 15 minutes, then serve.

FRITTATA *di* CIPOLLE
Onion Omelette

This is a delightfully Neapolitan recipe from Campania. I like to make it with red onions, as the colours – deep purple and brilliant yellow – are so attractive. If you can't get hold of red onions, don't worry; it will taste just as good. Serve as an antipasto or snack; it's also an excellent party dish.

SERVES 4

2 oz (50 g) piece prosciutto crudo *or* unsmoked bacon, sliced into strips

1¾ lb (800 g) onions, peeled and thinly sliced

6 leaves fresh mint, chopped

4 tablespoons olive oil

4 oz (100 g) lard *or* pork dripping *or* butter *or* margarine

salt and pepper

6 large eggs, beaten

2 tablespoons grated pecorino cheese

3 tablespoons grated Parmesan cheese

1 small handful fresh basil, finely chopped

3 canned tomatoes, drained, de-seeded and cut into strips

6–8 tablespoons vegetable oil

Fry the prosciutto or bacon, onions and mint together in 1 tablespoon of the olive oil and the fat, stirring from time to time, for about 10 minutes or until the onions are soft. Season to taste.

Beat the eggs with the cheeses and basil. Fry the tomatoes briefly in a separate pan with the remaining 3 tablespoons olive oil for about 10 minutes, then mix them into the eggs. Stir the cooked onions into the eggs as well.

Heat the vegetable oil in a pan large enough to take all the mixture. It should be so hot that a small piece of bread dropped into it sizzles instantly. Pour in all the mixture, press it down with a spatula, and cook it for about 6 minutes on one side. Slide it on to a plate and turn it over, return to the pan to cook for another 6 minutes and then slide it on to a serving plate. Serve cold (but not chilled).

FRITTATA AFFOGATA
Omelette Strips in a Tomato Sauce

I can remember eating this as a child at my grandmother's house. (The cook who made it for us then was Sardinian, but this dish is a speciality of Arezzo.) What I remember most vividly about meals with Grandma is that the napkins were of a size to cover a long skirt completely and when I was little they were big enough to envelop me altogether.

SERVES 4

4 large eggs, beaten
1 tablespoon plain white
  flour
salt and pepper
8 tablespoons olive oil
1 large onion, peeled and
  finely chopped
1 handful parsley, chopped
18 fl oz (500 ml) passata
large pinch dried mixed
  herbs
8 tablespoons freshly
  grated Parmesan cheese

Beat the eggs very thoroughly with the flour and seasoning. Heat half the oil in an omelette pan until sizzling hot and tip in the egg mixture in one or more batches, depending upon the size of your pan. The omelette should be quite thick – about 1½ inches (4 cm) – when cooked. Cook it on both sides like a pancake, then roll it up and slice across the roll to make strips.

In a separate saucepan, heat the remaining oil and fry the onion and the parsley for about 4 minutes or until the onion is soft. Add the passata and the mixed herbs and stir. Season and simmer for about 20 minutes. Slip the strips of omelette into the tomato sauce and heat through for about 5 minutes. Transfer to a warmed platter, sprinkle with the cheese and serve.

PEPERONI SOFFRITTI
con le UOVE
Scrambled Eggs with Sweet Red Peppers

This is a very ancient recipe from Puglia; its origins can be traced right back to the Daunian civilisation, to tribes which inhabited these rocky mountains in the mists of time. You need to use bright red peppers that are fleshy and juicy to achieve the right effect and, as always, fresh free-range eggs. Serve as a side dish or as a quick and delicious snack or antipasto.

SERVES 4

1 lb (450 g) juicy red
   peppers
3 large tablespoons olive oil
3 ripe tomatoes, peeled, de-
   seeded and chopped *or* 7
   cherry tomatoes, left
   whole
salt
2 large eggs, beaten

Wash and dry the peppers. Cut them open and discard the seeds and membranes. Slice them into neat strips. Fry them gently in a pan with the olive oil for about 6 minutes or until half-cooked. Add the tomatoes, stir and season with salt. When the tomatoes and peppers are both soft, pour on the eggs and cook very briefly, until just set. Serve at once, piping hot.

FORMAGGIO FRITTO
Fried Cheese with Eggs

An excellent dish from Friuli Venezia Giulia, served as an antipasto. In the original version, you would use one of the local mountain cheeses, but I have substituted mature Gouda or Cheddar very successfully.

SERVES 4

11 oz (300 g) cheese, cut in
   finger-thick slices
4 tablespoons coarse
   polenta flour
5 oz (150 g) unsalted butter
4 large eggs

Press the slices of cheese in the polenta flour to coat them thoroughly – as the flour is quite coarse it will easily embed itself in the cheese. Divide the butter between two frying-pans and bring them both to sizzling heat. Fry the eggs in one pan. In the other, fry the cheese for about 5 minutes or until the polenta coating is crisp. Serve the cheese and eggs together with bread.

CICORIA, CACIO e UOVA
Chicory, Cheese and Eggs

This is a speciality from the Abruzzi, and makes wonderful comfort food! It is actually very healthy and nourishing, a sort of cross between a soup and a vegetable dish.

SERVES 4

1 lb (450 g) Belgian chicory
  or curly endive, carefully
  picked over
salt
2 pints (1.2 litres) chicken
  or beef broth (see page
  289)
2 carrots, scraped and
  finely chopped
1 large onion, peeled and
  finely chopped
1 large stick celery,
  chopped
5 sprigs parsley, finely
  chopped
2 oz (50 g) lard mashed
  with 1 chopped onion
4 tablespoons olive oil
2 eggs, beaten
2 oz (50 g) pecorino cheese,
  grated

Wash the chicory very carefully, then boil it in plenty of salted water for about 10 minutes. Meanwhile, bring the broth to the boil, then add all the other chopped vegetables and the parsley. Fry the mashed lard and onion with the olive oil for about 8 minutes or until the onion is softened.

Drain the chicory and squeeze it dry lightly with your hands, chop it coarsely and add it to the frying onion. Stir-fry for about 5 minutes.

Beat the eggs and cheese together in the bottom of a soup tureen, then add the chicory and onion mixture and combine these ingredients with a fork. Pour in the broth, stir once and serve.

SCIATT
Cheese Fritters

This is a very old Lombard recipe, which has countless variations all over the region. The original recipe uses a local cheese which is not exported, but as a substitute I have used both Brie and firm mozzarella with immense success.

SERVES 4

7 oz (200 g) very fine rye flour

4 oz (100 g) plain white flour

salt

about 7 fl oz (200 ml) cold water

4 oz (100 g) Brie or mozzarella cheese, cut into large cubes

1 tablespoon Grappa

oil for deep-frying

Sift the 2 flours and a pinch of salt into a bowl. Make a well in the centre. Add the cold water gradually and beat until smooth. Let the batter rest for 1 hour, then add the cheese and the Grappa.

In a 12 inch (30 cm) deep pan, heat about 1½ inches (4 cm) oil until a piece of bread dropped into it sizzles instantly. Drop spoonfuls of the mixture into the oil – rather like making drop cookies, making sure that each spoonful contains cheese. Fry for about 5 minutes or until puffed and golden, then scoop out with a slotted spoon and drain on kitchen paper. Serve piping hot.

CACIU all'ARGINTERA
Silversmith's Cheese

Franca Colonna Romano, one of the greatest experts on Sicilian cuisine, gave me her recipe for this delicious dish over lunch at Lentini when we were invited to sample the Notabartolo wines. Legend has it that the dish was created by a silversmith who fell on hard times and was thereafter unable to afford meat. So he created this dish, which enabled him to enjoy the smell of 'meat' cooking even though it was not meat he ate, but simply cheese! Franca's recipe keeps the cheese soft and gooey – absolutely delicious. Serve with lots of crusty bread.

SERVES 4

1 lb (450 g) caciocavallo or mature Cheddar cheese
2 fl oz (50 ml) olive oil
1 large clove garlic, peeled and chopped
2 tablespoons red wine vinegar
large pinch dried oregano
salt and pepper

Cut the cheese into ½ inch (1 cm) thick wedges or slices. Heat the oil and fry the garlic until soft. Transfer the oil and garlic to a heatproof dish and place it over a pan of boiling water. Lay the cheese in the dish and cover with a lid. Heat until the cheese has softened, turning it over after about 4 minutes.

Transfer the melting cheese to a saucepan and place over a medium to high heat. Sprinkle with the vinegar and heat quickly to evaporate the alcohol. Remove from the heat, transfer to a warmed serving dish and sprinkle with oregano, salt and plenty of freshly ground pepper.

FONDUTA

When we visited Pinuccia Gaetani at her lovely cottage high in the mountains of Aosta, she made us a marvellous dish of polenta with Fonduta, using the wonderful Fontina cheese that is unique to this region. The grasses eaten by the mountain cattle give the cheese a very special flavour. The milk collected from all over the mountain pastures is turned into Fontina using an age-old recipe, and it is left to mature in deep tunnels bored right into the mountains themselves. We visited several of the cheese 'warehouses' and found a dank, dark, cold atmosphere, with water dripping through the rock surface and an unmistakable cheesy reek in the air.

The production of Fontina is second only to tourism as a mainstay of this region's economy, and almost every rural smallholding keeps cows for this purpose alone. I find it amazing to think of a product that is so much part of the land as an exportable commodity. Many wonderful recipes have been created from Fontina, but the most classic of all is the silky smooth Fonduta, just as Pinuccia made it for us.

For this recipe to be a success, all the ingredients must be at room temperature before you start cooking.

SERVES 4

1 lb (450 g) **Fontina cheese, cubed**

1 tablespoon **plain white flour** *or* 1 tablespoon **polenta flour**

7 fl oz (200 ml) **cold milk**

4 **egg yolks**

4 oz (100 g) **butter**

In a deep stainless steel saucepan, mix the cheese and the flour together thoroughly. Cover with the milk and leave to soften for about 30 minutes.

Drain the cheese, egg yolks and butter into the top half of a double boiler and stir constantly until the cheese has melted. The eggs must not be allowed to scramble. As soon as the Fonduta is velvety smooth and piping hot, serve it in hot soup plates or bowls with slices of toasted or fried bread, *grissini* (bread sticks) or polenta. You can also pour it over cooked pasta or make it into a risotto.

MEAT, GAME AND POULTRY

CARBONATA
Rich Brown Stew

This dish is absolutely typical of the Val d'Aosta, even though very similar recipes appear in Belgian cuisine and in Galician tradition. However, without going too far afield, you will find in Borgomanero what is considered by local cooks to be the ancestor of the dish, though here in a more rustic version, known as Tapulone and using either donkey or mule. It is believed to have been Tapulone which inspired the invention of Carbonata. The dish has many variations, even within the confines of tiny Val d'Aosta. In Saint Vincent the meat is cut into strips, whereas in Cervinia it is sliced thinly; some cooks add sugar, others add beer or vinegar. In Val d'Aosta this perfect cold-weather dish was originally made with meat preserved in salt and today would be served with piping-hot polenta. If you prefer, you can serve it with jacket potatoes.

SERVES 4

1¾ lb (800 g) good-quality chuck steak, cubed or cut into strips

3 tablespoons plain white flour

2 oz (50 g) unsalted butter

1 large onion, peeled and thickly sliced

about 1 bottle very heavy, strong red wine

salt and pepper

Toss the meat in the flour, then fry it in the butter in a deep flameproof casserole for about 6 minutes. Remove the meat from the casserole and put it on a plate. Fry the onion in the butter until soft, then return the meat to the casserole. Stir together and add about a quarter of the wine, simmer until the wine has been absorbed, then add more. Continue in this way for about 2 hours or until the meat is completely tender, adding as much wine as you need. Season generously with salt and pepper, in memory of the original dish which used salted beef. Serve very hot.

STRACOTTO
Pot Roast

When I was a child and lived by an unpolluted sea in Tuscany, I would spend more time in the water than out of it, swimming, fishing and sailing the long days of summer away. In September, when the days grew colder and the late summer storms turned the sea a deep violet colour, I would return home on my rickety bike in my wet swimsuit, teeth chattering in the darkening light. As I entered the house at a tremendous speed (I always ran everywhere in those days) the smell of supper would hit my nostrils and I knew for certain that soon I would be warm all over. This dish is exactly the sort of thing which would be simmering quietly on the stove, a nourishing, full-flavoured, magical pot roast, with meat so tender it melts in your mouth and with countless vegetables to make a thick gravy. I make it for my own children, but sadly the sea I knew and loved so well is now too polluted to swim in as we used to.

Serve the dish with mashed potatoes and a green vegetable such as spinach.

SERVES 4

3¼ lb (1.5 kg) braising steak *or* brisket, in a single piece

2–3 cloves garlic, peeled and cut into strips

2 oz (50 g) fat bacon, chopped

1 onion, peeled and chopped

1 carrot, scraped and chopped

1 stick celery, chopped

3 oz (75 g) butter

1¾ pints (1 litre) beef stock (see page 293)

salt and pepper

1 tablespoon tomato purée

Pierce the meat all over with the point of a sharp knife and insert the strips of garlic in the holes – adjust the amount to your taste. Mix the bacon, onion, carrot and celery together, place in a heavy flameproof casserole with the butter and fry for about 8 minutes. Then lay the meat on top and brown it all over. Pour about a third of the stock over the meat, season with salt and pepper, stir in the tomato purée and cover. Simmer on a very low heat for about 6 hours, adding a little more stock occasionally to prevent the dish from drying out.

When the meat is cooked, remove it from the casserole, place on a warmed platter and slice it thickly. If you like you can thicken the gravy by rubbing the cooked vegetables through a sieve and returning them to the casserole juices to heat through before pouring over the sliced meat to serve.

Parsley and Basil omelette (page 182)

Top: An open-air cupboard for drying cheese in Puglia. *Bottom:* Mozzarella hanging up to drip dry in Campania.

GULASCH TRIESTINO
Trieste Goulash

As it comes from the snowy region of Friuli, this spicy beef stew is a not-very-distant relative of the Magyar goulash which was so loved by Pablo Neruda. You can finish it off Hungarian-fashion with milk and semolina dumplings, dollops of yoghurt, mashed potato or boiled rice, all of which serve the purpose of putting out the fire in your mouth! Whereas in the south of Italy chilli pepper was used to cover up unsavoury smells and flavours and as a cure for everything from malaria to worms, here the 'hot' element is replaced by paprika and fresh green chillies cut into cubes. Beer is the ideal drink to serve with this dish.

SERVES 4

2 oz (50 g) bacon fat, chopped
3 large onions, peeled and thinly sliced
1 lb (450 g) stewing *or* braising steak, cut into 2 inch (5 cm) cubes
1 bouquet garni
3 potatoes, peeled and cut into 1½ inch (4 cm) cubes
1 tablespoon tomato purée diluted with a little warm water
¼ teaspoon paprika
2 small green chilli peppers, cut into cubes and de-seeded
18 fl oz (500 ml) hot meat stock (see page 293)
salt

Melt the fat in a deep flameproof casserole, add the onions and fry them for about 6 minutes or until softened, then add the meat, bouquet garni, potatoes, diluted tomato purée, paprika and chillies. Stir thoroughly and simmer slowly for 1½ hours or more (depending upon the quality of the beef) until the meat is completely tender and the potatoes soft, adding stock as you go along and stirring frequently. Season with salt at the end, just before serving.

BRASATO al BAROLO
Braised Beef with Barolo

'La Camilla' is one of the loveliest and most loved homes I have ever been in. Tastefully cluttered with hundreds of treasured family memorabilia, and scented with the unmistakable odour of faded upholstery and floor wax, it sits gracefully in acres of rich farmland. It was originally a monastery but was beautifully converted and is now run as a successful dairy farm, with many contentedly munching Friesians. The immense, rich, flat plain surrounding the house is made up of fields bursting with crops like maize and hay grass. We drove to 'La Camilla' to see Chiara and Anna Scavia, whose family farm it is. The girls obviously care passionately about the house and are happy to dispel much energy in baling hay and helping with the milking. Imelda is the family cook and has lived for many years in one of the cottages in the grounds. She gave us this delicious and very traditional Piedmontese recipe, made with a bottle of the region's most famous wine: Barolo.

SERVES 6

1 × 2 lb (1 kg) piece of beef suitable for pot roasting (such as shin or silverside)

1 large onion, peeled and quartered

1 large carrot, scraped and quartered

1 large stick celery, quartered

2 large bay leaves

1 teaspoon juniper berries

large pinch ground coriander

salt and pepper

1 bottle best-quality Barolo wine

1 beef stock cube (optional)

Trim and wipe the meat. Put all the vegetables, spices, seasoning and wine into a large bowl and stir briefly. Immerse the meat into this marinade and leave it to soak for about 10–12 hours.

Drain off and reserve the wine, straining it with care, and reserve all the vegetables and the spices. Heat the strained wine, with the stock cube if you are using it, over a very low heat.

Meanwhile, melt the butter or margarine with the oil in a large, deep pan and seal the meat all over in the hot fat. When it is well browned, pour the hot wine over the meat. Add all the vegetables and the spices, cover and simmer slowly for about 2 hours. Remove the meat and set aside.

Sieve all the vegetables to a purée with the liquid remaining in the pan. Return the meat to the pan, pour the purée over it and cover again. Simmer for a further 2 hours over a very low heat.

3 oz (75 g) butter *or*
  margarine
3–4 tablespoons olive oil

To serve, remove the meat from the pan and slice it thinly. Arrange it on a warmed platter and pour over the purée so that it almost completely covers the meat.

BISTECCA alla FIORENTINA
Florentine T-bone Steak

The perfect Fiorentina steak is made with Val di Chiana beef taken from a young animal and hung for at least 2 weeks. Alvaro Maccioni, who owns La Famiglia (my favourite restaurant in London), has a cousin who runs a restaurant at an olive oil co-operative near Pistoia. This restaurant is special to me, because it uncompromisingly serves the most Tuscan of Tuscan specialities. There are crostini (see page 76), thick pulse soups and rich salads made more filling by the addition of bread. Among all these dishes, there is the inimitable, deliciously tender and simply perfect grilled T-bone steak. If you decide to cook it on the barbecue, try some other simple Tuscan specialities too. For example, toast some bread lightly on either side over the embers, then rub it with garlic and sprinkle it generously with olive oil and salt. This is called Bruschetta and is delicious with a plate of salumi (see page 60), some olives, and plenty of Tuscan wine.

SERVES 4
2 very large T-bone steaks,
  weighing about 1½ lb
  (750 g) each
salt and pepper
1 teaspoon olive oil
  (optional)

Heat the grill or light the barbecue. When you have a really intense heat, lay the steaks side by side on the grill. Cook for just 2–3 minutes on the first side until the meat is darkened and sealed. (In Italy these steaks are always served rare, but you may cook them for longer if you prefer.) Turn the meat over, season generously with salt and pepper and cook the second side in the same way. If you wish, you may brush the cooked meat with a little olive oil to make it look shiny, just before serving. Serve at once.

MANZO alla CALIFORNIA
Beef California

Despite its rather odd name, this dish is very much a Lombard speciality.

SERVES 6

1 small onion, peeled and
  sliced
2 oz (50 g) butter
3 tablespoons plain white
  flour
2½ lb (1.25 kg) rump *or*
  chuck steak, cut very
  thick
½ wine glass red wine
  vinegar
8 fl oz (250 ml) meat stock
  (see page 293)
8 fl oz (250 ml) single
  cream
salt and pepper

In a heavy pan fry the onion in the butter for 5 minutes, then remove it with a slotted spoon and discard it. Flour the steak lightly and fry it in the onion-flavoured butter to seal it on both sides. When the steak is well browned, raise the heat and pour the vinegar over it. When this has evaporated, pour the stock and half the cream over the steak. Sprinkle with a little salt and pepper, lower the heat and cover. Simmer very slowly for 3 hours or until the meat is absolutely tender. Slice into thickish chunks, pour on the remaining cream and heat through. Serve very hot.

COSTATA alla PIZZAIOLA
Pizzaiola Steak

To me this epitomises the style of Campanian cookery – Neapolitan in particular. Such is the Neapolitans' love of the brilliant red tomato, which has become the most important symbol of their cuisine, that in dishes such as this one it is cooked as little as possible so as not to lose any of the bright colour, tangy flavour or scent. Naturally, the dish is best when made in its area of origin with freshly gathered, sun-warmed tomatoes, but it is still very good even when you use canned tomatoes or passata. It is the quintessential Neapolitan dish – quick and easy, bright and colourful, versatile and delicious. Any kind of meat can be used except lamb, but thinly sliced beef, veal or a well-flattened chicken breast will cook most quickly. It was cooked for us by a very charming friend we made on our travels – the Neapolitan surgeon Nello Oliviero, who invited us to his home for lunch. We enjoyed a wonderful meal in the family's beautiful flat – the dining room in particular has a really spectacular view over the bay of Naples, and the basil came from Nello's personal herb garden on the terrace. In fact, so keen was he to have fresh basil that he had part of the terrace covered with glass to help it grow!

SERVES 4

1½ lb (750 g) thinly sliced sirloin or rump steak *or* veal *or* chicken breasts, skinned

6 tablespoons olive oil

3 cloves garlic, peeled and crushed

1½ lb (750 g) canned tomatoes, sieved

2 tablespoons chopped parsley

3 tablespoons chopped basil

salt and pepper

Trim any gristle and fat off the meat, flatten it as much as possible with a meat mallet and set it to one side. Heat the oil in a frying-pan wide enough to take all the meat in a single layer, add the garlic and fry gently for about 3 minutes. Add the tomatoes, parsley and basil, stir and bring to the boil. Slip the meat into the tomato sauce, cook very quickly for about 5 minutes, sprinkle with salt and plenty of pepper and serve at once.

ABBACCHIO alla ROMANA
Roman Roast Lamb

There is something delightfully coarse about this dish, a far cry from prissy roast lamb with new potatoes, mint sauce and garden peas. This lamb comes in man-sized hunks and is drenched in oil, garlic and herbs: just made for 'eating as an experience' – holding the meat in your hands, with grease running down your chin. It is the distant, lingering flavour of the anchovy which marks the dish as uniquely Roman or Laziale. This is a race of people who are strong, full-blooded and very earthy, not lovers of the refined side of life!

Any cut of lamb is suitable, but you should include at least a small piece of breast. Roast potatoes and braised artichokes are good accompaniments.

SERVES 4

2 lb (1 kg) lamb on the bone, cut into chunks the size of a small apple
1 lamb's kidney, cubed
2 fl oz (50 ml) olive oil
knob of butter
salt and pepper
8 fl oz (250 ml) water
2 × 2½ inch (6 cm) sprigs rosemary
2 large anchovies preserved in salt, cleaned and boned, *or* 5 canned anchovy fillets, drained
4 cloves garlic, peeled
4–5 tablespoons red wine vinegar

Check the meat over carefully, wipe it with a clean, damp cloth and remove any splinters of bone. Set a wide, deep frying-pan over a low heat, pour in the oil, add the butter and heat for 5 minutes. Lay the chunks of lamb and the kidney in the fat, brown them all over, season generously with salt and pepper and lower the heat. Continue to cook the meat for about 45 minutes or until cooked through, turning over the pieces frequently and adding a little water occasionally to prevent it from drying out.

Meanwhile, strip the leaves from the rosemary sprigs and pound with the anchovies and garlic using a pestle and mortar. Alternatively, you can do this in a food processor. Add the vinegar, mix well and pour over the meat. Stir thoroughly and cook for a further 5 minutes before serving.

COSCIOTTO D'AGNELLO con UOVA e SUCCO di LIMONE

Dino Lazzaro's Lamb with Egg and Lemon Sauce

When Dino Lazzaro and I cooked this dish together in his nineteenth-century kitchen in L'Aquila, capital of the Abruzzi, we used a lovely old copper pot over the open fire. Dino is the L'Aquila representative of L'Accademia della Cucina Italiana, a lay organisation which helps to promote and inspire Italian cuisine at its best. He told me that the local lamb has a particularly good flavour because of all the wonderful wild herbs and grasses that grow in the mountains. As mutton and lamb have been the only meat available locally for so long, there are lots and lots of very different ways of cooking it; but in Dino's opinion this is one of the best recipes. I must say that the combination of egg and lemon juice works very well with the tender lamb, and the underlying sting of chilli pepper livens everything up. Be careful not to let the egg overcook and ruin the dish.

SERVES 4

1 small leg of lamb, boned and cut evenly into approximately 2½ inch (6 cm) chunks
1 clove garlic, peeled
3 tablespoons olive oil
½ dried red chilli pepper
1 wine glass dry white wine
salt
3 eggs
juice of 1 lemon

Put the lamb, garlic, oil and chilli into a deep pan and brown the lamb thoroughly all over. After about 10 minutes, during which time you must turn the meat frequently, remove the garlic and chilli. Now add the wine and raise the heat to evaporate the alcohol fumes for 2 minutes. Season with salt, cover and simmer for about 30 minutes or until the meat is cooked through.

Meanwhile, beat the eggs and lemon juice until well blended in a separate bowl. When the lamb is cooked, pour the egg mixture over the meat and stir the juices quickly until the egg is just set. Transfer to a warmed serving dish and serve at once.

PIGNATA alla MATERANA
Matera Lamb Stew

Until modern farming methods and various industries took over in the last 40 years or so, sheep were one of the main sources of income for the people of Basilicata. This recipe originated quite literally out in the fields where the shepherds would spend months and months tending their sheep. They were always on the move to find new pastures and would wend their way south to Lecce, where the annual sheep market took place at the end of the winter. In the original recipe for this lamb stew, the shepherds would have flavoured the dish with wild herbs and vegetables picked from around their camp and the ingredients would have varied according to what was available. As every animal was valuable, they would most probably have only used a sheep that had died of an injury or old age; there was no excuse for slaughtering an animal simply for food. The meat and vegetables would have been put into a traditional two-handled terracotta pot (the pignata*) and the opening sealed with wet clay or bread dough. Then the whole thing would have been buried in the hot embers of the camp fire to cook slowly for several hours. This dish was a luxury for the shepherds – probably one of the few hot meals they ever ate.*

In Matera, at Franco Ritella's restaurant, the chef makes this dish to his own recipe and lets it cook slowly in the mouth of his pizza oven. To make it at home, you'll need a clay or terracotta pot 4 inches (10 cm) in diameter and 12 inches (30 cm) deep. You can cover the top with crumpled foil instead of bread dough or clay, though it won't be quite so authentic!

SERVES 6

3 lb (1.5 kg) lamb or
  mutton, cut into large
  chunks
1 tablespoon sea salt
2 onions, peeled and
  quartered
2 carrots, scraped and
  quartered
1 head of chicory or curly
  endive, shredded
5 large potatoes, peeled
  and quartered

Pre-heat the oven to gas mark 4, 350°F (180°C).

Put all the stew ingredients into a clay pot, cover with cold water and close the opening completely with fresh, soft bread dough, wet clay or aluminium foil. Bake in the oven for 2 hours. When you serve the dish, remove and discard the bread or clay topping or foil at the table for maximum effect.

4 oz (100 g) salami, cubed
pinch chilli powder
4 ripe tomatoes, quartered
4 oz (100 g) soft pecorino
   or very mature Cheddar
   or Gouda cheese, cubed
1 stick celery, cut into 2
   inch (5 cm) chunks
a little bread dough to seal
   the pot (optional)

AGNELLO alle OLIVE
Lamb Casserole with Olives

This recipe is taken from La Cucina Molisana, *by Anna Maria Lombardi and Rita Mastropaolo of Campobasso. Their book, in two thick volumes, is one of my most treasured possessions and I reproduce their recipe here with their kind permission. The authors state: 'For lamb to be good it has to have the golden tooth, in other words it has to have eaten deliciously strong-tasting mountain herbs which only real shepherds know about.'*
Serve this dish with plenty of vegetables and bread.

SERVES 4–6

2¼ lb (1.2 kg) leg of lamb,
   boned and cut into small
   cubes
1 wine glass olive oil
1 thick slice belly pork, cut
   into small strips
1 clove garlic, peeled and
   sliced
1 glass dry white wine
salt
1 red chilli pepper, finely
   chopped
1 handful black olives,
   stoned

Trim the meat carefully. Pour the oil into a wide, shallow, flameproof casserole and arrange the cubed meat in the dish with the belly pork and the garlic. Cook over a high heat for a few minutes to seal the meat, then add the wine. Let the alcohol fumes evaporate for 2–3 minutes, then add salt and cover. Simmer for about 30 minutes, then add the chilli and the olives and stir. Transfer to a pre-heated oven at gas mark 4, 350°F (180°C), and cook for another 30 minutes. Serve at once, straight from the casserole.

UMIDO alla MARCHIGIANA
Pork Stew with Lemon Rind and Garlic

This wonderfully tangy pork casserole comes from the most jolly of all Italy's regions, the lovely Marche. I have adapted it over the years to suit cooking in Norfolk, and here give my adaptation instead of the original on the assumption that if I found it too complicated, you probably would too! I like to use pork fillet because it cooks more quickly than other cuts and is generally more tender. Other chunky pieces of pork such as hand or shoulder will do just as well, and are cheaper: for example, a hand can be skinned, boned and cut into chunks, and this cut is very tasty. When cubing the pork, be sure to cut an equal number of pieces for each serving. The dish is nice served with mashed potatoes, into which about 1 teaspoon of lemon rind is grated, and leeks.

SERVES 4

2 lb (1 kg) boneless pork, cut into equal-sized cubes about the size of a small apple

2 cloves garlic, peeled and finely chopped

finely chopped rind of ½ lemon

2 oz (50 g) prosciutto crudo *or* back bacon in a single piece, diced

5 oz (150 g) pancetta *or* streaky bacon, finely chopped

1 onion, peeled and chopped

1 carrot, scraped and chopped

1 stick celery, chopped

large pinch dried marjoram

1 large glass red wine

Pierce each cube of meat with a sharp pointed knife. Mix 1 of the chopped garlic cloves, the lemon rind and prosciutto or back bacon together and insert this mixture into the holes in the cubes of meat. Push it in deeply to prevent it escaping during the cooking. Put the chopped pancetta or streaky bacon into a heavy saucepan with the chopped onion, carrot, celery and remaining garlic clove and fry together for about 5–6 minutes. Lay the meat in the pan with the marjoram and brown it all over thoroughly. When it is well browned, add the wine and let it evaporate for 5 minutes. Then add the tomatoes and their juice and stir, add about one third of the stock, cover and simmer for about 1 hour, adding more stock as necessary (you may not need it all). Stir occasionally during the cooking time. When the meat is tender, season, mix in the butter and serve. The meat can be served with its sauce or separately – the sauce can be saved to dress pasta if you wish.

14 oz (400 g) canned
  tomatoes, de-seeded and
  chopped
about 1¾ pints (1 litre)
  meat stock (see page
  293)
salt and pepper
2 oz (50 g) butter

SALSICCE e FAGIOLI di ALVARO
Alvaro's Sausages with Beans

*This is the recipe for the traditional Tuscan dish of sausages with beans that
Alvaro Maccioni gave me. You really do need Italian sausages to make this
dish. They are much coarser in texture than a British sausage, with small
cubes of fat blended into the mixture. They are also quite strong in flavour
and usually have a fair amount of pepper as seasoning. These sausages are
available through good Italian delicatessens, though I know some people
have used fresh Greek sausages with some success. The only possible
alternative is to use very strong-tasting game sausages; this will give you the
powerful flavour if not the texture.*

SERVES 4

4 teacups dried white
  cannellini beans, soaked
  for 48 hours in cold water
½ teaspoon salt
6 cloves garlic, peeled
8 Italian sausages
  (preferably all pork)
4 tablespoons olive oil
4 fresh sage leaves
1 tablespoon tomato purée

Drain the beans and boil them in 4 pints (2.25
litres) fresh water for about 1½–2 hours or until
soft, then add the salt and 4 of the the garlic
cloves. Continue to cook for about 20 minutes.
Then add the sausages and cook for a further
15 minutes.

Heat the oil in a large frying-pan, crush the
remaining 2 cloves of garlic and fry them in the
oil for about 5 minutes. Remove the sausages
from the beans and add them to the frying-pan.
Turn them in the pan until brown, then add the
beans, the sage and the tomato purée.

Cover and simmer for 15 minutes, then serve.

LA CASOÊULA
Lombard Pork Stew

This is the recipe for Casoêula as prepared for me by Susanna Gelmetti and her mother in their lovely family home in the little town of Lodi, near Milan. Their kitchen clearly shows their real passion for cooking, and the house has an elegant style about it which made being there such a pleasure. The family and friends gathered around the table with me to enjoy this incredibly wintry stew with mounds of steaming polenta. It is said that the dish is of Spanish origin, although envious people from less prosperous parts of Italy say it was just the Lombard way of making a meal in one pot which left them plenty of time to get on with the serious business of earning money! As it is impossible to find certain types of Italian sausage in the UK, I have adapted this recipe very slightly. You can leave out the pig's trotters and ear if you like, but the result, though delicious, is obviously less authentic!

SERVES 8

- 2 pig's trotters (optional)
- 1 pig's ear (optional)
- 1 large onion, peeled and thinly sliced
- 1 tablespoon butter
- 1 tablespoon olive oil
- 2¼ lb (1.2 kg) pork ribs
- 1 lb (450 g) mild Italian sausages
- 1 lb (450 g) spicy Italian sausages
- 1 large glass dry white wine
- 1 lb (450 g) mixed carrots and celery, thinly sliced
- 1 heaped tablespoon tomato purée diluted with about 4 tablespoons meat stock
- salt and pepper
- 4½ lb (2 kg) Savoy cabbage
- 1 lb (450 g) pork loin, cubed

If using pig's trotters, split them open lengthways and singe the skin over a naked flame. Scrape off the hair and wash the trotters carefully. Do the same with the ear, if using. Put the trotters and ear in a saucepan, cover with plenty of boiling water and boil gently for 1 hour to remove most of the fat. Then drain them, slice into thin finger sticks and set aside until required.

Put the onion, butter and oil, ribs and both types of sausage into a very large pan. Place over a medium heat and brown thoroughly.

Pour over the wine and raise the heat for 2–3 minutes to evaporate the alcohol. Lower the heat and remove all the meats with a slotted spoon. Set them to one side, then put the carrots and celery into the same pan. Add the diluted tomato purée, season generously with salt and pepper, stir and cover. Leave to simmer for about 30 minutes, stirring occasionally.

Meanwhile, wash and prepare the cabbage, keeping the leaves whole but removing any hard white parts. Place in another large saucepan with only the water left on the leaves after washing. Cover the saucepan and set over a medium heat until the leaves have 'wilted'. Be careful: the leaves can easily stick to the bottom of the saucepan, so remove each one as soon as it is soft and drooping.

Transfer the cabbage to the pan in which the carrots and celery are cooking. Stir the vegetables together, then arrange all the cooked meat and the cubed pork loin on top. Cover, and shake the saucepan to make the cooking liquid cover most of the ingredients as much as possible. Do not stir again. Simmer for about 1 hour. Skim the fat which will rise to the top of the stew with a slotted spoon during this time.

MAIALE al LATTE
Pork Pot Roasted in Milk

This is a very unusual way of cooking pork from Friuli, but the finished effect is deliciously tender and tasty. It is another classic dish of my childhood. Serve with potatoes and a cooked vegetable such as carrots.

SERVES 4

2 lb (1 kg) leg of pork, boned
18 fl oz (500 ml) dry white wine
2 oz (50 g) butter
5 sage leaves
5 tiny sprigs rosemary
salt and pepper
1¾ pints (1 litre) milk

Put the meat in a non-metallic bowl, cover with the wine and leave to marinate in a cool place for between 6 hours and 2 days. The longer you leave it, the better the flavour and the more tender the meat will be. Remove the meat, dry it carefully with kitchen paper and brown it all over in a deep flameproof casserole with the butter and herbs. Season with salt and pepper, cover with the milk and place the lid on the casserole. Simmer slowly for about 3 hours. Remove the lid, raise the heat and let the liquid thicken for about 5 minutes. Set the meat on a warmed platter and slice thickly. Strain the milk and pour it all over the slices.

CIMA RIPIENA alla SANREMESE
Stuffed Veal in the Sanremo Style

The authentic Genoese recipe for this cannot be made without using the testicles of a young calf, but I have chosen the more prudish version, as made in Sanremo! The secret of the dish is that it should be colourful and bursting with lots of different flavours and textures. In some households the finished veal roll is cooled, sliced and fried, but I prefer it cold in thick slices. The dish needs to be cooked a day in advance and is quite complicated, so save it for very special Sunday lunches in summertime. It is quite a nice touch to serve with it salads made of the same vegetables that are in the stuffing – carrots, lettuce, celery and pine kernels. A couple of days before you intend making the dish, explain to your butcher the cut of veal you require and he/she should be able to prepare it for you.

SERVES 8

3½ pints (2 litres) cold water

1 large onion, peeled and studded with 3 cloves

1 large raw carrot, scraped, and 1 boiled carrot, cubed

1 stick celery

3 sprigs parsley

1 clove garlic, peeled

2½ lb (1.25 kg) veal breast in a single piece, split open like a sack so that it is easy to stuff

3 tablespoons fresh breadcrumbs

3 tablespoons grated Parmesan cheese

4 cos lettuce leaves, shredded

1 tablespoon pine kernels

salt and pepper

Pour the water into a very deep saucepan, add the onion, the raw carrot, celery, parsley and garlic and bring to a gentle boil. This is the stock in which the meat will cook.

Meanwhile, make sure that the veal forms a sack which you can easily fill with the stuffing ingredients. The cut should be at the point of the breast so that it is pocket-shaped and needs only to be split open on the end where the butcher cut it for you. Wash and dry the meat.

Mix together the breadcrumbs, Parmesan, shredded lettuce, boiled carrot and pine kernels and season with salt and pepper. Spoon this mixture into the pocket in the meat and pack it down quite tightly. Sew up the open end of the breast with white cook's string. Lower the stuffed meat carefully into the boiling stock, cover and boil gently for 2 hours. Drain and leave to cool completely overnight.

Slice before serving.

VARIATION

Coat the slices of stuffed veal in egg and breadcrumbs and fry in olive oil until golden.

SCALOPPINE alla PERUGINA
Perugina Escalopes

Although escalopes are almost always veal, you can also use well-flattened chicken or turkey breast or even very thinly sliced 'minute' steak (beef). The Italian housewife would be lost without her fettina, *a thin slice of meat which cooks very quickly and is extremely versatile. This recipe, one of the more elaborate ways of cooking escalopes, is a splendid dish from the glorious Umbrian university city of Perugia. It goes well with boiled potatoes and a green salad.*

SERVES 4

8 × ¼ inch (5 mm) thick slices veal *or* chicken breast *or* turkey breast *or* tender beef, total weight about 1 lb (450 g)

2-3 anchovies preserved in salt, cleaned and boned *or* 4-6 canned anchovy fillets, drained

2 oz (50 g) prosciutto crudo

1 chicken liver, washed and trimmed

2 teaspoons capers, rinsed and dried

1 clove garlic, peeled

1½ fl oz (30 ml) olive oil

juice and grated rind of ½ lemon

6 sage leaves

salt and pepper

Trim and flatten the meat as much as possible. Chop together the anchovies, prosciutto, chicken liver, capers and garlic. Put this mixture into a wide frying-pan with the oil, lemon juice and rind and the sage leaves and fry for about 8 minutes. Lay the meat on top, season generously with salt and pepper and cook on both sides for about 6 minutes (or less, depending upon how thin the meat is). Arrange the meat and the sauce together on a warmed platter and serve at once.

VITELLO TONNATO
Veal in a Tuna Fish Sauce

This is a great Piedmontese favourite of mine for outdoor summer lunches on those rare occasions when we actually get a summer in England! It is a dish that never fails to create a good impression. I serve it with three or four different salads, including a potato salad and some tender green beans in a vinaigrette dressing. The quantities given below may easily be increased to feed a larger party, but remember that a very big joint of veal easily dries out if roasted whole, so it is best cut into two or more pieces.

SERVES 4

4 tablespoons plus about 10 fl oz (300 ml) olive oil

1½ lb (750 g) best-quality roasting veal, in a single piece

1 glass dry white wine

salt and pepper

2 bay leaves

1 clove garlic, peeled

8 celery leaves

2 eggs *or* 2 egg yolks

juice of ½ lemon

2 tablespoons white wine vinegar

2 heaped tablespoons capers, drained but *not* rinsed (if in vinegar) and finely chopped

7 oz (200 g) canned tuna fish in oil, drained and flaked

2 anchovies preserved in salt, cleaned, boned and finely chopped *or* 4 canned anchovy fillets, drained and finely chopped

Pre-heat the oven to gas mark 4, 350°F (180°C).

Heat the 4 tablespoons oil in a large frying-pan, put in the meat and seal on all sides. Take the meat out of the pan and lay it in a roasting-tin with the wine, salt, pepper, bay leaves, garlic and celery leaves. Place in the oven and roast for 45 minutes, basting occasionally. Remove the meat from the roasting-tin and allow to cool completely.

Meanwhile, make a basic mayonnaise with 2 whole eggs if using a food processor (or with 2 egg yolks only if working by hand), up to 10 fl oz (300 ml) oil and the lemon juice (see page 290). Stir in the vinegar, capers, tuna and anchovies. Season to taste with salt and pepper.

Cut the cooled, cooked meat into neat, thin slices and arrange them on a serving platter. Pour over the sauce to cover completely, garnish with capers, lemon slices, parsley sprigs and olives if you wish and chill until required.

Pollo alla Marengo (page 219)

Capriolo in Salsa con i Mirtilli (page 226)

capers, lemon slices,
   parsley sprigs and olives
   to garnish

COSTOLETTE alla MILANESE
Milanese Veal Chops

Called Cotoleta *in Milanese dialect, this is the dish which Vincenzo Buonassisi, one of Italy's most famous and best loved cookery experts, cooked for me at his home in Milan. Signor Buonassisi is one of my great heroes, a legendary figure in Italian gastronomy whom I was somewhat awestruck and stunned to meet. I have always admired his wealth of knowledge and expertise from afar and was delighted to discover that he is as charming and amenable as he is knowledgeable.*

Costolette alla Milanese is a delightful quick dish, perfect for suppers or lunches, excellent hot or cold. If it is served hot, fried potatoes and tomato salad are good accompaniments. I like to serve it cold as a party dish – in fact, it seems to taste better when eaten without a knife and fork!

SERVES 4

4 veal chops, cut to equal
   thickness
salt
2 eggs, well beaten
10 tablespoons fresh,
   coarse breadcrumbs
4 oz (100 g) unsalted butter
lemon wedges to garnish

Flatten the meat slightly with a meat mallet and sprinkle with salt. Dip the chops into the egg, keeping the bone handle out of the egg. Then dip them into the breadcrumbs and press down hard with the heel of your hand to make the breadcrumbs stick firmly all over the meat, but obviously not on the bone. Melt the butter in a heavy-bottomed frying-pan until foaming, then fry the chops for about 3 minutes on each side. The end result must be golden and crisp on the outside and moist and tender on the inside. Serve hot or cold, with lemon wedges.

VITELLO alla SARDA
Veal Cooked in the Sardinian Style

Veal is not very much in evidence among all the mutton and horsemeat on the meat stalls in the covered market in Cagliari, but this is because it is a fairly new element in the local cuisine – though no less valid because of it. After all, the locals have only recently begun to be able to afford such luxuries! If you would like a cheaper alternative, a boned and rolled turkey breast also works very well.

SERVES 4

1¼ lb (500 g) piece stewing veal *or* turkey breast
3 tablespoons plain white flour
6 tablespoons olive oil
1 tablespoon capers, rinsed and dried
1 glass dry white wine
2 thin slices from a carefully peeled lemon
1 onion, peeled and chopped
1 carrot, scraped and chopped
1 handful parsley, chopped
1 large clove garlic, peeled and chopped
salt

Roll the meat lightly in the flour. Pour the oil into a deep flameproof casserole with a tight-fitting lid and heat on top of the stove for about 2 minutes. Add the meat and brown all over to seal it. Add the capers, wine, lemon slices, onion, carrot, parsley and garlic. Sprinkle with about 3 pinches salt, cover with aluminium foil and place the lid on the top. Simmer very slowly on top of the stove or in a pre-heated oven at gas mark 4, 350°F (180°C), for about 2 hours.

Remove the meat from the casserole, slice it and arrange it on a warmed platter. Strain the juices in the casserole, pushing the vegetables through the sieve to make a smooth sauce. Heat this through and pour it over the sliced meat. Serve at once.

POLPETTE NELLA FOGLIA di LIMONE

Meatballs in Lemon Leaves

Eleonora Consoli made these delicious meatballs for me at Lentini, cooking them on a grill layed over the embers of a lemon-wood fire. At Lentini there is no shortage of lemon trees, as they grow alongside the oranges and vines in wildly Sicilian, passionate profusion. In the UK it is less easy to find lemon trees. However, sometimes you can find clementines or tangerines on sale with a branch of leaves attached, and some people grow citrus trees in their home, so perhaps you can get around the problem. In any case, the object of using the leaves is to impart a vaguely lemony scent and flavour to the meat, but I have experimented with making the dish with no leaves and as long as you fry the meatballs in olive oil, squeeze lemon juice over them and serve them hot, they are absolutely scrumptious.

SERVES 4

14 oz (400 g) minced veal or beef or turkey or chicken

4 oz (100 g) dry breadcrumbs

4 oz (100 g) caciocavallo or Parmesan cheese, grated

1 large egg

salt and pepper

3 tablespoons chopped parsley

½ wine glass cold water

lemon leaves or juice of ½ lemon and 1 teaspoon grated rind plus about 6 tablespoons olive oil

Mix the meat, breadcrumbs, cheese, egg, salt, pepper and parsley together very thoroughly, then blend in the water gradually. Mix with your hands for a few minutes, then shape the mixture into small balls about the size of a large walnut and press them slightly flat with your palms. Sandwich each one between 2 lemon leaves (if using), securing them with 2 wooden cocktail sticks. Grill them over a moderate heat on a barbecue or under a grill until the leaves begin to burn slightly, turning them over after about 4 minutes.

If you have no lemon leaves, fry the meatballs in about 6 tablespoons olive oil, drain them on kitchen paper and sprinkle with the lemon juice and grated rind.

Serve the meatballs very hot.

RAMBASICI
Birds Hiding in the Cabbage Patch

This dish comes from the area around Trieste. It originated in neighbouring Yugoslavia, where stuffed cabbage leaf recipes are popular. There are many variations on the basic theme. Here is my favourite – it's very easy to make and might even persuade your children to eat cabbage! The important thing is to start off with a very fresh, green, crisp Savoy. Mashed potatoes, red cabbage and sautéed mushrooms are nice with this.

SERVES 4–5

1 medium Savoy cabbage
salt and pepper
11 oz (300 g) lean minced
    pork
11 oz (300 g) lean minced
    beef
2 oz (50 g) parsley, chopped
2 cloves garlic, peeled and
    finely chopped
2 hard-boiled eggs, shelled
    and finely chopped
2 slices brown bread, cut
    into very small cubes
2–3 slices salame, cut into
    small squares
paprika
6 tablespoons vegetable oil
    or 4 tablespoons butter
1 large onion, peeled and
    sliced
10 fl oz (300 ml) warm
    meat stock (see page
    293)
1 heaped tablespoon dry
    breadcrumbs
1 heaped tablespoon grated
    Parmesan cheese
2 tablespoons olive oil

You will need only the large outer cabbage leaves for this recipe: select them carefully, wash thoroughly and blanch for 1 minute in boiling salted water. Arrange the leaves on a clean work-surface, spread out flat and ready to fill.

Mix together the minced meats, parsley, garlic, hard-boiled eggs, bread and salami. Season to taste with salt, pepper and paprika. Put 1 tablespoon of this mixture into the centre of each leaf. Roll up the leaves, close them with a couple of wooden cocktail sticks and set them aside. You should end up with about 12 rolls.

Heat the vegetable oil or butter in a wide pan and fry the onion in it until well browned. Remove the onion from the pan and put in the rolls in a single layer. Pour in about half the stock, bring to a low simmer and cook for about 15 minutes, then add the rest of the stock and continue cooking for another 15 minutes or so.

Fry the breadcrumbs and Parmesan together in the olive oil in a separate pan until the breadcrumbs are crisp. Arrange the hiding birds on a warmed platter, scatter with the fried breadcrumb mixture and serve at once.

ROGNONE in UMIDO
Roman Kidney

Offal features plentifully in Roman food, far more than anywhere else in Italy, which is probably why Roman cuisine has never become as famous as the cuisines of Naples or Tuscany! Offal is not everyone's favourite food and therefore very few recipes using it have been included in this collection. One of them is this delicious kidney casserole, which has the added advantage of being very quick to make. It is nice served with mashed potatoes and a green vegetable.

SERVES 4

1 lb (450 g) calf's kidney *or* lamb's kidneys

2 strips belly pork, cubed

1 large onion, peeled and sliced

14 oz (400 g) canned tomatoes, drained, de-seeded and coarsely chopped

3 tablespoons dry white wine

salt and pepper

3 tablespoons chopped parsley

Cut the kidney into neat, thin slices with a very sharp knife. Remove the hard, fatty core in the centre and any other bits of fat round the outside. Place it on its own in a wide, deep frying-pan over a medium heat and allow it to release its liquid, stirring constantly to prevent sticking. Remove the pan from the heat when no more liquid is forthcoming. Tip the sliced kidney into a colander set on a plate and let it drain for about 20 minutes.

Place the belly pork and onion in the pan and fry gently together for about 8 minutes or until the onion is golden, then add the drained tomatoes and cook for 15 minutes. Add the kidney, pour on the wine and cook for 10 minutes more, stirring frequently. Season generously with salt and pepper and transfer to a warmed platter. Sprinkle with chopped parsley and serve immediately.

FEGATO alla VENEZIANA
Liver and Onions Venetian-style

This is my own version of this dish, as cooked for me and my family more times than I care to remember by the best Venetian cook I have ever met. Beppino learned to cook in the restaurants of Milan, but never lost his traditions and original recipes. I can still see the long white platter with its mountains of soft, red onions, surmounted by tender slices of liver, being carried into the dining room with immense pride and joy. When I cook this at home I get the onions ready well in advance as this part of the recipe takes the longest. They can then be re-heated and the liver put in with them to cook briefly at the last moment, which makes it a perfect dinner-party dish.

SERVES 4

1¼ lb (500 g) calf's *or* lamb's liver, cut into very thin slices

1½ lb (750 g) onions (preferably red)

2½ fl oz (65 ml) vegetable oil

1 oz (25 g) butter

1 handful parsley, finely chopped

1 glass dry white wine

salt and pepper

Trim the liver with care, pulling off the transparent, rind-like skin from around each slice. Peel and slice the onions evenly and very thinly (a food processor does this very well and easily) and rinse them briefly under cold running water. Fry the onions in the oil and butter with the parsley over a very low heat for 1 hour, covered, until shiny and soft. Stir frequently to prevent sticking or burning. Then raise the heat and lay the liver in the onions. Brown it quickly on both sides and pour the wine over as it browns; the liver will be cooked in 5 minutes. Season it with salt and pepper, remove from the pan and keep warm. Tip the cooked onions on to a warmed platter, arrange the liver on top and serve at once.

CODA alla VACCINARA
Oxtail Stew

This is one of Rome's most famous and traditional recipes. At the end of the last century, the people of Rome developed a unique series of dishes, made from the offal and scraps from the central abattoir at Testaccio on the outskirts of the city. This cuisine was based exclusively on the use of meat which was shunned by the upper classes, but eaten out of necessity by the men and women who worked at the abattoir and lived in its vicinity. These dishes live on, with the delicious Coda as one of the most popular. Here is my own recipe for it.

SERVES 4–6

4½ lb (2 kg) oxtail, cut into thick chunks
4 tablespoons sunflower oil
1 large carrot, scraped and finely chopped
1 large onion, peeled and chopped
1 clove garlic, peeled and chopped
1 handful parsley, chopped
1 large glass white or red wine
2 tablespoons tomato purée diluted with 18 fl oz (500 ml) hot water
1 head tender celery, cut into small sections
salt and pepper

Wash the oxtail and put it into a saucepan. Cover with water and bring to the boil. Boil fast for about 15 minutes, then drain.

Heat the oil and fry the chopped carrot, onion, garlic and parsley for about 5–8 minutes or until the carrot and onion are soft. Add the oxtail and brown it all over. Add the wine and cook for about 2–3 minutes to let the alcohol evaporate, then add the diluted tomato purée and stir. Cover and simmer slowly for 4–5 hours or bake in the oven at gas mark 2, 300°F (150°C). Add the celery, stir and cover again. Simmer for a further 30 minutes or until the celery is completely soft. Season to taste and serve immediately.

IL POLLO alla CACCIATORA di ANTONIETTA
Antonietta's Chicken Casserole

The Delle Fratte family live at Zagarolo, a small town in the province of Rome. They keep chickens, rabbits and doves, have a small vegetable plot and are almost self-sufficient. Antonietta, the mother of the family, adores cooking and I cannot visit them without feeling as though I have put on about 3 kilos in weight! When we last visited them, she made us this delicious and very simple chicken casserole. The fact that it was a free-range chicken, lovingly tended by Antonietta, helped to make it taste extra special. Serve with roast potatoes and a green salad.

SERVES 4

3 tablespoons sunflower oil
8 small chicken joints
2 tablespoons white wine vinegar
2 cloves garlic, peeled
2 tablespoons fresh rosemary leaves
salt and pepper
1 large glass dry white wine

Heat the oil in a wide, deep frying-pan. Add the chicken and turn it quickly in the oil to brown it all over. Sprinkle with the vinegar and continue to heat for about 3 minutes to evaporate the fumes.

Meanwhile, pound the garlic, rosemary and salt and pepper in a mortar with a pestle. Alternatively you can do this in a food processor or on a chopping board with a very heavy knife. Sprinkle the mixture over the chicken, stir and add the wine. Allow the fumes from the alcohol to evaporate for about 2 minutes, then cover tightly with a lid. Simmer slowly for about 30 minutes. The chicken should be well browned and crisp on the outside, moist and tender on the inside.

POLLO GRILLETTATO alla ROMANA

Roman Chicken Stew

The Lazio is one of the few areas where chicken is eaten in any quantity worth mentioning – 'Alas,' say the Italian cardiologists, 'not enough white meat is eaten in this country!' Rabbit can be cooked in exactly the same way for an equally delicious dish.

SERVES 4–6

1 × 3 lb (1.5 kg) chicken, jointed

2 oz (50 g) prosciutto crudo, coarsely chopped

4 tablespoons chopped parsley

3 tablespoons olive oil

1 large glass white wine

1 large clove garlic, peeled and chopped

large pinch dried marjoram

1 lb (450 g) canned tomatoes, drained and de-seeded

½ chicken stock cube *or* 4 tablespoons very concentrated chicken stock (see page 292)

salt and pepper

8 slices from a French stick loaf, cut at an angle to give the largest possible slice

Wash and dry the chicken joints. Fry the prosciutto and parsley together in the oil for about 5 minutes over a low heat. Add the chicken joints, raise the heat and brown them well all over. Sprinkle the wine over the chicken, then add the garlic and marjoram. Add the tomatoes, stock cube or stock and salt and pepper. Cover and simmer for 30 minutes, stirring occasionally.

Toast the bread and arrange it around the edges of a serving platter. Put the chicken in the centre of the circle, pour all its sauce over and serve at once.

POLLO alla MESSINESE
Messina Chicken

Meat is virtually non-existent in Sicilian cooking – who needs meat when you have a wealth of fish, fruit and vegetables, fantastic pasta, delicious rice dishes, pastries and ice-creams? The few meat dishes that do crop up are usually fairly elaborate, or at least they are often dressed with a fancy sauce. This is certainly the case with the boiled chicken recipe which follows, in which the humble fowl is turned into something very memorable by the addition of a clever, rich sauce. The dish would originally have been made with a boiling fowl, so don't feel that you have to buy an expensive bird.

SERVES 4

1 × 3 lb (1.5 kg) chicken, suitable for boiling
1 leafy stick celery
4 large sprigs parsley
4 large sprigs basil
salt
1 egg yolk *or* 1 whole egg
3½ fl oz (100 ml) olive oil
juice of ½ lemon
3½ oz (90 g) canned tuna in oil, drained
2 anchovies preserved in salt, cleaned and boned, *or* 4 canned anchovy fillets, drained
1 heaped tablespoon capers, lightly rinsed and dried
1 tablespoon white wine vinegar (optional)
lemon slices and olives plus extra parsley and capers to garnish (optional)

Check over the chicken, trim off fat and skin as required, wash it and lay it in the bottom of a deep pan. Cover with enough cold water to come about 1½ inches (4 cm) over the chicken. Remove the chicken from the water and set it aside. Put the celery, parsley, basil and ½ teaspoon salt into the water and bring to the boil, then slide the chicken into the water. Cover and simmer for about 1½ hours or until the chicken is cooked through, then remove it from the heat and leave it to cool completely in its cooking juices.

Meanwhile, make a basic mayonnaise with the egg, olive oil and lemon juice. If you are using a food processor, use 1 whole egg; if you are working by hand, use only 1 egg yolk (see page 290). Chop the tuna, anchovies and capers together, then stir into the mayonnaise. Taste and add vinegar if you like a sharper flavour; and add salt to taste also, remembering that the mixture will already be quite salty. Stir very thoroughly, then set aside.

Remove the cooled chicken from its cooking juices (which you can reserve for use in another dish), carve and arrange on a serving dish. Cover with the mayonnaise and decorate with lemon slices, olives, parsley and capers.

POLLO alla MARENGO
Chicken Marengo

This is a dish created by one of Napoleon Bonaparte's chefs, who cooked it on the camp stove on the battlefield at Marengo (near the town of Alessandria) for Napoleon and his generals when the fighting was over. They were situated a long way from the supply wagon and therefore the ingredients were what the cook could collect from the immediate surrounding area.

SERVES 4

1 × 2½ lb (1.25 kg) chicken, jointed

1 small glass plus 4 tablespoons olive oil

4 tablespoons plain white flour

salt and pepper

1 lb (450 g) canned tomatoes, de-seeded and chopped

5 basil leaves, tied together with white cotton

1 glass plus 8 fl oz (250 ml) dry white wine

1 clove garlic, peeled and crushed

4 oz (100 g) mushrooms, thinly sliced

4 large uncooked prawns (optional)

4 slices white bread

4 eggs

1 handful parsley, finely chopped

juice of 1 lemon, strained

Wash the chicken joints and pat them dry with kitchen paper. Heat the small glass of oil in a wide, deep pan. Flour the chicken, season with salt and pepper and fry it in the oil until brown all over. After about 15 minutes add the tomatoes, basil and glass of wine to the cooking chicken. Then add the crushed garlic, sprinkle with a little salt, stir and cover. Cook for a further 15 minutes. Add the mushrooms, cover again and cook for another 10 minutes.

Meanwhile, pour the 8 fl oz (250 ml) wine into a small saucepan, add 2 pinches of salt and heat to boiling point. Add the prawns, cook for 5 minutes, then drain and set aside.

Heat the 4 tablespoons oil in a separate frying-pan and fry the bread in it until crisp and golden. Remove and set aside. Fry the eggs in the same frying-pan.

Scatter the chicken with the parsley, pour over the lemon juice and stir. Remove the chicken from the pan and arrange on a large, warmed platter. Surround with the mushrooms and put the fried bread around these. Put an egg on each slice of bread, then lay the cooked prawns on top of the eggs. Serve at once with Napoleonic flair!

'STRACCI' di SELLA di CORNO
Sella di Corno 'Rags'

This delicious and very special dish comes from the little village of Sella di Corno in the Aquila province. It's quite lengthy and fussy to prepare, so do reserve it for a really special occasion. Despite this, the dish is actually quite inexpensive. It is called 'Rags' because the pancakes are wrapped around the filling like cloths.

SERVES 4

1 onion, peeled and finely chopped

1 stick celery, finely chopped

11 oz (300 g) minced chicken *or* turkey breast

salt and pepper

3½ oz (90 g) butter *or* lard plus extra for greasing

14 oz (400 g) canned tomatoes, sieved, *or* passata

3 large eggs, beaten

1 heaped tablespoon plain white flour

1 tablespoon olive oil

2¼ fl oz (60 ml) cold water

4 tablespoons vegetable oil

5 oz (150 g) mozzarella or scamorza cheese, cubed

2 tablespoons warm melted butter

3 tablespoons grated pecorino or Parmesan cheese

Mix together the onion and celery with the minced chicken or turkey in a bowl. Add salt and pepper. Melt half the butter or lard until sizzling, pour it over this mixture and stir together very carefully. Tip the mixture back into the pan in which you melted the fat and sizzle it gently for just a few minutes.

Put the other half of the butter or lard in a second pan, heat until sizzling, then pour in the sieved tomatoes or passata, season with salt and pepper, stir and simmer for 10 minutes. Pour half of the tomato sauce on to the meat and continue to simmer gently for 40 minutes, stirring frequently. Simmer the remaining tomato sauce for only 15 minutes before removing it from the heat.

Beat the eggs with the flour, olive oil, a little salt and the water until you have a completely smooth batter. Heat a small pan suitable for making pancakes and, using the vegetable oil, make as many pancakes as you can out of this batter. You should be able to get 8 out of it quite easily.

Pre-heat the oven to gas mark 5, 375°F (190°C). Cover each pancake with some of the minced meat mixture, dot with mozzarella or scamorza cubes and roll closed. Lay them all in a well-buttered, ovenproof dish, pour over the remaining tomato sauce, pour the warm melted butter over that, sprinkle with the grated cheese

and place in the centre of the oven for 8
minutes. Remove from the oven, rest for 3
minutes, then serve.

CAPPONE RIPIENO alla MANFREDA
Stuffed Roast Capon

---

*This Christmas, why not try capon as an alternative to turkey? It has a
milder flavour, is more digestible and juicy than turkey and won't leave you
with a fridge full of left-overs for 10 days. In Rome, where this recipe comes
from, capon is often served on New Year's Eve. Ask the butcher to bone the
bird for you. Excellent either hot or cold, this dish is traditionally served with
peas, tomatoes, fried courgettes, sautéed mushrooms and stewed artichokes.
You can cook pheasant, guinea fowl, chicken, turkey, duck, goose and
partridge with the same delicious stuffing; I particularly like it with wood
pigeon too.*

SERVES 8–10

1 × 10 lb (4.5 kg) capon,
   boned
11 oz (300 g) minced veal
   or pork
4 oz (100 g) prosciutto
   crudo, cubed
4 oz (100 g) ham, cubed
4 oz (100 g) mortadella,
   rind removed and cubed
about 1 liqueur glass
   Marsala wine
4 hard-boiled eggs
salt and pepper
8 tablespoons olive oil
2 oz (50 g) butter

Pre-heat the oven to gas mark 4, 350°F (180°C).
   Lay the boned bird out as flat as possible on
a wooden board. Remove a little of the meat
from the breast and cut it into thin strips. In a
bowl mix together the minced and the cubed
meats, pour in the Marsala and stir carefully.
Add more Marsala if the mixture is a little dry.
Shell the eggs and separate the whites from the
yolks. Chop the whites finely and mix with the
meats. Season with salt. Quarter the yolks. Put
the Marsala-flavoured mixture into the bird,
laying the strips of breast and the quarters of
egg yolk in among it. Close the capon and sew
it up with cook's string, repairing any tears.
Place it in a roasting-tin, pour over the oil and
dot with the butter. Sprinkle with salt and
pepper and roast in the oven for 2½ hours,
basting occasionally. Remove the bird from the
oven and let it rest for 6 minutes before carving.

ARROSTO RIPIENO
Stuffed Turkey Roll

Stuffings are important in the cuisine of Emilia Romagna – distinctly flavoursome, thanks to the use of local salumi such as prosciutto, mortadella, pancetta and so on, as well as great snowy hills of Parmigiano Reggiano (Parmesan cheese) – famous everywhere for its delicious flavour and piquancy.

Ask your butcher to prepare the turkey breast for you – it needs to be flattened so that it's about ½ inch (1 cm) thick and will roll up easily. If you ask him/her politely, your butcher might also give you a piece of elasticated net to hold the roast together, and show you how to use it. Serve the dish with sautéed potatoes and salad.

SERVES 4-6

2 large eggs
3½ oz (90 g) Parmesan cheese, grated
salt and pepper
4½ oz (120 g) butter
1½ lb (750 g) spinach
1 × 1¾ lb (800 g) boned turkey breast, flattened to a thickness of ½ inch (1 cm)
4 oz (100 g) pancetta *or* bacon, thinly sliced
4 tablespoons vegetable oil
1 tumbler cold water

Beat the eggs and half the cheese together with a little salt and, using about one third of the butter, cook the mixture to make a plain, flat, pancake-shaped omelette. Put it to one side until required.

Wash and check over the spinach carefully. Steam it until soft, then toss it in a pan with the rest of the cheese, about half the remaining butter and a little salt and pepper for about 5–6 minutes. Set this aside also.

Lay the turkey out on a wooden board, flatten it and trim it carefully, then lay the pancetta or bacon on top. Lay the omelette on top of the bacon and the spinach on top of that. Roll up like a Swiss roll and sew closed with thick, white cook's string. Then tie it up in a net as for a normal stuffed roast.

Heat the remaining butter and the oil into a heavy flameproof casserole, brown the turkey roll all over in it, then pour on the water and season generously with salt and pepper. Cover tightly and cook over a low heat for 1 hour 10 minutes, adding a little more water occasionally to prevent the dish from drying out. Serve hot or cold, in thick slices.

In the flat plains of the Veneto duck is cooked and eaten a great deal in a great many recipes. On the whole, they eat more poultry in this region than in any other. There are two Venetian recipes for this delicious stuffed duck, one boiled and one roast. I give them both as an encouragement to British cooks to make more use of this tasty bird.

ANATRA col PIEN 1
Venetian Boiled Duck with Garlic Stuffing

Serve this dish with green beans, boiled potatoes and cooked radicchio.

SERVES 6

1 × 4½ lb (2 kg) oven-ready duck
1 onion, peeled and cut in half
1 carrot, scraped and cut in half
1 stick celery, cut in half
salt
3½ pints (2 litres) cold water
1 handful parsley, finely chopped
2 cloves garlic, peeled and finely chopped
4 oz (100 g) duck *or* chicken livers, trimmed, washed and finely chopped
1 rasher bacon, finely chopped
½ teaspoon grated nutmeg
2 eggs
4 tablespoons grated Parmesan cheese
3–4 tablespoons fresh breadcrumbs

Wash the duck inside and out and dry it carefully. Put the onion, carrot, celery and a little salt into a saucepan large enough to take the duck when it is covered in the water. Pour in the cold water and bring to a gentle boil.

Mix together the chopped parsley and garlic, the duck or chicken livers, bacon, nutmeg, eggs, Parmesan and a pinch of salt. Stir thoroughly and add enough breadcrumbs to make a thickish consistency, rather like stiff porridge. Spoon this inside the duck and press it down lightly with the back of a spoon. Sew up the bird with white cook's string and lower it into the simmering water with the vegetables. Cover and continue to simmer for about 2 hours or until the duck is tender and cooked through.

Remove the bird from the water, undo the stitches and split it open. Slide out the stuffing and slice it into neat rounds. Joint the bird carefully and arrange both the duck and the stuffing on a warmed serving platter.

ANATRA col PIEN 2
Venetian Roast Duck with Macaroon Stuffing

I have eaten this on many occasions when I used to go to Conegliano to visit my cousin and to hunt for treasures at the antique fair in Asolo. Although it is not vital to use a boned duck for this recipe, it does make carving it so much easier – ask your butcher to bone it for you.

SERVES 6

4 oz (100 g) veal escalope *or* chicken breast, minced

4 oz (100 g) plus 1 rasher bacon, finely chopped

1 duck liver *or* 2 chicken livers, trimmed, washed and chopped

2 tablespoons olive oil

1 handful parsley, finely chopped

1 stale, white bread roll, crusts removed, grated

4 amaretti biscuits *or* 2 macaroons, crumbled

5 tablespoons Marsala wine

1 tablespoon grated Parmesan cheese

salt and pepper

1 egg yolk

1 × 4½ lb (2 kg) oven-ready duck, boned

3 tablespoons vegetable oil plus extra for greasing

2 sprigs rosemary, leaves removed and chopped

1 bottle dry white or red wine

Pre-heat the oven to gas mark 4, 350°F (180°C).

Mix together the minced veal or chicken, the 4 oz (100 g) chopped bacon, duck liver or chicken livers, olive oil, parsley and breadcrumbs. Stir the crumbled amaretti biscuits or macaroons into the Marsala until mushy, then pour this into the minced meat mixture. Stir in the Parmesan, season to taste with salt and pepper and bind it all together with the egg yolk. Lay the duck on a wooden board, spoon this mixture into it and sew it closed with white cook's string.

Blend together the vegetable oil, a little salt, the chopped rosemary leaves and chopped bacon rasher. Put the stuffed duck into a lightly oiled roasting-tin and spread the rosemary mixture all over it. Place in the oven and roast for about 1½ hours, basting frequently with the wine. (You are not really meant to use it all, though you can if you like. Whatever doesn't go on the cooking duck can be drunk with the finished dish.)

Remove the duck from the oven, transfer to a warmed platter and carve before serving with Salsa peverada into which 4 amaretti biscuits or 2 macaroons have been crumbled.

Peperoni in Padella (page 243)

Above: Mushroom policemen in
Trento, hard at work! *Below:* Wild
mushrooms on sale in Pistoia.

To serve
1 quantity Salsa peverada
   (see page 283)
4 amaretti biscuits *or* 2
   macaroons, crumbled to
   a fine dust

QUAGLIE in TEGAME
Quail Casserole with Peas

This delicious dish of quails cooked in white wine with peas comes from the Marche. It is definitely the recipe for anybody who has wanted to try quails but has never known how, or wondered if they were a bit tricky. The Marche can boast many wonderful wines, but none is more famous than the Verdicchio from the town of Iesi; if possible, use it in the dish and drink it with the finished result. An alternative to quails is poussins or chicken breasts. Serve with boiled new potatoes and a green vegetable.

SERVES 4
8 quails *or* 4 chicken
   breasts *or* 2 poussins
5 oz (150 g) fat cut off
   prosciutto crudo, ham or
   bacon
12 fl oz (350 ml) dry white
   wine (preferably
   Verdicchio)
11 oz (300 g) canned
   tomatoes, drained, de-
   seeded and chopped
salt and pepper
2 lb (1 kg) fresh peas
   (shelled weight) *or* frozen
   peas
4 tablespoons water

Check over the quails, removing any remaining feathers. Wash and dry them (or the chicken breasts or poussins, if using), then put them in a shallow flameproof casserole with half the ham or bacon fat. Brown carefully all over, add a little wine and begin to cook them, covered, adding more wine as you go along. After about 15 minutes, add the tomatoes and season to taste with salt and pepper. Cover and continue to cook for a further 10–15 minutes.

In a separate pan, cook the peas with the rest of the fat and the water until soft. Then add the peas to the quails, mix together thoroughly, heat through for 5 minutes and serve at once.

CAPRIOLO in SALSA con i MIRTILLI

Venison Casserole with Blueberry Sauce

This is very much a recipe of Italy's cold north, a region heavily influenced by its Austrian past. It uses myrtleberries – small, blue berries which grow very close to the ground and are extremely hard work to pick. In Tuscany we have always eaten them on mountains of sweet, dense vanilla ice-cream, their tartness clashing delightfully on the tastebuds, but up here in Alto Adige they use them for all kinds of savoury recipes, including the one which follows. I have never seen a myrtleberry in the UK (although I am sure they must grow somewhere) so I have substituted blueberries, which are even available in my local supermarket in deepest East Anglia. If you cannot find fresh blueberries, or if you can't be bothered to make the required sauce, buy a pot of good-quality myrtleberry or blueberry jam and use that instead.

Both the myrtleberries and the dumplings are traditional accompaniments, but you can, of course, serve the casserole with whatever you wish. Boiled or roast potatoes make a very passable alternative to the dumplings. A good selection of freshly cooked green vegetables has the advantage of cleansing the palate and aiding the digestion, but do remember that this does not apply to members of the cabbage family. On the other hand, few things blend better with gamy flavours than well-cooked red cabbage with apple. When gathering the fir tree spears which are an optional addition to the dish, choose the soft, fresh, green sprouts about 2–3 inches (5–7.5 cm) long – do not try to use hard, sharp tips because they will ruin the dish.

SERVES 6

For the Casserole

2 lb (1 kg) venison, boned and cut into 3½ inch (9 cm) cubes

1¾ pints (1 litre) red table wine

2 bay leaves

8 juniper berries

3–4 soft young sprigs from a fir tree (optional)

Cover the cubed venison with the red wine in a large, non-metallic bowl. Rub each herb, including the juniper berries and fir tree sprigs (if using), lightly between your palms and drop into the wine: this will help release the natural oils and so flavour the marinade more strongly. Leave the venison to marinate in a cool place for at least 1 day, preferably 2. Remove the meat with a slotted spoon, drain it carefully, reserving the marinade, and toss in the flour.

Fry the onion and the bacon together in a large flameproof casserole for 8 minutes or

4 inch (10 cm) sprig
  rosemary
4 tablespoons plain white
  flour
1 large onion, peeled and
  thinly sliced
3 oz (75 g) fat bacon,
  coarsely chopped
salt and pepper
10 fl oz (300 ml) single or
  double cream

For the Canederli (Dumplings)
5 oz (150 g) unsalted
  butter, creamed
1 lb (450 g) stale white
  bread
4½ oz (120 g) plain white
  flour
5 large eggs
10 fl oz (300 ml) milk
3 tablespoons chopped
  parsley
salt
pinch nutmeg

For the Blueberry Sauce
1 lb (450 g) blueberries
  (preferably unripe)
5 fl oz (150 ml) red wine
½ cinnamon stick
4 cloves
14 oz (400 g) granulated or
  preserving sugar

until the onion is soft. Add the meat, mix
together and season with salt and pepper. Cook
slowly for about 3 hours, adding a little of the
wine from the marinade from time to time.

When the meat is completely tender (the
cooking time will vary slightly according to the
age of the animal), remove it from the pan and
arrange it on a warmed platter. Stir the cream
into the liquid in the pan, bring to the boil just
to thicken it, then pour all over the cooked
meat. Serve with Canederli and Blueberry
Sauce or accompaniments of your choice.

To make the Canederli (Dumplings)
Make sure the butter is fluffy and soft before
you start to prepare the dumplings. Grate the
bread and blend it into the butter with a
wooden spoon. Add all the other ingredients
one at a time – flour, eggs, milk, parsley, salt
and nutmeg – and mix them together lightly so
as to incorporate as much air as possible. Shape
them into meatball shapes about the size of
golfballs. Bring a wide, shallow pan of salted
water to the boil, slide in the dumplings and
boil them for 15 minutes. Remove with a
slotted spoon, arrange on a warmed platter and
serve with the casserole.

To make the Blueberry Sauce
Wash the blueberries carefully and discard any
bruised or rotten ones. Place them in a
stainless-steel pan with the wine, cinnamon and
cloves. Set the pan over a medium heat and
bring the wine to the boil; as soon as it is
boiling, tip in the sugar. Mix together
thoroughly, turn down the heat and simmer for
30 minutes, stirring frequently. Serve hot or
cold in a sauceboat with the casserole. The
sauce may also be preserved in tightly sealed,
sterilised jars for up to 6 months. It also goes
well with other game dishes.

LEPRE in DOLCE e FORTE
Tuscan Sweet and Sour Hare

This rather peculiar but very traditional Tuscan speciality was doubtless created in the kitchens of Florence during the Renaissance and taken to France on the occasion of twelve-year-old Caterina de' Medici's marriage. The French now claim it as their own, but even in French it retains an Italianised name. Only hare will work for the dish: do not attempt to substitute rabbit. Serve with plenty of green vegetables, boiled potatoes in their skins dressed with a little olive oil, and Chianti to drink. The dish is eaten the day after it is cooked, allowing the flavours time to develop.

SERVES 6

1 large hare, hung head down for several days
5 cloves garlic, peeled
2 small sprigs rosemary
2 large onions, peeled and chopped
2 large carrots, scraped and chopped
3 sticks celery, finely chopped
1 handful parsley, finely chopped
1 handful basil, finely chopped
3 bay leaves
6 sage leaves
5 tablespoons olive oil
salt
1 large glass Chianti wine
11 oz (300 g) canned tomatoes, de-seeded and chopped
18 fl oz (500 ml) hot game stock (see page 293)
3 Cavallucci (Tuscan almond biscuits) *or* stale

Skin the hare and cut it into joints, reserving only the more meaty parts for this recipe. Wash it carefully, pat it dry and lay it in a deep flameproof casserole. Crush 3 of the garlic cloves and add them with the rosemary to the casserole. Set it over a medium heat on top of the stove and shake to prevent the hare from sticking. As soon as the hare starts exuding liquid, remove the joints from the casserole and set them aside. Discard the garlic and rosemary.

Rinse the casserole, return it to the heat and put in the chopped onions, carrots, celery, parsley, basil, bay leaves, sage and olive oil. Chop the remaining 2 cloves garlic and add those also. Fry together for about 10 minutes over a lowish heat, stirring constantly. Lay the hare joints in this mixture, brown them on all sides and sprinkle with salt. Pour the wine over the joints and continue heating until it evaporates, then add the tomatoes and their juice and stir. Cover and cook for about 1½ hours, adding a little hot stock occasionally to prevent the casserole from drying out. The finished dish must be quite 'wet'.

In a separate saucepan mix the Cavallucci or ratafias, pine kernels, sultanas, candied peel, drinking chocolate powder and sugar together.

ratafias, thinly sliced
4 oz (100 g) pine kernels
2 oz (50 g) sultanas
2 oz (50 g) mixed candied
  peel, chopped
2 oz (50 g) drinking
  chocolate powder
1 tablespoon granulated
  sugar
3 tablespoons red wine
  vinegar

Add about 8 tablespoons cold water and cook over a low heat, stirring, for about 10 minutes, then remove from the heat and put in the vinegar. Pour this mixture all over the hare, stir and cook for a further 10 minutes. Remove from the heat and allow to cool overnight.

On the following day heat the casserole through again and serve piping hot.

PERNICI con LENTICCHIE
Partridge and Lentil Casserole

Game is an integral part of the Sardinian food scene, a fact which might surprise most visitors who see this glorious island only in the summer time, when its landscape is parched and river beds dried up. When the island is rich and green, however, all kinds of delicious game, from baby wild boar to plump pheasant, finds its way into the pot.

If you cannot get partridges, use poussins.

SERVES 4
5-7 oz (150-200 g) brown
  lentils, soaked overnight
  in cold water
salt and pepper
5 tablespoons olive oil
1 large onion, peeled and
  sliced
2 very plump partridges *or*
  poussins, jointed
1 tablespoon tomato purée
1 bay leaf

Drain and rinse the lentils, cover with fresh cold water in a saucepan and bring to the boil. Boil for 5 minutes, drain, rinse and cover again with fresh cold water. Add 2 pinches of salt and simmer for about 45 minutes, then drain, reserving the cooking liquid.

Pour the oil into a deep flameproof casserole, heat it and lightly brown the onion in it. Add the partridges and seal all over. Put in the lentils and about half their reserved cooking liquid, the tomato purée and the bay leaf. Simmer, uncovered, for about 40 minutes (depending upon the age of the birds), stirring frequently and adding more of the cooking liquid from the lentils. (The sauce should be fairly thick.) Season to taste. Arrange on a warmed platter and serve at once.

LEPRE in SALMÌ – VAL d'AOSTA

Hare Casserole Val d'Aosta

This ancient speciality crops up here and there all over Italy, but its real home is in the Dolomites. It is sumptuously rich and calls for two whole bottles of aged red Barbera, so make it for special occasions. Rabbit or even chicken can be substituted for the hare if you wish. As it is fairly heavy, I like to serve it with a cool starter like prosciutto and figs, and follow it with a crisp salad to cleanse the palate.

SERVES 8

1 × 4½ lb (2 kg) hare, gutted and hung for about 8 days, then skinned and jointed, *or* rabbit *or* chicken

18 fl oz (500 ml) red table wine *or* water

2 carrots, scraped and cut into small pieces

4 sticks celery, cut into pieces the same size as the carrots

2 large onions, peeled and thickly sliced

4 bay leaves

2 sticks cinnamon

10 black peppercorns

2 bottles well aged Barbera *or* other good-quality strong red wine

4 oz (100 g) unsalted butter

salt

8 fl oz (250 ml) meat stock (see page 293)

1 large white truffle, cleaned (optional)

Wash the hare, rabbit or chicken in the table wine or water (this removes the sour 'gamy' smell and taste) and lay it in a deep, non-metallic bowl. Discard the washing wine or water. Put the vegetables on top of the meat, then add the bay leaves, cinnamon and peppercorns. Pour over the Barbera wine and leave in a cool place for 48 hours.

Remove the meat, strain the marinade and reserve it. Put the vegetables from the marinade into a flameproof casserole with the butter and fry for 10 minutes. Add the meat, season with salt and brown all over. Now pour in the marinade, cover and simmer very slowly on top of the stove for about 1½ hours or until all the wine has been absorbed. When there is no wine left, add the stock, stir and cook for a further 45 minutes. (If using rabbit or chicken, reduce the cooking time by 30 minutes and 15 minutes respectively.) When the meat is cooked through and all the vegetables soft, remove the meat and strain the remaining contents of the casserole, pushing the vegetables through the sieve. Return the meat to the casserole, pour over the resulting gravy and cool overnight.

Re-heat the casserole in a bain-marie until piping hot. If using a truffle, shave it lightly all over the top of the dish just before serving.

VEGETABLES & SALADS

CARCIOFI alla TRIESTINA
Trieste Artichokes

Friuli Venezia Giulia has very few recipes for vegetables. Here is the one I like the best, using tender, fresh artichokes. This recipe crops up in very similar forms in other parts of Italy, but it would appear that it originally came from the very windy city whose name it bears. It makes a very good antipasto dish.

SERVES 4

4 globe artichokes

juice of ½ lemon

6 tablespoons fresh
    breadcrumbs

2 tablespoons chopped
    parsley

2 cloves garlic, peeled and
    finely chopped

3 tablespoons grated
    Parmesan *or* Cheddar
    cheese

salt and pepper

3 canned anchovy fillets,
    drained and finely
    chopped (optional)

6 tablespoons olive oil

about 10 fl oz (300 ml) cold
    water

Remove and discard all the hard exterior leaves of the artichokes. Cut off the hard stalks, peel them until you get to the tender part and drop them into a basin of cold water to which you have added the lemon juice to prevent them from discolouring. Cut off all the sharp points on the artichokes, open them out widely with your hands (to look like flowers), remove and discard as much of the choke as possible without splitting them, and drop them into the lemon water also. Leave them there for 20 minutes, then drain and dry them thoroughly.

Mix together the breadcrumbs, parsley, garlic, cheese and seasoning, and the anchovies if using. Put a little of this mixture inside each artichoke and arrange them upright in a single layer in a saucepan. Put the stalks in with them. Pour the oil over them and the water around them. Sprinkle with a little salt and pepper, cover loosely and stew gently for about 40 minutes or until the artichokes are tender and all the water has evaporated.

INSALATA di ARANCE
A Salad of Oranges

Eleonora Consoli prepared this lovely fresh orange salad to eat with her lemony meatballs (see page 211). It is a very traditional Sicilian dish that can be made easily anywhere. Perfect for eating in hot weather, the salad may be served either as an antipasto to prepare the palate for what is to follow, or as a side dish with meat, poultry or fish. I also like to serve it on its own after a game course as it cleanses the mouth perfectly and removes the slightly cloying effect of game on the digestive system.

It is important to note that the salad cannot be dressed in advance and left to stand, although you can of course prepare the shallots and oranges ahead. A leek or a small onion can be used instead of the shallots.

SERVES 4

2 large shallots

6 oranges (2 of which should preferably be blood oranges)

6-8 tablespoons olive oil

salt and freshly ground black pepper

Peel the shallots, slice them thinly and set them aside. Peel the oranges carefully, removing as much of the pith as possible. Slice them neatly and arrange them in a salad bowl or a deep dish. Scatter the shallots on top, then add the oil, salt and plenty of freshly ground black pepper. Toss together quickly and serve at once.

SALADA'D COCONJ
Mushroom Salad

Although the original Piedmontese recipe calls for wild mushrooms, any kind works well except porcini. You must be sure to use a good strong dressing with plenty of flavour, even if you leave out the anchovies. The salad makes a good starter or accompaniment.

SERVES 4

14 oz (400 g) wild or cultivated mushrooms, very thinly sliced

1 egg, hard-boiled

Arrange the sliced mushrooms on a platter. Shell the egg, remove the yolk and chop it finely – save the white for another dish, perhaps sandwiches. Chop the parsley and the anchovies together, stir them into the oil and

1 handful parsley

2 anchovies preserved in
salt, cleaned and boned,
or 4 canned anchovy
fillets, drained

½ wine glass olive oil

juice of 1 lemon

1 clove garlic, peeled

pepper

add the chopped egg yolk and lemon juice.
Crush the garlic clove with the heel of your
hand, put the crushed clove on the end of a
fork and beat the oil with this fork until it is of
a rich, smooth texture. Season with a little
pepper, pour the dressing over the mushrooms
and serve immediately: this is not a salad that
can wait around.

INSALATA di RADICCHIO alla VICENTINA
Radicchio Salad Vicenza-style

*Treviso radicchio, the most special of them all, is unfortunately seldom seen
in the UK. It has long, narrow leaves and a particularly good flavour.
While growing it is dug out so that it is blanched by frost and becomes
exceptionally crisp. Originally a type of Venetian endive, it was cleverly
developed by a Flemish botanist called Van den Boor. This delicious salad
has one of those full-bodied dressings they like using in the Vicenza province.
It is excellent with grilled steak.*

SERVES 4

4 heads radicchio
(preferably Treviso)

2 oz (50 g) bacon fat, finely
chopped

3 tablespoons red wine
vinegar

salt and pepper

Wash the radicchio, dry the leaves and arrange
them in a salad bowl. Heat the fat in a frying-
pan until absolutely sizzling, pour in the
vinegar and let it evaporate quickly. Cool
slightly, then pour all over the radicchio.
Sprinkle with salt and pepper and serve
immediately, before the fat congeals on the
leaves.

ASPARAGI alla MILANESE
Asparagus Cooked in the Milanese Style

The asparagus of Lombardy is more phallic in appearance and pulpier than that found anywhere else. It has a deep purple tinge which singles it out from other types. This dish makes a wonderfully simple lunch. The eggs can be omitted if you wish, or poached instead of fried.

SERVES 4

3¼ lb (1.5 kg) asparagus, stems scraped

salt

4 oz (100 g) butter

4 eggs

4 oz (100 g) Parmesan cheese, grated

Tie the asparagus into bundles with cook's string, put it into a deep saucepan with the tips pointing upwards and pour in enough water to come three quarters of the way up the stems. Add a pinch of salt, place the lid on the saucepan, bring to the boil and simmer for 9 minutes or until the asparagus is tender.

Meanwhile, melt the butter in a frying-pan until foaming. Break the eggs carefully into the very hot butter and fry them until just set, spooning butter over the yolks constantly. Sprinkle the eggs with a little salt.

Arrange the cooked asparagus like the spokes of a wheel, with the points facing inwards, on a warmed platter. Lay the fried eggs in the centre of the dish, pour the butter all over the asparagus tips and the eggs, scatter Parmesan over everything except the inedible ends of the asparagus and serve at once.

MELANZANE alla PARMIGIANA
Aubergines Cooked in the Style of Parma

This is not to be confused with the gloriously rich, colourful and sumptuous dish from Campania, in which aubergines mingle with mozzarella, tomato and basil to create an incredible explosion on your tastebuds. This is a dish which is no less exciting, but is rather less sensuous, having a more sedate air about it. I like both enormously, and both recipes are included in this collection. This dish is very much easier to make than the Campanian one, which is one of those 'lots-of-work-but-very-much-worth-the-effort' recipes. Serve it with bread as an antipasto or as a main course with jacket potatoes and other vegetable dishes of your choice.

SERVES 4

4 aubergines

salt and pepper

1 onion, peeled and thinly sliced

4 oz (100 g) prosciutto crudo di **Parma** *or* unsmoked back bacon, cubed

2 tablespoons butter

2 tablespoons vegetable oil

5–6 canned tomatoes, drained, de-seeded and coarsely chopped

Peel the aubergines and cut them into slices about ½ inch (1 cm) thick. Bring a large pan of salted water to the boil, toss in the aubergines and cook them for about 5 minutes. Drain them, dry each one with kitchen paper and leave to dry out, preferably on a clean cloth on a tray placed on a sunny windowsill.

In a flameproof casserole, fry the onion and ham or bacon together in the butter and oil until the onion is soft and golden. Add the tomatoes and season with salt and pepper. Simmer for about 5 minutes, then add the aubergines and cover. Simmer very slowly for 1 hour. Arrange on a warmed platter and serve hot.

FAGIOLI all'UCCELLETTO
Classic Tuscan Bean Stew

The Tuscans have been famous as bean eaters for centuries and many recipes for cooking these delicious pulses have originated from the region. The dishes do require fresh beans for the best results, but I think the dried variety works rather well too. This dish is excellent both as an antipasto and an accompaniment.

SERVES 6

3¼ lb (1.5 kg) dried haricot, kidney, cannellini or butter beans, soaked overnight in cold water, *or* canned beans, drained

3½ fl oz (100 ml) best-quality Tuscan olive oil

4 fresh sage leaves *or* ¼ teaspoon dried sage

2 cloves garlic, peeled

salt and pepper

1 lb (450 g) canned tomatoes, de-seeded and chopped

If using dried beans, drain them and rinse thoroughly in cold water. Put them in a saucepan and cover with fresh cold water. Bring to the boil, boil fast for 5 minutes, drain, rinse and return to the pan. Cover again with fresh cold water, return to the boil and simmer for about 1 hour or until tender – the cooking time will vary according to the type of bean.

Heat the oil in another pan and add the sage, garlic and a large pinch of pepper. Fry for about 5 minutes or until the garlic is golden. Drain the cooked beans and add them to the sage and garlic. If using canned beans, add them at this point also. Stir together and add the tomatoes and their juice. Season to taste with salt and pepper and cover. Simmer very slowly for about 20 minutes, making sure the end result is not too dry – add a little water during cooking if necessary.

VERZOLINI della VIGILIA
Christmas Eve Cabbage Leaves

This dish comes from the Val Taro area in the province of Parma where it is eaten on Christmas Eve. As it is a magro *(lean) dish containing no meat, it is suitable for such important holy days. I don't know why one is supposed to make exactly 27 of these on Christmas Eve. However, it is part of the local tradition; and around Christmas time all local traditions, including the pagan ones, are upheld. Serve it for lunch or supper with a tomato salad.*

MAKES 27

1¼ lb (500 g) large whole cabbage leaves, separated

salt and pepper

3 oz (75 g) stale white bread, crusts removed

10 tablespoons milk

7 oz (200 g) Parmesan cheese, grated

3 eggs, beaten

4 oz (100 g) fresh breadcrumbs

2 oz (50 g) butter

6-7 tablespoons vegetable oil

1 onion, peeled and chopped

2 tablespoons tomato purée

12 fl oz (350 ml) meat stock (see page 293)

Wash and trim the cabbage leaves. Bring a large pan of salted water to the boil, toss in the leaves and simmer for 8 minutes. Meanwhile, cover the stale bread with the milk and leave it to soak. Drain the cabbage leaves, select the 27 best ones and lay them out flat on a work-surface. Chop the remaining leaves finely.

Remove the bread from the milk, squeeze it dry in your hand and put it in a bowl. Add the Parmesan, eggs, fresh breadcrumbs, a little salt and pepper and the chopped cooked cabbage and mix well. Spoon about 1 heaped tablespoon of the mixture on to each cabbage leaf. Roll up and close the leaves and secure with cook's string or wooden cocktail sticks.

Heat 1 oz (25 g) of the butter with 4 tablespoons of the vegetable oil in a frying-pan until sizzling and fry the cabbage rolls until lightly browned all over. In a separate pan, fry the onion in the remaining butter and oil until the onion is soft and golden. Add the tomato purée and 5 tablespoons of the stock, stir, season with salt and simmer for a few minutes. Lay the cabbage leaves in this mixture, cover and simmer for 1 hour, adding more meat stock if necessary. Lift the rolls out of the pan and remove the string or the cocktail sticks. Arrange the rolls on a warmed dish, pour over any cooking liquid remaining in the pan and serve.

CAVOLO ROSSO
Red Cabbage

This is a really wonderful dish to serve with pork or game. In Trentino they still call this vegetable Rotkhol, and indeed it does sound more authentic in German! I like it very much with roast pheasant or goose.

SERVES 4

2 lb (1 kg) red cabbage, shredded
1 large onion, peeled and thinly sliced
3 oz (75 g) Speck *or* smoked prosciutto *or* smoked streaky bacon
2 tablespoons olive oil
2 oz (50 g) butter
1 glass strong red wine
salt and pepper

Prepare the cabbage, making sure that it is clean. In a large pan, fry the onion gently until soft with the Speck, smoked prosciutto or smoked streaky bacon in the olive oil and butter, stirring frequently. Then add the wine and the cabbage, stir, season with salt and pepper and cover so that the cabbage loses none of its colouring. Cook slowly with the lid on the pan, stirring occasionally, for about 35 minutes or until the cabbage is of the texture you like – the longer you leave it, the mushier it will become. Serve piping hot.

VARIATION
Dice a crisp, sour apple and add it to the cabbage about half-way through the cooking time for extra flavour.

GOBBI al FORNO
Baked Umbrian Cardoons

This dish is rather like a layered lasagne but uses cardoons instead of pasta. It is a great pity that this delicious winter/spring vegetable (the stems of the plant are eaten) is not grown more extensively in the UK: it is enjoyed all over Umbria, the Abruzzi and Lazio. If you have never seen or cannot get cardoons, thick celery – as white as you can find – is the only possible substitute. Serve as a lunch or supper dish with a salad and plenty of crusty bread.

1¾ lb (800 g) cardoons *or*
  thick sticks white celery
juice of ½ lemon
2 oz (50 g) butter plus extra
  for greasing
4 tablespoons olive oil
1 large onion, peeled and
  chopped
11 oz (300 g) minced beef
  or pork *or* lamb
1 oz (25 g) dried porcini
  mushrooms, soaked for
  15 minutes in tepid
  water, drained and
  chopped, *or* 4 oz (100 g)
  fresh mushrooms, thinly
  sliced
5 oz (150 g) canned
  tomatoes, drained, de-
  seeded and coarsely
  chopped
8 fl oz (250 ml) chicken or
  meat stock (see page
  293)
salt and pepper
oil for deep-frying
3 tablespoons plain white
  flour
2 eggs, beaten
4 oz (100 g) Fontina *or*
  mozzarella *or* Edam
  cheese
4 oz (100 g) Parmesan
  cheese, grated

Prepare the cardoons or celery. Remove any stringy bits, cut into sections no more than 3½ inches (9 cm) in length and wash very carefully. In the case of the cardoons, drop the cut vegetables into a basin of cold water to which you have added the lemon juice to prevent them from turning black – like artichokes, they have a very high iron content. This is not necessary if you are using celery.

Heat the butter and olive oil in a pan and fry the onion in it until soft. Add the minced meat, brown it all over, add the drained mushrooms, then stir in the tomatoes. Add about three quarters of the stock, season with salt and pepper and cover. Leave to simmer for about 45 minutes or until reduced and thickened.

Pre-heat the oven to gas mark 6, 400°F (200°C).

Heat the oil for deep-frying until a piece of bread dropped into it sizzles instantly. Dry the cardoons or celery sticks carefully, toss them in flour, then in beaten egg, and fry them until crisp and well browned. Drain them very thoroughly on kitchen paper and sprinkle lightly with salt.

Cut the Fontina, mozzarella or Edam into ½ inch (1 cm) cubes. Butter an ovenproof dish about 9 inches (23 cm) square. Arrange a layer of fried cardoons or celery on the bottom of the dish, cover with a layer of meat sauce and sprinkle with cubed and grated cheese. Lay another layer of cardoons or celery on top and continue to layer the dish as described until you have used up all the ingredients, including the remaining stock, finishing with a layer of cubed and grated cheese. Bake the dish in the centre of the oven for 15 minutes or until it is heated through and all the cheese has melted.

PISELLI col GUANCIALE
Peas with Bacon

Guanciale is the cheek or jowl of the pig which, in the opinion of most Italians, makes the best possible bacon. Next best is pancetta, Italian bacon made from belly pork. If you cannot get either of these, you can use very good-quality, unsmoked, preservative-free back bacon, as fat as possible. In this delicious dish, proving once again how much the Lazio cuisine favours vegetables, peas are carefully stewed with guanciale until full of flavour. Fresh peas are, of course, best, but you can use frozen petits pois.

SERVES 4

2 lb (1 kg) fresh peas in pods *or* 1 lb (450 g) frozen petits pois, thawed

5 oz (150 g) guanciale *or* pancetta *or* good-quality fat back bacon

1 onion, peeled and finely sliced

2 oz (50 g) unsalted butter

1 wine glass meat or chicken stock (see page 292)

salt and pepper

If using fresh peas, shell them, wash them and set aside. Divide the guanciale, pancetta or bacon into fat and lean parts and chop each finely. Fry the onion until soft in half the butter and the chopped bacon fat. Add the peas and stock, stir and simmer for about 10 minutes, stirring frequently. Then add the lean guanciale, pancetta or bacon, the rest of the butter and plenty of salt and pepper. Simmer for another 5–10 minutes and serve immediately.

Insalata di Radicchio alla Vicentina
(page 233)

Top: The soil in the south of Italy may be completely parched, but it will still yield perfect tomatoes. *Bottom:* The glory of the island of Capri – the delectable Insalata Caprese.

TORTINO di ZUCCHINE alla FIORENTINA

Florentine Baked Courgettes

When I was growing up in Tuscany, the kitchen garden was always overflowing with courgettes, their brilliant yellow flowers betraying their hiding places under the big, spreading leaves. This very easy dish became a great favourite with us all, because it is perfect for summer meals. It is light yet nourishing, and feeds a lot of people quite cheaply. You can also use potatoes, aubergines or artichokes instead of courgettes. For a lighter dish, use only five eggs.

SERVES 4

4 very large or 8 small courgettes, topped, tailed and cut lengthways into ¼ inch (5 mm) slices

2–3 tablespoons plain white flour

about 7 fl oz (200 ml) sunflower oil plus extra for oiling

8 eggs, beaten

4 tablespoons milk

salt and pepper

large pinch dried marjoram

1 handful parsley, finely chopped

about 4 oz (100 g) Parmesan cheese, grated

1 heaped tablespoon fresh white breadcrumbs

Coat the courgette slices lightly in flour on both sides. Heat the oil in a wide pan until a small piece of bread dropped into it sizzles instantly. Fry the courgettes until crisp and golden on the outside and soft all the way through. Remove with a slotted spoon or fish slice and drain carefully on kitchen paper.

Pre-heat the oven to gas mark 5, 375°F (190°C). Oil the bottom and sides of a large ovenproof dish. Arrange a layer of courgettes on the bottom of the dish. Beat together the eggs, milk, salt and pepper, herbs and half the cheese. Pour about one third of this mixture over the layer of courgettes. Cover with another layer of courgettes and continue in this way until you have used up all the courgettes and the egg mixture. Scatter the remaining cheese and the breadcrumbs over the top and bake in the oven for 20 minutes or until firm all the way through but not rubbery. Serve hot or just warm.

ZUCCHINE al GUANCIALE
Courgettes with Bacon

Sadly, this is one of those recipes which has fallen into disuse and risks being forgotten forever in its native Marche. It results in very soft courgettes which are excellent with chicken dishes. See the introduction to Piselli col guanciale (page 240) for information about this superior bacon and recommended substitutes.

SERVES 6

12 small, tender courgettes

salt and freshly ground black pepper

7 oz (200 g) guanciale *or* pancetta *or* good-quality back bacon, cut into thin strips

1 very large onion, peeled and sliced

1 tablespoon olive oil *or* butter (optional)

1½ oz (40 g) parsley, chopped

3 cloves garlic, peeled and finely chopped

1 lb (450 g) canned tomatoes, drained, de-seeded and coarsely chopped

Peel the courgettes carefully to remove all the green skin. Slice them into discs ¼ inch (5 mm) thick and put them in a colander. Place the colander in the sink, sprinkle the courgettes with plenty of salt and leave for 1–3 hours to allow their juice to drain away. Then rinse the courgettes and dry them carefully.

Fry the guanciale, pancetta or bacon together with the onion until the onion is browned and soft. (Use 1 tablespoon oil or butter if the guanciale is not very fat.) Mix in the parsley and garlic and cook for a further 10 minutes. Add the tomatoes and the courgettes, mix thoroughly and cook gently for a further 20 minutes, stirring frequently. Season with plenty of pepper just before serving.

PEPERONI *in* PADELLA
Sautéed Peppers

Peppers always remind me of Rome. There is something about their colours which conjure up what it is like when the Rome football team wins a game – the entire city becomes a mass of flapping red and yellow flags. The sensuous texture of peppers is also very Roman – 'heavy-handed elegance' describes it rather well. Not for the Roman palate the delicate flavours of subtle herb and cream, no place here for shallots – bring on the garlic! No Roman cook has ever had time to spare in fussing over a stove: there are always far more important things to be done. So a recipe like this one, very simple, very easy, delicious and strong-flavoured, is about as typically Roman as you can get. Serve it as an antipasto or accompaniment; it also makes a wonderful omelette filling.

SERVES 4

4 firm, juicy, green, red or
    yellow peppers
4 tablespoons olive oil
1 large onion, peeled and
    chopped
3 cloves garlic, peeled and
    chopped
6 canned tomatoes, de-
    seeded and coarsely
    chopped
salt

Put the peppers on the end of a fork, hold them over a naked flame, such as a lit gas ring or a candle, or under a grill, and singe the skin all over so that it blisters and blackens. Rub it off under cold running water. Cut the peppers in half, remove and discard the seeds and the inner membranes and cut each half into about 6 pieces.

Heat the oil in a pan and fry the onion and garlic until the onion is soft but not coloured. Add the tomatoes and their juice, simmer for about 10 minutes, then add the peppers. Season with salt, stir and cover. Simmer for 20 minutes, stirring frequently. Serve hot or cold.

ZUCCA FRITTA
Fried Pumpkin

In this recipe, slices of pumpkin are cooked in a coating of egg and breadcrumbs rather like Cotolette alla milanese. It is excellent served as a light lunch with a fairly sour salad to offset the sweetness of the pumpkin.

SERVES 4–6

1¼ lb (500 g) pumpkin, rind removed

salt

18 fl oz (500 ml) milk

2 eggs, beaten

3 tablespoons plain white flour

4 tablespoons stale breadcrumbs

4 oz (100 g) butter

2 tablespoons oil

De-seed the pumpkin and cut it into ¾ inch (2 cm) slices. Put the slices in a saucepan, sprinkle with salt, cover with milk and bring to the boil. Simmer until tender, drain and set aside to cool.

Add a little salt to the beaten eggs. Put the flour and breadcrumbs on separate soup plates. Heat the butter and oil in a heavy pan. Quickly dip each slice of pumpkin into flour, then into egg, then into breadcrumbs, and fry in the hot butter and oil until crisp and brown on both sides. Drain on kitchen paper and serve.

RADICCHIO in PADELLA
Pan-roasted Radicchio

There are several ways of cooking radicchio: you don't have to save it exclusively for salads. This recipe is ideal for a quick lunch with grilled steak or chops.

SERVES 4

4 heads radicchio

2 oz (50 g) butter *or* 2½ fl oz (65 ml) olive oil

salt and pepper

Wash and dry the radicchio and cut it into halves or quarters, depending upon its size. Melt the butter in a heavy pan (or, if using oil, heat it slightly) and lay the radicchio in it. Cook on either side for about 4 minutes or until just tender. If you cover the pan, the radicchio will be soft; if you leave the pan uncovered, it will be crisp – the choice is yours. Sprinkle with salt and pepper and serve at once.

RADICCHIO ROSSO di TREVISO alla BIRRA

Radicchio in Beer Batter

The radicchio of Treviso is very special. It has long, smooth leaves with pointed tips, a deep, burgundy red colour, startlingly white veins and a very crisp, crunchy texture. Although hard to find, it is sometimes available in the UK. Failing that, you can use the more common, rounded variety from Chioggia. I have also made this dish with Belgian endive with equally good results. Serve it as a side dish with a simple meat course such as grilled steak, or as an interesting hot antipasto.

I was given this recipe at the delightful Agriturismo al Sile, near Treviso, where radicchio is the main crop grown. They have about twenty different recipes for delicious radicchio dishes and contributed two of them to this collection.

SERVES 8

4 large heads radicchio, trimmed and quartered
1 large egg, beaten
1 level tablespoon plain white flour
pinch salt
10 fl oz (300 ml) beer
oil for deep-frying

Wash the radicchio, dry it carefully and set it to one side.

Beat the egg, flour, salt and beer together to make a batter. Let the batter stand for 1 hour, then immerse the radicchio in it.

Heat the oil until a small piece of bread dropped into it sizzles instantly. Take the radicchio quarters out of the batter, allow the excess to drip off, then fry each one quickly in the hot oil until crisp and golden. Scoop them out with a fish slice or slotted spoon and drain thoroughly on kitchen paper. Serve at once.

SCORZONERA in UMIDO
Stewed Scorzonera

Scorzonera is a very peculiar-looking vegetable which tastes delicious. Prepare it as you would a carrot, but drop each root into a basin of cold water with added lemon juice as you finish scraping it. This improves the flavour and texture and prevents discolouration. The dish is excellent for a light lunch or supper, served with a salad.

SERVES 4

1¾ lb (800 g) scorzonera *or* carrots *or* parsnips

juice of 1½ lemons

4 tablespoons olive oil

4 tablespoons chopped parsley

1 onion, peeled and finely chopped

1 tablespoon plain white flour

12 fl oz (350 ml) hot vegetable *or* chicken stock (see page 292)

3 egg yolks

salt and pepper

Prepare the scorzonera, cutting it into finger-sized pieces and dropping it as you work into a basin of cold water to which you have added the juice of ½ lemon. (If you are using carrots or parsnips, you don't need to soak them in this way.) Heat the olive oil in a pan, add the parsley and onion and fry until the onion is soft. Add the scorzonera (or carrots or parsnips), stir and cook for about 10 minutes. Sprinkle in the flour, mix well and add about half the stock. Cover and simmer until the vegetable is cooked through – for about 1 hour in the case of scorzonera, less time for carrots and parsnips – adding stock as required.

Beat together the egg yolks with the juice of 1 lemon and any remaining stock, season and pour over the vegetable. Stir through and allow the eggs to scramble before serving.

RAPE alla TRENTINA
Trentino Turnips

Turnips, potatoes, cabbage, gherkins, red cabbage and something called a cabbage-turnip – these are the vegetables of Trentino and Alto Adige. Visualise the average market stall in southern Italy, bursting with colours and textures, sweet and erotic peppers, aubergines, courgettes, mountains of salad in incredible colours, every hue of green, orange, red, yellow, purple.

Then think of these dull white turnips, these pasty white, green and purple cabbages that stand like sentinels in neat rows – endless fields of soon-to-be-Sauerkraut! And yet the flavours of this region are fantastic.

Here is a Trentino recipe for the humble turnip which transforms it into something delicious, worthy of any Italian kitchen, in whatever region. Turnips cooked in this way taste really superb with lamb and mutton dishes.

SERVES 4

2 lb (1 kg) small turnips, peeled
salt and pepper
½ wine glass olive oil
½ tablespoon granulated sugar

Cover the turnips with water, add a little salt and bring to the boil. Cook gently for about 10 minutes or until tender, drain and cool. Slice the turnips into thin strips about half the width of your little finger. Pour the oil into a saucepan, heat it for about 3 minutes, then add the sugar. Allow it to caramelise slightly, add the turnips, stir and season with pepper. Cook for a further 10 minutes and serve.

CIAMBOTTA

Calabrian Summer Vegetable Casserole

This is a typical dish of the south, where aubergines grow in wild profusion in raging heat and arid conditions. In Calabria I have eaten variations on this dish many times, either as an antipasto or with meat or fish dishes.

SERVES 4–6

2 large, tender, juicy peppers (any colour)
2 large or 4 small ripe tomatoes
3 medium aubergines
3 medium potatoes
1 large onion, peeled and finely sliced
3 sticks tender celery, cut into chunks
5 tablespoons olive oil
5 large green olives, stoned

Wash and de-seed the peppers and cut each one into about 8 pieces. Dip the tomatoes in boiling water for 1 minute, then plunge into cold water, peel, de-seed and quarter. Peel the aubergines and potatoes and cut into even-sized chunks about 2½ inches (6 cm) or less across. Fry the onion and the celery in the olive oil until the onion is soft but not browned. Add the other vegetables and the olives. Season and stir together, cover and simmer for about 40 minutes or until all the vegetables are cooked. Stir frequently during cooking and add water if the dish seems to be getting too dry. Serve piping hot.

VERDURE in INTINGOLO
Italian Vegetable Casserole

This delicious Italian version of ratatouille always re-kindles arguments about whether France taught Italy to cook or vice versa! The recipe below is from romantic Mantua in Lombardy and makes a lovely antipasto or accompaniment to an omelette.

SERVES 4

14 oz (400 g) onions, peeled and sliced

4 oz (100 g) butter

3 tablespoons vegetable oil

3 large yellow and red peppers, de-seeded and cut into strips

1 large courgette, peeled and cut into thin rounds

11 oz (300 g) canned tomatoes, drained and coarsely chopped

1 stick celery, chopped

4 tablespoons white wine vinegar

salt and pepper

Fry the onions in the butter and oil until soft but not browned. Add the peppers, courgette, canned tomatoes, celery and vinegar. Stir well, season with salt and pepper and cover. Simmer very slowly for 40 minutes, stirring frequently and adding a little water if necessary. Serve piping hot.

VERDURE RIPIENE di PATATE
Vegetables Stuffed with Potatoes

This delightful dish of vegetables stuffed with mashed potato flavoured with Parmesan cheese, garlic, basil and oregano comes from the city of Sanremo. It is very filling so can be served for lunch or supper along with a good salad. You can eat it either hot or cold. I like to prepare it for parties and serve it cold with salads because it is inexpensive to make and more original than other kinds of party food.

SERVES ABOUT 8

about 1½ lb (750 g) vegetables suitable for stuffing (such as large basil or dark green lettuce leaves, peppers, courgettes, large onions, aubergines, tomatoes or celery sticks)

2 lb (1 kg) potatoes, peeled and cut into chunks

1 handful basil, chopped

1 handful parsley, chopped

2 cloves garlic, peeled and chopped

3 tablespoons olive oil plus extra for oiling

4 oz (100 g) Parmesan *or* Cheddar cheese, grated

4 eggs

salt and pepper

large pinch dried oregano

3 tablespoons breadcrumbs mixed with 2 tablespoons grated Parmesan *or* Cheddar cheese

Prepare the vegetables for stuffing. Peppers, tomatoes, celery sticks and basil and lettuce leaves can be stuffed raw, but courgettes, aubergines and peeled onions must be lightly boiled for about 3 minutes, then cut in half or quartered and made into a shape that can be filled. When all the vegetables are ready, set them to one side.

Boil the potatoes in water until soft, mash them and mix in the chopped herbs, garlic, 3 tablespoons olive oil, cheese and eggs and season with salt and pepper. Stuff the prepared vegetables with the mixture; in the case of basil or lettuce leaves, roll them up around the filling and secure each one with a wooden cocktail stick.

Pre-heat the oven to gas mark 5, 375°F (190°C). Arrange the stuffed vegetables in an oiled ovenproof dish and scatter with the dried oregano and breadcrumbs mixed with cheese. Bake in the oven for about 5 minutes in the case of stuffed basil or lettuce leaves, 15 minutes in the case of other vegetables, or until heated through and well browned. Serve hot or cold.

DESSERTS

CASSARULATA di GELATO
Ice-cream Cassata

This is the original recipe for the most traditional ice-cream of them all: a real Sicilian Cassata. If you dislike pistachio ice-cream, you can use vanilla instead, but you are breaking with tradition.

SERVES 8

4 oz (100 g) mixed candied
  fruit, finely chopped
4 tablespoons liqueur (such
  as Cointreau)
5 oz (150 g) whipped cream
1¼ lb (500 g) best-quality
  pistachio ice-cream
1 egg white
2 oz (50 g) icing sugar,
  sifted
chopped and whole
  candied fruit to decorate

Cover the chopped candied fruit with the liqueur and leave to soak for about 10 minutes. Have ready a 2 pint (1.2 litre) bombe mould, pudding basin or similar-shaped vessel (preferably metal) and keep this and the cream in the refrigerator until required; keep the ice-cream in the freezer. When the mould is absolutely ice-cold, line the inside completely with the pistachio ice-cream using the back of a spoon which you should dip in cold water from time to time as you work. Put the lined mould in the freezer.

Strain and dry the candied fruit. Whip the egg white and icing sugar together, fold into the whipped cream, then carefully stir in the candied fruit. Use this mixture to fill the centre of the lined mould. Smooth the surface and put it back into the freezer at a temperature of −4°F (−18°C) for at least 3 hours. Also chill the platter on which you plan to serve the dessert.

Shortly before you want to eat the Cassata, remove the mould from the freezer, dip it into cold water to loosen the dessert, turn it out on to the chilled platter, slice into 8 sections, decorate with chopped and whole candied fruit and serve at once.

La CASSATA SICILIANA di PINO CORRENTI

Pino Correnti's Sicilian Cassata

This recipe comes from Pino Correnti's amazingly theatrical dining club, deep in the heart of Catania. It is reproduced by kind permission of the author from his book Il Libro d'Oro della Cucina e dei Vini della Sicilia *(published in Italy by Mursia). Here is Pino's introduction to the recipe: Cassata was born of the union between the Arab culinary legacy (the word cassata comes from the Arabic* quasat, *meaning big round bowl) and conventional Sicilian cake and pastry making. Five centuries ago, after the Arabs left Sicily, the custom of preparing cassata had become so popular that in 1575 the religious authorities of Mazara del Vallo were forced to prohibit the local nuns from making it, so as not to distract them from their religious duties during Holy Week.*

SERVES 4

1¼ lb (500 g) very fresh ricotta cheese

11 oz (300 g) icing sugar, sifted

1 teaspoon vanilla essence

3 tablespoons rum *or* liqueur

3 tablespoons cooking chocolate, splintered

3 tablespoons chopped mixed candied peel

11 oz (300 g) basic sponge cake (see page 300), cut in thin slices

6 tablespoons basic custard (see page 300)

To decorate

flakes of chocolate, candied fruit, glacé fruit, silver balls, sugared almonds, rice paper flowers, coloured dragees

Push the ricotta through a sieve, then blend it lightly with the icing sugar until it is of the consistency of lightly whipped cream. Flavour it with the vanilla essence and rum or liqueur. Mix in the chocolate splinters and candied peel. Line a 6 inch (15 cm) bowl or pudding basin with aluminium foil or baking parchment, then line it with slices of sponge cake, using the custard to make it stick. Pour the ricotta mixture into the lined bowl, smooth the top carefully and cover with more cake slices. Put a plate on the top and press it down, then place it in the refrigerator for about 2–3 hours. Turn the cassata out on to a plate and decorate it as much as possible with chocolate flakes, candied fruit and so on to make it look like the wonderfully Baroque Sicilian dessert that is famous all over the world. Chill until required.

ICE-CREAM

It is a great Italian tradition to eat an ice-cream cone as you stroll along the street carrying out one of the Italians' favourite pastimes: people-watching. However, ice-cream can only really be made successfully at home if you have an ice-cream machine. If you want to make good ice-cream, I would recommend you invest in one: there are several models on the market at various prices.

Once you have mastered the basics, any number of flavours can be created. To a water-based ice, you can add any kind of fruit – strawberry, mango, lemon or melon, for example – and whipped cream. To a custard-based ice, add a flavouring such as ground hazelnuts or chocolate and whipped cream for the richer, more fattening *mantecato*. All ice-cream machines come with recipes and instructions to set you on your way, turning your kitchen into a private *gelateria*!

DOLCE di RICOTTA
Ricotta Pudding

This is a very good, easy-to-make, stand-by pudding if you are fortunate enough to have a good supplier of fresh ricotta. In the summer I serve it with a bowl of sliced peaches dusted with sugar and in winter with sliced oranges or poached dried apricots. You can use whipped cream cheese instead of ricotta if you wish.

SERVES 4

14 oz (400 g) very fresh
  ricotta *or* cream cheese
2 oz (50 g) icing sugar,
  sifted
3 egg yolks
4 tablespoons dark rum
1 tablespoon Marsala wine
7 fl oz (200 ml) whipping
  cream, whipped until
  fairly stiff

If you are using cream cheese instead of ricotta, whip it to give it a lighter texture. Mix together the ricotta or whipped cream cheese, icing sugar and egg yolks until you have a light, smoothly blended mixture. Stir in the rum and the Marsala, then carefully fold in the whipped cream. Pour the mixture into individual bowls or stemmed glasses, put in the refrigerator and chill for 3 hours. Remove from the refrigerator just before serving, accompanied by some light, plain biscuits such as langues de chat.

TORTA di RICOTTA
Sardinian Ricotta Cake

Although ricotta cakes in various guises appear all over Italy, my favourite is this one, also from the beautiful island of Sardinia. You must be certain to use the freshest ricotta for this dessert, or alternatively use whipped cream cheese. What I like most about this cake is its light, lemony flavour and its rather odd texture. It should be crisp on the outside, and soft and slightly custard-like on the inside. It is perfect for afternoon tea, or to serve at the end of a meal with some sparkling wine.

SERVES 6-8

11 oz (300 g) very fresh ricotta *or* cream cheese

11 oz (300 g) granulated *or* caster sugar

3 egg yolks, beaten with 4 tablespoons milk

3 oz (75 g) finest possible plain white flour, sifted twice

grated rind of 1 large lemon

3 level teaspoons baking powder

3 egg whites, chilled

1 walnut-sized piece butter for greasing

4 tablespoons icing sugar

Pre-heat the oven to gas mark 3, 325°F (160°C).

If you are using cream cheese instead of ricotta, whip it first to lighten it. Whisk the ricotta or whipped cream cheese lightly with a balloon whisk for about 10–15 minutes, gradually adding the sugar, until the mixture is fluffy. (If you use an electric hand beater it will take less time.) Continue to whisk, blending in the egg yolks and milk, then the flour, the lemon rind and baking powder. Whisk the chilled egg whites into stiff peaks and carefully fold them into the ricotta mixture. Butter a 12 inch (30 cm) cake tin generously. Pour the mixture into the cake tin and level it out smoothly with a spatula or the back of a spoon. Bake in the oven for about 45 minutes–1 hour or until a long, thin, metal skewer pushed into the centre of the cake comes out perfectly dry and clean. Do not worry if the middle of the cake sinks a little: this is quite normal. Remove the cake from the oven, turn it out on to a wire rack and leave to cool completely. Sift the icing sugar all over the cake and serve.

SUSPIRUS
Sardinian Sighs

There are few more pleasant ways to end a meal than by lingering slowly over a glass of Sardinian Mirto (the local sweet liqueur made with myrtle) and picking and choosing from a selection of little cakes. The most romantically named of all the cakes in this book are these delicious, light, golden, almond cakes.

MAKES ABOUT 15 CAKES

2 tablespoons plain white
  flour for dusting
7 oz (200 g) blanched
  almonds
2 egg whites, chilled
7 oz (200 g) caster sugar
1½ teaspoons vanilla
  essence

Pre-heat the oven to gas mark 2, 300°F (150°C). Flour a baking sheet using all the flour.

Chop the almonds finely or whizz them in a food processor until pulverised. Whisk the chilled egg whites until stiff, fold in the sugar, the vanilla essence and the almonds. Using 2 dessertspoons, scoop up lumps of the mixture and push them on to the floured baking sheet, well spaced apart. Bake in the oven for about 25 minutes or until golden-brown and crisp. Remove from the oven and transfer to a wire rack to cool before serving.

La CROSTATA di FRUTTA di ALVARO
Alvaro's Fruit Flan

Alvaro Maccioni has a sweet tooth. When he talks about cakes and desserts, his eyes light up and he becomes tremendously passionate about the subject. This very simple Tuscan fruit flan is made in exactly the same way as his mother used to make it for him when he was a boy. You can use ordinary shortcrust pastry if you wish, but the result is by no means the same. Alvaro serves the flan at his restaurant in Chelsea and after eating it there I asked him what makes it so light and soft, yet moist and crumbly. He says that the secret lies in beating the dough with a whisk to make it light and airy. The pastry base must have a caky, soft texture, and not be biscuity and crisp; if the texture is right, it will become wonderfully gooey while absorbing the juices exuding from the fruit which soak through the cream.

SERVES 4

For the pastry
1 lb (450 g) plain white
  flour, sifted
8 fl oz (250 ml) milk
¾ oz (20 g) baking powder,
  sifted
6 tablespoons olive oil (*not*
  extra virgin but refined),
  plus extra for greasing
4 oz (100 g) caster sugar

For the topping
about 1¼ lb (500 g) fruit
  (blackberries,
  blueberries, strawberries,
  raspberries, redcurrants,
  blackcurrants *or* cherries
  or peaches)
15 fl oz (450 ml) whipping
  cream
icing sugar

Pick over and hull the fruit and keep it in separate piles until required.

Next make the pastry. Pre-heat the oven to gas mark 4, 350°F (180°C). Blend all the pastry ingredients together quickly with a whisk, working the dough as little as possible but making sure that everything is properly amalgamated and incorporating as much air as possible into the mixture. When it is smooth and even, pour it into an oiled 10 inch (25 cm) shallow cake or flan tin. Bake in the oven for about 30 minutes or until a wooden cocktail stick inserted in the centre comes out dry and clean. Remove from the oven and cool on a wire rack until required. If necessary, cut the top off the cooled pastry base to make it slightly concave: in this way the topping will sit on it much more easily.

Prepare the fruit for the topping. If you are using cherries, stone them; if using peaches, peel and stone them and cut into small cubes. Whip the cream until it forms soft peaks, then gradually beat in 5 tablespoons icing sugar (or more or less if you prefer). Spread this all over the pastry base in an even layer.

To complete the flan, arrange the fruit on top of the cream. Sift with more icing sugar and put the flan in the refrigerator for 6–24 hours. Remove the flan from the refrigerator and allow it to return to room temperature before serving.

ZELTEN TRENTINO
Trentino Fruit Cake

A very rich, quite heavy fruit cake, made with equal amounts of fruit and cake dough and not for those with a delicate digestive system. Trentino housewives are very good at making this delicious cake, which is traditionally prepared at Christmas time in every small town and village of the region.

MAKES 2 LARGE CAKES

1 lb 6 oz (700 g) plain white flour, sifted
1½ oz (40 g) dried yeast
about 8 fl oz (250 ml) warm milk
4¾ oz (135 g) blanched almonds
4¾ oz (135 g) shelled walnuts
4 oz (100 g) candied lime *or* lemon *or* chopped mixed peel
4 oz (100 g) dried figs
4 oz (100 g) sultanas
4 oz (100 g) pine kernels
2 measures rum *or* grappa
6 coriander seeds, crushed
4 oz (100 g) unsalted butter
3 egg yolks
3 oz (75 g) caster sugar
grated rind of 1 orange

Measure 7 oz (200 g) of the flour into a bowl, mix it with the yeast and add as much milk as you need to create a soft, pliable dough. Cut a cross on the top, cover with cling film and put in a warm, draught-free place to rise for about 1 hour or until doubled in size.

Meanwhile, set aside 1 tablespoon almonds and 1 tablespoon walnuts; mix the remainder together and chop them finely. Slice the candied lime or lemon and the figs very finely. Mix these with the sultanas, pine kernels, rum or grappa and coriander. Leave the mixture to macerate for 1 hour, then drain carefully.

Remove the risen dough from the bowl, add to it 7 oz (200 g) of the remaining flour and knead together, adding milk as necessary to create a soft, smooth, elastic dough. Put it back in the bowl, cover and return to a warm, draught-free place to rise again.

Work about 3½ oz (90 g) of the butter into a cream with 2 of the egg yolks and the sugar, adding the yolks one at a time and blending the ingredients together with precision.

When the dough has risen to twice its original volume, turn it out on to a clean work-surface, blend in the butter mixture using your hands, and add the remaining milk and 4 oz (100 g) of the remaining flour. Put the last 4 oz (100 g) flour into a clean bowl, add to it the grated orange rind, the chopped almonds and

'Tocco' di Nocci (page 284)

Top: Aceto Balsamico, an indefinable
passion for the men of Modena. *Bottom:*
Hot work in September when it's time
to pick the grapes for Lambrusco in
Emilia Romagna.

walnuts and the drained, macerated fruit. Add the flour and fruit mixture to the dough and knead together very energetically, banging it hard on the work-surface. When it is smooth and elastic, shape it into 2 almond shapes and place each one on a baking sheet greased with the remaining butter. Scatter with the reserved unchopped almonds and walnuts. Beat the remaining egg yolk and brush the cakes with it. Set them aside to rest for 30 minutes.

Pre-heat the oven to gas mark 4, 350°F (180°C). When the cakes have rested, place them in the oven and bake for about 1 hour or until a knife inserted into the centre comes out clean. Remove from the oven and cool on wire racks. Wrap in lightly greased foil to mature for 7–8 days before eating. Serve very thinly sliced.

SOFFIATO alla TRENTINA
Trentino Meringue Trifle

This is one of my great standbys, a very simple store-cupboard pudding which everybody loves. It is a biscuity custard with a meringue topping.

SERVES 4–6

9 oz (250 g) basic sponge cake (see page 300) or boudoir biscuits

rum

1¼ pints (750 ml) custard (see page 300)

7 oz (200 g) amaretti biscuits or macaroons, crushed

4 egg whites

5 tablespoons caster sugar

1 tablespoon alchermes or sweet vermouth

Soak the sponge or biscuits with rum and arrange them on the bottom of a pretty ovenproof dish. Cover with half the custard. Soak the amaretti biscuits or macaroons in rum and set aside.

Pre-heat the oven to gas mark 5, 375°F (190°C). Beat the egg whites until completely stiff and fold in the sugar and the alchermes or vermouth. Spoon this on top of the custard layer, cover with the remaining custard and sprinkle with the soaked amaretti biscuits. Place in the oven to cook for 20 minutes or until golden on top. Serve immediately.

TORTA di PERE
Pear Tart

When I visited my friend Vitti Gabrielli in Vattaro, near Trento, during the filming of the television series Italian Regional Cookery, *she made this delicious pear cake to a traditional local recipe. The whole region is covered in fruit trees, mainly apples, pears and cherries – quite different in appearance from the citrus-fruit-clad fields of the south.*

SERVES 4

9 oz (250 g) plain white flour, sifted, plus extra for dusting

4 oz (100 g) caster sugar

4 oz (100 g) unsalted butter, cubed, plus extra for greasing

1 egg and 1 egg yolk, beaten

2 teaspoons baking powder, sifted

1 teaspoon vanilla essence

about 4 tablespoons grappa *or* brandy

pinch salt

1 tablespoon breadcrumbs

3-4 tablespoons apricot jam

2 oz (50 g) amaretti biscuits, crumbled

about 1½ lb (750 g) ripe pears (preferably William), peeled and thinly sliced

½ teaspoon ground allspice

4 oz (100 g) sultanas

2 oz (50 g) pine kernels

2 oz (50 g) caster sugar

milk sweetened with sugar

Pre-heat the oven to gas mark 3, 325°F (160°C).

Pile all the flour on the centre of a clean work-surface, make a hole in the middle with your fist and add the sugar, butter, egg and egg yolk, baking powder, vanilla, grappa or brandy and salt. Knead everything together with your hands to make a soft dough and roll it into a ball. Remove one quarter of the dough and set it aside.

Butter an 11 inch (28 cm) shallow cake tin, dust with flour and breadcrumbs then cover with the apricot jam and crumbled amaretti. Roll out the larger piece of dough to line the base and sides of the tin. Cover it with the pears and scatter over the allspice, sultanas, pine kernels and caster sugar. Roll out the reserved dough into sausage shapes and place one round the edge of the flan. Flatten the rest to a thickness of about ¼ inch (5 mm) and lay them on top to form a lattice pattern. Put the tart in the oven and bake for about 40 minutes or until cooked through and browned on top. About 10 minutes before the end of the cooking time, remove it from the oven and brush the top very generously with sweetened milk: this will keep the cake softer. Serve cold.

CHARLOTTE alla MILANESE
Milanese Charlotte

This superb apple Charlotte is one of my most favourite puddings. Our apple trees produce a glut every single year, without fail, and I am always trying out new ways of cooking them in order to use them up. Everyone in my family loves this one.

SERVES 6–8

1¾ lb (800 g) crisp eating apples (such as Spartan or Cox)

5 oz (150 g) granulated sugar

2 teaspoons grated lemon rind

½ glass dry white wine

1½ oz (40 g) butter

1 stale French stick, thinly sliced and crusts removed

5 oz (150 g) sultanas *or* raisins, soaked in warm water for 15 minutes, drained and dried

2 tablespoons pine kernels

1 wine glass dark or white rum

Peel, core and slice the apples, put them in a saucepan with 4½ oz (120 g) of the sugar, the lemon rind, wine and enough water just to cover. Cook on a low to medium heat until the apples are starting to fall apart, transfer to a bowl and allow to cool completely.

Pre-heat the oven to gas mark 4, 350°F (180°C). Blend the butter with the remaining sugar and spread some of it generously around the sides and across the bottom of a 10 inch (25 cm) round Charlotte mould or soufflé dish (not a ring mould), reserving the remainder of the mixture. Line the bottom and sides of the mould completely with the slices of bread, reserving enough to cover the top of the pudding. Fill the centre almost to the top with layers of apples, sultanas and pine kernels. Spread the reserved bread slices with the remaining butter and sugar mixture and use to cover the top of the Charlotte. Place the pudding in the oven to bake for 1 hour.

Remove the cooked Charlotte from the oven, turn it out on to a platter, pour over the rum and set it alight. Carry it, flaming, to the table and serve.

FORTI
Almond Ginger Biscuits

The original recipe for these biscuits dates from the sixteenth century and was revised in the first half of the eighteenth century to include cocoa. There is only one pastry shop left in the Veneto where you can buy them ready-made – in Bassano at L'Antica Offelleria Toffano. The bakers use a secret original recipe which they are determined will remain secret, but here is an interpretation which makes a passable approximation. The biscuits keep very well for several months in tightly closed tins.

MAKES 40-50 BISCUITS

9 oz (250 g) molasses *or* treacle

9 oz (250 g) granulated sugar

2 oz (50 g) butter *or* margarine, softened and cubed, plus extra for greasing

2 eggs, beaten, and 1 egg white

9 oz (250 g) unblanched almonds

6 tablespoons very sweet wine (such as Sauternes or Moscato)

4 oz (100 g) unsweetened cocoa powder

1 teaspoon ground cinnamon

1 teaspoon ground cloves

½ teaspoon ground ginger

½ teaspoon finely ground black pepper

1 tablespoon warm milk

1 teaspoon salt

14 oz–1 lb (400–450 g) plain white flour, sifted

Put the molasses or treacle, granulated sugar, butter or margarine and whole eggs into a bowl. Mix together thoroughly with a balloon whisk. Pound or process 7 oz (200 g) of the almonds to a fine powder and add them to the mixture. Mix in the wine, cocoa powder and all the spices including the pepper. Mix the salt with the milk and blend this in also. Add the flour gradually until the mixture reaches a thick consistency that is not too stiff; use your hands to knead it. Cover the bowl with cling film and put it in the refrigerator to rest overnight.

Pre-heat the oven to gas mark 4, 350°F (180°C). Butter one or more baking sheets. Roll out the biscuit mixture one piece at a time into thick cylinder shapes with a diameter of 2½ inches (6 cm). Cut each cylinder into neat circles about ¾-1 inch (2–2.5 cm) thick. Push a hole about 1 inch (2.5 cm) in diameter in the centre of each one – you can do this very easily with your thumb or alternatively use a very small pastry cutter. Arrange the biscuits on the baking sheet(s) in neat rows about 1½ inches (4 cm) apart.

Pound or process the remaining almonds and blend them with the icing sugar. Beat the egg white until just foaming and combine it with the almond mixture. Brush the biscuits with the

2 tablespoons icing sugar
2–4 tablespoons sugar
   crystals

egg white mixture using a pastry brush and scatter with the sugar crystals. Bake in the oven for about 15 minutes. Remove from the baking sheet(s) with a spatula, cool on wire racks and store in tightly closed biscuit tins until required. The biscuits will be quite soft when freshly baked and will gradually harden as they cool (their name means 'hard'). As they cool, the flavour of the molasses or treacle intensifies.

NEAPOLITAN CAKE-MAKING

Naples has a great tradition of cake-making. Most of the more recent recipes came via France, because the Bourbon kings and queens would have their cooks – locally called *monsu*, meaning *monsieur* – sent from Paris to cook at court. Gradually, desserts which were created at the Court of Naples found their way into the general Neapolitan tradition.

However, there are a few cakes that are typically Neapolitan, in the sense that they were created for Neapolitans by Neapolitans. Two of the most famous, Sfogliatelle and Zeppole, were created by a man named Pintauro and there is a lovely story behind these cakes. Pintauro was a successful but unhappy restaurateur: deep down, he felt himself to be a pastry chef. Eventually he persuaded his rather nagging wife, Carmela, to let him convert the restaurant into a pastry shop, with windows opening out on to the street, selling cakes to the passers-by. This was the first commercial pastry shop in Naples – until this time, pastries had only been made at home and in

monasteries and convents. Pintauro's first creation was the Sfogliatelle: a very light, crisp, fan-shaped pastry, filled with ricotta blended with lemon rind, candied orange peel, sugar and eggs. Pintauro was tremendously successful. Thereafter people would remark on another's good fortune by saying, 'You're just like Pintauro.'

But eventually the shop went bust. Carmela was furious: the restaurant and the shop were gone, they were broke. So Pintauro shut himself away in the kitchen to think up another plan. Finally, he came up with Zeppole – circular buns of baked or fried choux pastry, filled with a fine egg custard and topped with a liqueur-soaked cherry. News of these new cakes spread like wildfire, and the King himself went to the re-opened shop to eat one. So impressed was he that he rewarded Pintauro's efforts with a medal in the shape of a cross. Looking across at his nagging wife, Pintauro said, 'Your Majesty, this is the lightest cross I have ever had to bear!'

TORTELLI di MARMELLATA
Breakfast biscuits

In Emilia Romagna these delicious sweet versions of stuffed pasta are traditionally made and eaten at carnival time. You can buy them ready-made during the weeks before Lent in good pastry shops throughout the region, where people on their way to work stop for breakfast, dunking tortelli in huge bowls of foamy, milky coffee.

MAKES ABOUT 20 PUFFS

1 lb 2 oz (475 g) plain white flour, sifted, plus extra for dusting

grated rind of 1 lemon

9 oz (250 g) granulated sugar

1 teaspoon vanilla essence

2 teaspoons baking powder, sifted

3 large eggs

5 oz (150 g) butter, softened and cubed, plus extra for greasing

3 tablespoons liqueur such as Strega or Galliano (optional)

about 6 tablespoons white wine *or* cold water

1 lb (450 g) thick cherry *or* apricot *or* peach jam

6 tablespoons icing sugar for dusting

Pre-heat the oven to gas mark 5, 375°F (190°C).

Put the flour on to a board or clean work-surface. Make a hole in the centre with your fist and put in the lemon rind, sugar, vanilla and baking powder. Mix all these ingredients together with your hands. Shape back into a hill shape, make another hole in the centre with your fist and break the eggs into the hole. Add the butter and the liqueur (if using). Knead all this together thoroughly with your hands. Alternatively, prepare the dough in a food processor. If the mixture appears too dry and stiff, add a little wine or water.

Roll out the dough on a floured board or work-surface to a thickness of ¼ inch (5 mm). Arrange teaspoons of jam on half the rolled-out dough at a distance of 2 inches (5 cm) from each other. Fold the rolled-out dough without jam on it over the dough with the jam on it and press down around each covered mound of jam with your fingertips. Do this very carefully, otherwise the jam will ooze out during cooking. Cut round each mound of jam with an upturned glass or pastry cutter. Butter 2 baking sheets and dust with flour. Arrange the jam puffs on the baking sheets in neat rows about 1½ inches (4 cm) apart. Bake in the oven for 20 minutes or until golden-brown. Allow to cool and dust with icing sugar before serving.

TORTA di PAPARELE alla VERONESE
Veronese Pasta Ribbon Cake

This delicious cake from Verona is very similar to the Greek and Turkish cake called katayif, *an obvious result of Venetian travels around the Mediterranean, when all kinds of foreign recipes and ingredients poured into the port of Venice, and from there were introduced into the cuisine of the region and then the entire country. There are many variations of pasta cake cooked all over Italy, but this is by far the nicest in my opinion.*

MAKES 1 × 9 inch (23 cm) CAKE

12 oz (350 g) plain white flour, sifted

2 oz (50 g) butter, melted, plus extra for greasing

3 large eggs

pinch salt

7 oz (200 g) almonds, finely chopped

7 oz (200 g) caster sugar

grated rind of 1 lemon and 2 tablespoons lemon juice

6 tablespoons liqueur *or* apple juice

Measure out 11 oz (300 g) of the flour and put it on a board or clean work-surface. Plunge your fist into the centre to make a hole. Pour the melted butter into the hole, then break the eggs into it and add a pinch of salt. Knead all this together to make a soft dough. Roll it out as thinly as possible and set aside.

Pre-heat the oven to gas mark 4, 350°F (180°C). Butter a 9 inch (23 cm) cake tin thoroughly and dust it with the remaining flour. In a bowl mix the almonds, sugar and lemon rind together thoroughly.

Cut the dough into fine, even-sized ribbons with a sharp knife. Arrange a layer of these in the bottom of the cake tin, scatter with the almond mixture, sprinkle with the liqueur or apple juice and cover with another layer of pasta ribbons. Continue in this way until you have used up all the ingredients, ending with a layer of pasta ribbons. Cover the top of the cake carefully with a sheet of buttered baking parchment and bake in the oven for 55 minutes. Remove from the oven and sprinkle with the lemon juice. To aid removal from the tin, run a knife round the edge of the cake, loosen it and ease it out carefully. Place it on a platter and serve warm or cold. It will be moist and quite chewy.

MARITOZZI con la PANNA
Roman Buns Stuffed with Whipped Cream

I can remember my mother buying me one of these whenever we went out shopping together. With hindsight I don't know if I would have done the same for my own children because the cream has an uncanny way of splurging all over your face and down your front – most inelegant in smart Roman boutiques! However, it remains one of my all-time favourite treats. Traditionally, these buns were served to guests during Lent, with a glass of white wine but without the cream. To make them at home you need to allow a whole day.

MAKES 6–8 BUNS

2 oz (50 g) bread dough, fully risen (see page 294)
11 oz (300 g) plain white flour, sifted
pinch salt
6 tablespoons olive oil
2 eggs
1 tablespoon caster sugar
about 3 tablespoons hot water
4 oz (100 g) sultanas, soaked in warm water for 15 minutes, drained and dried
2 oz (50 g) pine kernels
2 oz (50 g) mixed candied peel, finely chopped
14 oz (400 g) whipped cream, sweetened with 5 tablespoons caster sugar

Put the bread dough on a clean work-surface. Using your hands, blend 4 oz (100 g) of the flour with the dough. Add the salt, 1 tablespoon of the oil and 1 of the eggs. Knead all this together, then place it in a bowl, cover it with a thick napkin and put it in a warm place to rise for 4 hours.

When the dough has risen, take it out of the bowl and put it back on the work-surface. Knead in the remaining flour, 4 more tablespoons of the oil, the sugar, and the remaining egg. Knead together thoroughly, adding enough warm water to make a fairly soft and workable but not sticky dough. Knead in the sultanas, pine kernels and candied peel. Work this dough for about 20 minutes, then shape it into long ovals. Oil one or more baking sheets with the remaining 1 tablespoon oil, lay the buns on the sheet(s) and leave in a warm place to rise for another 6 hours.

Pre-heat the oven to gas mark 4, 350°F (180°C), and bake the risen buns for 15 minutes. Remove from the oven and cool on a wire rack. Split the buns open and fill to bursting with the sweetened whipped cream. Arrange on a platter and serve.

CASSATA ABRUZZESE
Abruzzi Pudding

This delicious Abruzzese dessert calls for two ingredients which could not be more local: torrone *(nougat) and Centerbe liqueur. Naturally, you can substitute ready-made nougat and any other liqueur of your choice provided that it is aromatic and powerful, such as Benedictine or Chartreuse. The dessert consists of layers of liqueur-soaked sponge with differently flavoured whipped cream in between each layer. Needless to say, it's very rich!*

SERVES 12

1½ lb (750 g) whipped cream, divided into 3 equal portions

4 egg yolks

7 oz (200 g) plus 4 tablespoons icing sugar, sifted

4 oz (100 g) nougat, finely chopped

2 oz (50 g) unsweetened cocoa powder

2 oz (50 g) plain cooking chocolate, flaked

2 oz (50 g) almonds, chopped

2 oz (50 g) unsalted pistachios *or* walnuts, chopped

about 14 oz (400 g) basic sponge cake (see page 300), round or oblong, cut horizontally into 4 pieces

Centerbe *or* other liqueur to taste

12 glacé cherries, halved

Make sure that the cream is whipped very stiffly and keep each of the 3 portions chilled in a separate bowl until required. Beat the egg yolks with the icing sugar until pale yellow, light and foamy, then fold one third of this mixture into each bowl of whipped cream. Fold the nougat into the first bowl of cream and egg mixture, the cocoa powder and chocolate into the second bowl, and the nuts into the third. Set aside 1–2 tablespoons of each flavoured cream to coat the finished pudding.

Arrange the first of the 4 pieces of cake on a platter and sprinkle liberally with the Centerbe or other liqueur. Cover with the nougat cream. Soak the second piece of cake, lay it on top of the nougat cream and cover with the chocolate cream. Soak the third piece of cake, lay it on top of the chocolate cream and cover with the almond and pistachio cream. Soak the last piece of cake and lay it on the top of the final layer of cream. Mix the reserved cream together and spread this over the top and sides of the cassata. Place it in the fridge and leave to chill for several hours or overnight.

Just before serving, decorate the cassata with the glacé cherries and dust with the 4 tablespoons icing sugar. Covered with aluminium foil or cling film, this dessert keeps perfectly in the fridge for up to 3 days.

TORRONE al CIOCCOLATO
Abruzzese Chocolate Nougat

This nougat is as typical of the city of L'Aquila as the fountain with the ninety-nine spouts, each one representing one of the ninety-nine castles which used to stand on these hills, and the glorious Basilica di Collemaggio, which has the only holy door outside the Vatican. The original recipe is a well-kept secret, still made by one or two small local factories and sold commercially all over the world. It has provided a useful source of calories for expeditions to the North and South Poles, and to areas around the Equator, because it has the miraculous property of not changing texture, no matter what the ambient temperature might be. It is always soft and chewy and delicious. Here is a recipe for a humble home-made version which you may like to try for a Christmas treat. It keeps for up to a year.

MAKES ENOUGH FOR
ABOUT 8

**14 oz (400 g) granulated
sugar**
3 fl oz (85 ml) cold water
**10 oz (275 g) plain cooking
chocolate, flaked**
11 oz (300 g) honey
3 egg whites
**1½ lb (750 g) shelled
hazelnuts, toasted and
skin rubbed off**
rice paper

Put 1½ oz (40 g) of the sugar into a saucepan with half the water, place on a medium heat and reduce to a smooth syrup, stirring continuously. Stir in the chocolate until it is completely melted. Put the honey in another saucepan over a medium heat and stir continuously until one drop placed in a glass of cold water crystallises instantly: the honey is now ready to use. Keep the honey and the chocolate mixtures warm.

Put the egg whites in a bowl placed over a pan of very hot but not boiling water and whisk until they form soft peaks. Melt the remaining sugar in another saucepan with the rest of the water until it has become syrup, transfer it to a large bowl and stir in the honey. Fold in the beaten egg whites, then the chocolate mixture and finally the hazelnuts. Lay rice paper on a baking sheet and spread the nougat mixture over it to a thickness of ¾ inch (2 cm). Cover it completely with rice paper and leave it to set until just solid. Cut it into shapes (traditionally oblongs) with a sharp knife and store in a securely closed jar or tin until required.

CICERCHIATA
Umbrian Carnival Cake

This very sticky, honey-smothered cake, which consists of little fried balls of dough stuck together, is made in Abruzzi and Molise to such an extent that many cooks of those regions claim that it actually belongs to them! This is, however, untrue, but then good ideas always travel far and wide – or at least they do when they are about food.

SERVES ABOUT 6

3 large eggs
2 tablespoons olive oil
2 tablespoons liqueur
grated rind of ½ lemon
about 11 oz (300 g) plain
    white flour, sifted
oil for deep-frying
1 lb (450 g) honey
4 oz (100 g) blanched
    almonds, cut into strips
3 oz (75 g) glacé cherries,
    chopped
coloured sugar crystals and
    vermicelli or other tiny
    cake sweets to decorate

Beat the eggs in a bowl and add the olive oil, liqueur and lemon rind. Blend in as much flour as necessary to make a soft but not sticky dough. Knead it with your hands, then divide it up and roll it out into pencil-sized sticks. Cut the sticks into ¼ inch (5 mm) pieces and roll these on a board under the palm of your hand to make them into pellets.

Heat the oil for deep-frying until a piece of bread dropped into it sizzles instantly. Fry all the dough pellets in the oil until crisp and brown, then remove and drain on kitchen paper until required.

Melt the honey in a large saucepan until dark-coloured and completely liquid. Test whether it is ready by putting one drop into a glass of cold water: if it hardens, it is ready to use. Put the fried dough pellets and the almonds and glacé cherries into the honey and stir thoroughly with a large spoon. Turn this mixture out on to a marble work-surface or large china platter and shape it into a ring with your hands – you will get very sticky! Scatter with sugar crystals and vermicelli or tiny cake sweets, transfer to another clean platter and serve.

ZUCCOTTO
Sponge Cake, Chocolate and Cream Mould

This is one of those classics which looks incredibly difficult to make but, though time-consuming, is actually very easy and absolutely scrumptious. It is a mould of sponge cake filled with chocolate and cream. During my childhood in Italy we always had this at home for birthdays, holy days and anniversaries. The fiddly decorating bit with the paper cut-out can be ignored, although it is traditional.

SERVES 6–8

3 oz (75 g) blanched almonds

3 oz (75 g) shelled hazelnuts

1 × 10 inch (25 cm) basic sponge cake (see page 300), cut in half horizontally

6 tablespoons brandy

4 tablespoons sweet liqueur

1¾ pints (1 litre) whipping cream

2 tablespoons chocolate drops or chips

2 tablespoons chopped mixed candied peel *or* glacé fruit

4 oz (100 g) plain cooking chocolate, melted

5 oz (150 g) icing sugar, sifted

2 tablespoons unsweetened cocoa powder

Chop the almonds coarsely. Toast the hazelnuts until dark brown under a grill, then rub off the skins. Chop the hazelnuts also. Cut the top crust and the sides off the cake and reserve for use in another dish; slice the cake itself in half horizontally. Line with aluminium foil a bowl large enough to take both the cake and the cream when whipped. Press the cake into the bowl to line the bottom and sides, breaking it into pieces as necessary and using the brandy and liqueur to soak it and make it stick. Set aside.

In another bowl whip the cream until stiff, fold in the almonds, hazelnuts, chocolate drops or chips and candied peel or glacé fruit. Divide the cream in half and stir the melted chocolate into one half. Sweeten each portion of cream with 2 oz (50 g) icing sugar, folding it in carefully. Line the bottom and sides of the cake-lined bowl with the white cream, then fill in the hollow with the chocolate cream. Smooth the surface flat. Place the bowl in the refrigerator for a minimum of 2 hours.

Meanwhile, draw a circle slightly larger than the bowl on a sheet of stiff paper. Draw a line across the diameter to create 2 half-circles. Draw another line to create quarters and another to create eighths. Number the 8 wedges 1 to 8 and cut out wedge numbers 2, 4, 6 and 8.

Shortly before serving turn the dessert out on to a platter. Remove the foil and, using a sieve, dust the Zuccotto with the remaining icing sugar. Lay the cut-out circle of paper on the top. Dust the 4 wedges that are not covered by paper with the cocoa powder. Remove the paper circle carefully. You now have the traditional design on the pudding – it is meant to look like a small pumpkin, which is what Zuccotto actually means. Chill until required.

TORTA di MELE
Apple Cake

From the glorious city of Ferrara comes this wonderfully simple and delicious apple cake, an absolute must for a tea-time treat. The apple remains juicy and slightly chewy in contrast to the sponginess of the cake.

SERVES 6

2 large eggs

5 oz (150 g) caster sugar

6½ oz (185 g) plain white flour, sifted

4 fl oz (120 ml) milk

grated rind of ½ lemon

1 heaped teaspoon baking powder, sifted

2 oz (50 g) butter, cut into small pieces, plus extra for greasing

3 tablespoons stale breadcrumbs

2 lb (1 kg) apples (any sort except Bramley), peeled and thinly sliced

2 tablespoons granulated *or* light brown sugar

Pre-heat the oven to gas mark 4, 350°F (180°C).

Beat the eggs until light and fluffy, adding the sugar gradually, then fold in the flour, milk, lemon rind and baking powder. The mixture should be quite runny. Butter a 10 inch (25 cm) cake tin thoroughly, then dust with the breadcrumbs. Turn the tin upside down to remove all the loose breadcrumbs and discard them. Pour the cake mixture into the tin, arrange the apples on the top, dot with 2 oz (50 g) butter, sprinkle with the granulated or light brown sugar and bake in the oven for 55 minutes. Remove from the oven and cool completely before removing from the tin and serving.

TORTELLI di CARNEVALE alla MILANESE
Milanese Carnival Cakes

Traditionally these fluffy fried cakes would be eaten during carnival time and also on 19 March, Father's Day or the Feast of the Carpenters, commemorating the most famous carpenter and one of the most well known of all parents, St Joseph. In the Bible St Joseph is described as being qualified as a carpenter and cook of fried food; in fact, carpenters of his era apparently often 'moonlighted' in this way. It would appear that in Lombardy the master carpenters would hand out dishes of these fritters to their apprentices on 19 March, and they are still eaten on that day.

MAKES ABOUT 2 DOZEN CAKES

10 fl oz (300 ml) milk
10 fl oz (300 ml) cold water
pinch salt
½ teaspoon bicarbonate of soda
3 oz (75 g) granulated sugar
1 teaspoon vanilla essence
4½ oz (120 g) unsalted butter
½ teaspoon grated lemon rind
½ cinnamon stick
10 oz (275 g) plain white flour, sifted
8 eggs
2 egg yolks
1 tablespoon dark rum
2½ pints (1.5 litres) sunflower *or* other oil for deep-frying
4 oz (100 g) icing sugar, sifted

Put the milk and water in a saucepan with the salt, bicarbonate of soda, sugar, vanilla, butter, lemon rind and cinnamon. Set over a medium heat and bring to the boil, remove from the heat, discard the lemon rind and cinnamon and briskly stir in the flour. Return to the heat and continue to stir vigorously for 10 minutes or until the mixtures comes away from the sides of the pan easily. Remove from the heat and cool slightly. While the mixture is still tepid, begin to beat in the eggs and egg yolks, one at a time, always making sure that each one is completely absorbed before adding the next. Stir in the rum and set aside to rest for about 3 hours.

Heat the oil in a deep-fryer until a piece of bread dropped into it sizzles instantly. Drop spoonfuls of the mixture into the hot oil, using one spoon to scoop up the mixture and a second to push it off into the oil. If you don't crowd the pan, the cakes will turn themselves over as soon as they are done on one side; otherwise you will have to turn them. When they are well puffed and golden, lift them out of the oil with a slotted spoon and drain on kitchen paper. Dust with icing sugar and serve at once, piping hot.

BUNET PIEMONTESE
Piedmontese Bunet

Of all the puddings Giorgio Rocca serves at his restaurant, Da Felicin, in Monforte d'Alba, the most traditionally regional is the smooth, dark, delicious Bunet. The flavour and texture of the amaretti biscuits combined with the egg custard make it different from any other chocolate pudding I have ever tasted and, since I first ate it with Giorgio, Bunet has become a great favourite in my home.

SERVES 8

1¾ pints (1 litre) milk

9 oz (250 g) amaretti or ratafia biscuits or slightly stale macaroons

1 tablespoon drinking chocolate powder

5 oz (150 g) caster sugar

6 large eggs, beaten

1–2 teaspoons instant coffee powder

6 tablespoons granulated sugar

2 tablespoons cold water

Put the milk and the amaretti or ratafia biscuits or macaroons in a saucepan. Bring to the boil, remove from the heat and break up the biscuits completely with a wooden spoon. Stir in the chocolate powder. In a bowl beat the caster sugar and eggs together until pale and fluffy, then slowly fold them into the milk mixture. Stir carefully to amalgamate perfectly, adding the coffee powder.

Pre-heat the oven to gas mark 3, 325°F (160°C).

Put the granulated sugar and water into a small saucepan and heat until the sugar has caramelised. Coat the bottom of 4–6 small moulds with the caramel. Divide the milk mixture evenly between the moulds and place them all in a roasting tin. Pour enough water around the moulds to come half-way up their sides and bake in the oven for about 30 minutes or until a knife inserted into the centre of a mould comes out dry and clean. (The cooking time will vary slightly according to the shape and size of the moulds.) Remove from the oven, allow to cool and serve cold, preferably chilled.

PANNA COTTA
Boiled Cream Pudding

Among the selection of Piedmontese desserts that Giorgio Rocca serves on a big plate to end the meal, Panna cotta is one of the most memorable. This version of a basic custard is very thick and creamy, with a rich, smooth flavour and a very silky, slippery texture. It should be quite pale yellow in colour and must always be slightly chilled when served. It's very easy to make and is absolutely wonderful to eat. I like to serve it with a dish of soft fruits like raspberries, loganberries or stewed gooseberries to give a contrast of flavours.

SERVES 6–8

1¾ pints (1 litre) single or
    double cream
9 oz (250 g) caster sugar
1 teaspoon vanilla essence
6 tablespoons milk
1 sachet gelatine powder
6 tablespoons granulated
    sugar
2 tablespoons cold water

Put the cream, caster sugar and vanilla into a saucepan and set it over a low heat. Heat until just below boiling point, stirring to melt the sugar completely. Bring the milk to the boil in a separate pan, dissolve the gelatine in it completely and stir it into the very hot cream. Bring the mixture to the boil, stirring continuously. As soon as it boils, remove it from the heat.

Put the granulated sugar and water into another saucepan and place over a medium heat. Allow this mixture to boil until caramelised, then quickly coat the bottom and sides of 6–8 small moulds with it. Divide the cream mixture evenly between the moulds, cool and then chill in the refrigerator for at least 1 full day. Remove from the refrigerator and allow to return almost to room temperature before serving.

VARIATION
Add a fruit liqueur of your choice to the cream mixture.

Too good to eat! Sardinian cakes are real
works of art.

Top: Is there anything more Italian than real ice cream? *Bottom:* Siena has been famous for its sweetmeat industry for centuries.

LE CASTAGNOLE di ANTONIETTA

Antonietta's Castagnole

These crisp, sweet fritters are served in the Delle Fratte household in Zagarolo in the province of Rome either as a simple dessert or as a snack. In either case they are delicious and very easy to make. Antonietta herself is an expert at making them all come out evenly. Here is her own recipe.

MAKES ABOUT 12

2 eggs
6 tablespoons milk
6 tablespoons granulated sugar
2 teaspoons baking powder, sifted
1 teaspoon vanilla essence
6 tablespoons cooking oil
grated rind of ½ lemon
about 6 tablespoons plain flour, sifted
1¼ pints (750 ml) oil for deep-frying
4 tablespoons icing sugar, sifted

Beat together the eggs, milk, granulated sugar, baking powder, vanilla, 6 tablespoons cooking oil and lemon rind until smooth and creamy. Add as much flour as is necessary to make a soft but not sticky dough. Heat the oil for deep-frying until a small piece of bread dropped into it sizzles immediately. Using a spoon dipped in cold water, scoop up spoonfuls of the mixture and drop them into the hot oil. Fry until puffed and golden, turning the pan to make the fritters come out well rounded. Lift them out of the oil with a slotted spoon and drain on kitchen paper. Dust with icing sugar and serve warm or cold.

ZABAGLIONE
Whipped Marsala Custard

The most important thing to remember about this light, very alcoholic and fluffy Piedmontese egg custard is that you must never abandon it while it cooks! If you want to serve it hot, you'll have to leave the table and stay in the kitchen with it for a solid 25 minutes until it is ready. If your guests are boring you to death, this may not be such a bad thing; however, if they are people whose company you enjoy, you may be better off serving it chilled! If you do decide to serve the Zabaglione chilled, please be sure that it is properly cooked before you chill it, otherwise it might separate and the result will be disastrous. Serve with a selection of light biscuits, such as langues de chat.

SERVES 4

4 egg yolks
4 tablespoons sugar
4 tablespoons cold water
4 tablespoons Marsala wine

Put all the ingredients into the top half of a double boiler over hot but not boiling water, on a low to medium heat. Using a balloon whisk, beat energetically and evenly, always in the same direction, for about 18–20 minutes or until the mixture achieves a smooth, foamy consistency. It should be thick and creamy but very light, like semi-melted ice-cream. If you overcook it, it will become like scrambled eggs; if you undercook it, the liquid will separate from the egg yolk. Take great care and remember to remove it from the heat every now and again while it cooks. Do not stop whisking.

When the Zabaglione is ready, pour it into stemmed glasses and serve, or cool and chill in the refrigerator until required.

Variation: Sapajean (Lombard Zabaglione)

This variation of the Piedmontese Zabaglione is from Lombardy, where they use white or red wine instead of Marsala, and a final touch of lemon juice to reduce the sweetness of the dessert. A much heavier result is achieved with red wine, whereas white wine produces a very lightly flavoured and coloured pudding.

SERVES 4

4 large eggs
4 tablespoons caster sugar
4 tablespoons dry white *or* red wine
juice of 1 small lemon, strained

Put a large saucepan of water to heat on the stove and keep it just below boiling point; you will cook the dessert over the hot water. Break the eggs into a very clean copper or stainless-steel, heavy-bottomed, 1¼ pint (750 ml) saucepan and cover with the sugar. Away from the heat, beat vigorously with a balloon whisk or electric hand-held beater for 15–20 minutes or until the eggs are pale and fluffy and have doubled in volume. Beat in the wine, 1 teaspoon at a time, then set this saucepan over the saucepan of almost-boiling water on the stove. Beat continuously with a balloon whisk for 15–20 minutes as you would for a normal Zabaglione. As soon as the texture is right (it should be like a light mousse and just beginning to stick to the bottom of the pan), remove it from the heat and whisk in the lemon juice. Keep whisking and return to the heat to thicken again and heat through: this will take 1–3 minutes. Then remove it from the heat and pour into individual bowls or long-stemmed glasses to serve. You can eat this dessert either hot or chilled.

NOTE
An interesting way of serving Sapajean is as the filling in a hollowed-out panettone (a large Milanese Christmas cake available from all good delicatessens from November onwards). To fill an average-size panettone, you will need

triple the quantity given above. Cut the top off the panettone and scoop out most of the centre. Pour the piping-hot Sapajean into the resulting hollow and replace the lid. Serve at once for a memorable end to any meal.

CAFFÈ VALDOSTANO
Val d'Aosta Coffee

Cesare Pinuccia and François Gaetani gave me this 'friendship cup' to drink on my last visit to their home in Bianaz in Val d'Aosta. The Grolla (the wooden bowl from which you drink the coffee) has several spouts. It is apparently very important not to change direction when passing round the Grolla, and the coffee must be drunk to the very last drop. (I think it's just an excuse for getting extremely drunk!)

SERVES 4

4 small cups coffee
2 small cups grappa
½ cup Cointreau *or* other liqueur
1 strip orange rind
1 strip lemon rind
sugar to taste

Pour the boiling-hot coffee into the Grolla, then add all the other ingredients and stir. Light the grappa with a match: this will cause a transparent blue flame to shoot up. Put the lid on the Grolla immediately and pass it round the table. Each person drinks from the Grolla as a sign of friendship.

SAUCES

IL PESTO
Fresh Basil Sauce

If you could choose one thing which says everything there is to say about Ligurian cooking, this sauce would have to be it! You can use it on any pasta shape you like, stir it into soups, pour it over boiled potatoes or use it as a dip with breadsticks. It is one of my very favourite sauces, a real Italian original, though copied by the French who have renamed it Pistou *– but they've always had problems with languages!*

There are many variations on the basic sauce: some people use walnuts, others like using pine kernels; I have seen some cooks put creamy milk junket into the sauce and others who chop smoked bacon very finely and then stir that in. Like all the best recipes, it has been enjoyed enough for cooks to want to improve upon it over the decades. What is essential in any version is large amounts of fresh basil; and by this I mean at least 4 handfuls for the quantities given below, more if possible. The Genoese will tell you that the most vital point about this sauce is the instruments used to make it – you should have a marble mortar with a wooden pestle. Failing this, you will have to use a food processor.

MAKES ENOUGH TO DRESS
1¼ lb (500 g) PASTA

36 leaves fresh basil,
  washed but not bruised,
  dried carefully
large pinch rock salt
2 cloves garlic, peeled and
  cut in half
1 handful pine kernels
2 tablespoons grated
  Parmesan cheese
about ½ wine glass best-
  quality olive oil
salt and pepper

If you use a pestle and mortar, remember to press the basil leaves against the sides: do not bang downwards as usual. Put the basil, salt and garlic into the mortar or food processor and reduce to a smooth green purée. Add the pine kernels and cheese and blend these in also, then begin to add the oil a little at a time, until you have reached a smooth, creamy texture. Season with salt and pepper and use as required.

BATTUTO
Flavoured Pork Fat

Roman cuisine has flavoured pork fat as the basis of its many soups and stews. The habit has now spread round the country.

You need to begin with what the Italians call lard and what in the UK is called raw dripping. Your butcher should be able to supply you with some. If you cannot get any you can use the fat cut off ham instead.

5 tablespoons raw dripping
1 large onion, peeled and chopped
1 handful parsley, chopped
3 sticks celery, finely chopped

Chop all the ingredients together until you have a sort of paste. Use at the beginning of a recipe instead of oil or butter when these are required for frying other ingredients.

SALSA al CREN
Horseradish Sauce

This piquant sauce made from horseradish root is very popular in the north, both in Alto Adige and in Friuli Venezia Giulia. The Alto Adige version is very similar to the British sauce we all know, so I have opted for the recipe from Friuli Venezia Giulia, even though it was originally an Austrian recipe.

SERVES 4
4 oz (100 g) fresh horseradish, scrubbed
2 oz (50 g) butter
2 oz (50 g) stale bread, grated
2 teaspoons sugar
2 tablespoons meat stock (see page 293)
½ teaspoon English mustard (optional)
salt and white pepper

Grate the horseradish. This will make your eyes water, so when you've done it, allow yourself time to recover!

Melt the butter in a saucepan, then stir in the bread and sizzle for a few minutes until lightly browned.

Then add the horseradish and the sugar, mix together, pour in the stock and add the mustard, if using. Bring to the boil, season to taste and serve as required.

SAUSSE di AVIJE
Honey Bee Sauce

This delicately piquant no-cook sauce marries perfectly with any boiled meat. Try it with boiled brisket or chicken with steamed potatoes, a green vegetable and some salad for a delicious supper. In Piedmont, where this sauce comes from, boiled meats are very popular.

SERVES ABOUT 4

6 walnuts, shelled

2 tablespoons meat stock
  (see page 293)

1 heaped tablespoon
  French mustard

1 wine glass runny honey

Blanch the walnuts and rub off their thin inner skins. Pound them to a powder by hand with a pestle and mortar or in a food processor. Stir the stock into the walnut powder, then mix in the mustard and honey. Blend all the ingredients very well and serve as required.

AGLIATA PICCANTE
Ligurian Garlic Sauce

This sauce is the one for serving with plain boiled fish of any variety from trout to prawns. It was copied from a French equivalent from the port of Marseilles and reached the shores of Italy via the sailors, no doubt about that.

If you wish to increase the quantity, allow 1 clove of garlic per person.

SERVES 4

4 large cloves garlic, peeled

8-10 tablespoons olive oil

1 slice white bread, crusts
  removed

2 tablespoons sharp red or
  white wine vinegar

salt and pepper

Crush the garlic to a purée using a pestle and mortar or food processor. Stir in the oil, a little at a time, depending upon how much sauce you require. Soak the bread in the vinegar until sopping wet, then stir this into the sauce too. It should have the consistency of thin mayonnaise. Season with salt and lots of pepper and use as required.

SALSA di TARTUFI
Umbrian Black Truffle Sauce

If you are lucky enough to have a black truffle at your disposal, you could do a lot worse than turn it into this fantastic sauce. In Umbria it is spread on small slices of toasted bread and eaten hot as an antipasto or served with freshly poached trout with a squeeze of lemon.

MAKES ENOUGH FOR 2
SMALL TROUT OR ABOUT 10
THIN SLICES TOASTED
FRENCH BREAD

1 peach-sized black truffle, cleaned
3 tablespoons olive oil
pinch salt
1 clove garlic, peeled and very finely chopped
1 anchovy preserved in salt, cleaned and boned, *or* 2 canned anchovy fillets, drained

Cut the truffle into fine strips and reduce it to a purée in a food processor or by hand with a pestle and mortar. Pour the oil into a small saucepan and heat it slightly, then add the truffle and stir without letting the mixture bubble or boil. Stir in the salt and the garlic. Just before serving the sauce, mix in the anchovy. The sauce should be quite runny with occasional lumps of truffle. Blend the ingredients evenly and use the sauce as required.

SALSA GHIOTTA
Greedy Guts Sauce

This is an Umbrian sauce which is served with all types of roast game, but especially with pigeon.

MAKES ENOUGH FOR 2
AVERAGE-SIZED ROAST
PHEASANTS

8 fl oz (250 ml) red wine
8 fl oz (250 ml) white wine
2 oz (50 g) prosciutto crudo *or* unsmoked back bacon, finely chopped

Put all the ingredients into a saucepan, stir thoroughly and bring to a low boil. Simmer until reduced to about 8 fl oz (250 ml). Transfer to a sauce boat and use as required.

rind of ½ lemon, finely
   chopped
3 fresh sage leaves
1 × 1½ inch (4 cm) sprig
   fresh rosemary
3 cloves garlic, peeled and
   crushed
6 juniper berries
salt and pepper
1 wine glass red wine
   vinegar
½ wine glass olive oil
2 chicken livers, trimmed,
   washed, dried and finely
   chopped

SALMORIGLIO
Sicilian Oil and Lemon Sauce

This sauce is used in Sicily and all over the south of Italy for brushing over food that is cooking on a grill. It imparts a delicious lemony flavour and prevents the food from drying out. It can be used for fish or meat, and is very simple to make. It can also be poured all over the cooked food just before you take it to the table.

SERVES ABOUT 6
GENEROUSLY

8 fl oz (250 ml) best-quality
   olive oil
juice of 2 lemons
1 teaspoon dried oregano
2 cloves garlic, peeled and
   chopped
1 tablespoon chopped
   parsley

Whisk the oil until it begins to thicken. Whisk in the lemon juice, then the oregano and the garlic and finally the parsley: the sauce should be thick and creamy. Keep it warm on the top half of a double boiler on a very low heat and use as required.

VARIATION

Beat together 8 fl oz (250 ml) olive oil with the juice of 2 lemons, 1 heaped teaspoon dried oregano, 2 peeled and chopped cloves of garlic and salt and pepper to taste.

RAGÙ alla BOLOGNESE
Bolognese Sauce

This is the original and best version of this much-loved sauce. It requires a great many ingredients and a lot of time, but it is worth all the effort. Use it to fill cannelloni, to dress plain boiled pasta or to layer in Lasagne. It freezes very well for up to 6 weeks.

SERVES 4

6 tablespoons olive *or* vegetable oil

1 onion, peeled and finely chopped

1 carrot, scraped and finely chopped

2 sticks celery, finely chopped

1 clove garlic, peeled and finely chopped (optional)

2 oz (50 g) fat prosciutto crudo *or* fat streaky bacon, finely chopped

1 oz (25 g) dried porcini mushrooms, soaked in warm water for 15 minutes, then drained (optional)

1 lb (450 g) lean minced beef

1 large glass red wine

1 tablespoon tomato purée diluted with ½ wine glass warm water

salt and pepper

Heat the oil and fry the onion, carrot, celery and garlic together until the onion is soft and transparent. Add the prosciutto or bacon, stir and simmer for about 4 minutes. Then add the drained mushrooms (if using) and the beef. Brown the beef carefully, without letting it go crisp, then pour in the wine and raise the heat to evaporate the alchohol. Pour in the diluted tomato purée and stir carefully. Season to taste and cover. Simmer very very slowly for about 4 hours, adding water or stock if necessary and stirring frequently. The sauce is best left overnight to allow the flavours to develop and reheated when required.

SUGO FINTO
Fake Meat Sauce

A legacy of Ancient Roman cuisine, when only the very rich could afford meat, this recipe uses the fat from ham to give the sauce some richness.

MAKES ENOUGH FOR
1¼ lb (500 g) PASTA
½ onion, finely chopped
1 carrot, finely chopped
1 stick celery, finely
  chopped
1 handful parsley, finely
  chopped
2 oz (50 g) fat from ham,
  finely chopped
3 tablespoons tomato purée
  diluted with 1 glass of
  meat stock (see page 293)
salt and pepper

Fry the chopped vegetables and parsley with the ham fat until the onion is transparent and soft. Add the diluted tomato purée, season and stir. Simmer for about 30 minutes, or until the fat begins to separate from the sauce. Use hot as required.

SALSA PEVERADA
Venetian Sauce for Roast Game

SERVES 4
3 anchovy fillets, boned
  and finely chopped
4 oz (100 g) chicken livers,
  trimmed, washed and
  finely chopped
2 rashers unsmoked back
  bacon, finely chopped
grated rind of 1 lemon
1 clove garlic, peeled
½ wine glass olive oil
1 tablespoon white wine
  vinegar
salt and pepper

Simmer all the ingredients except the vinegar, salt and pepper on a gentle heat until soft and cooked through. Stir frequently to achieve as smooth a texture as possible. Sprinkle with the vinegar, season and stir. Serve hot with roast game or chicken.

'TOCCO' di NOCCI
Ligurian Walnut Sauce

Another lovely Ligurian sauce, made with walnuts and olive oil and cream cheese. Normally used to dress the local version of stuffed pasta, it is also very good as a dip or with freshly made tagliatelle.

MAKES ENOUGH FOR
1¼ lb (500 g) PASTA

1 lb (450 g) unshelled
  walnuts
1 thick slice white bread,
  crusts removed
5 tablespoons cold milk
1 clove garlic, peeled
salt and freshly ground
  black pepper
3 tablespoons olive oil
4 tablespoons cream cheese

Shell the walnuts, blanch them in boiling water and rub off their thin inner skins. Cover the bread in the milk and leave to soak. Reduce the walnuts to a fine powder using a pestle and mortar or food processor. Squeeze the bread dry in your fist, then blend it into the powdered walnuts (this will prevent them from exuding any oil which would give a bitter taste). Crush the garlic to a smooth purée with the flat of a knife and stir it into the bread and walnuts, add salt and pepper and then the oil and cream cheese. Stir very thoroughly to achieve as smooth and well blended a sauce as possible. Use as required.

SALSA al POMODORO
Basic Tomato Sauce

You can use this to enrich and enliven all kinds of sauces, soups and stews. It will keep in the fridge for about 4 days and in the freezer for 1 month. Then use it rather like a stock cube or as a sauce in its own right for pasta, risotto or casseroles. To this basic sauce you can add flaked tuna fish, stoned and chopped olives, mushrooms or anything else which takes your fancy.

MAKES ENOUGH FOR
1¼ lb (500 g) PASTA

3 tablespoons olive *or*
  vegetable oil *or* butter *or*
  margarine

Heat the oil or fat and fry the carrot, onion, celery and herbs until the onion is soft and transparent. Add the tomatoes and stir thoroughly. Season with salt and pepper and simmer, covered, for about 30 minutes.

1 carrot, scraped and finely
  chopped
1 onion, peeled and finely
  chopped
1 stick celery, finely
  chopped
2 tablespoons chopped
  fresh mixed herbs *or*
  parsley
1 × 14 oz (400 g) can
  tomatoes, drained, de-
  seeded and puréed
salt and pepper

AULIVI CUNSATI
Sicilian Olive Sauce

You need to leave this sauce to marinate for about 3 days, so be sure you have time at your disposal. It is delicious with cold meats or grilled fish.

SERVES 4

14 oz (400 g) green olives,
  stoned and crushed
2 oz (50 g) fresh dill,
  chopped
4 cloves garlic, peeled and
  crushed
15 leaves fresh mint
salt
4 oz (100 g) small inner
  sticks celery with leaves,
  chopped
8 tablespoons olive oil
4 tablespoons red wine
  vinegar
½ red chilli pepper, de-
  seeded and finely
  chopped

Put the olives into a bowl, add the dill, garlic, mint and a pinch of salt; cover with water and leave to soak for 3 days. Drain and add the celery, olive oil and vinegar, then the chilli. Stir it all together thoroughly and use as required.

PEPERONI sott'ACETO
Pickled Peppers

Peppers are also preserved in vinegar to keep for the wintertime. Although you can buy these ready-made in jars, the home-made version is a thousand times nicer.

MAKES 1 LARGE JAR
4 firm peppers
good-quality white wine
  vinegar

Wash and halve the peppers, remove the seeds, and cut in half again. Leave them in the open air in a warm, preferably sunny place, for about 2 hours – a conservatory is ideal. Place them in a large sterilised glass jar, cover completely with good-quality white wine vinegar and seal tightly. Place in the larder until required. They will be ready to use after 2 months.

MELANZANE sott'OLIO
Aubergines Preserved in Olive Oil

In the south of Italy, virtually everything which grows during the summer is preserved in oil for use during the winter. Tomatoes are sun-dried and then kept in jars of oil; peppers, mushrooms, aubergines and onions too end up like this so they can be enjoyed all year round.

Using the same method you can also preserve a mixture of vegetables: aubergines, carrots, cauliflower, onions, celery, fennel and gherkins, all cut into small pieces. Serve them as an antipasto with cured meats and pickles.

MAKES ABOUT 8 × 1 lb
(450 g) JARS
4 aubergines
salt
red chilli pepper, de-seeded
  and chopped
red wine vinegar
olive oil
dried oregano

Slice the aubergines and lay them in a bowl. Cover with salted water, then place a plate on top and a weight on top of that and leave for 24 hours. Drain and squeeze dry carefully without breaking the slices too much. Arrange them in layers in a sterilised glass jar or several jars, with a sprinkling of chilli, vinegar and oil (to taste) in between each layer. Be sure to fill the jar completely and that the final layer is properly submerged in oil. Seal the jar or jars tightly and keep in the larder or a dark cupboard until required. The aubergines will be ready to use after about 1 month but will keep for up to a year.

SALSA al DRAGONCELLO
Tarragon Sauce

Tarragon has been famous for centuries for its medicinal properties and for its culinary uses. It has a delicious, bitter-sweet taste which makes it perfect for using with meats and chicken. In Siena, where this recipe comes from, it is used a lot with boiled beef. The plant is a member of the Compositae *family and all parts of the herb are edible, including the stalks which are used to make delicious vinegar.*

MAKES ENOUGH TO SERVE WITH AN AVERAGE-SIZED CHICKEN FOR 4 PEOPLE

1½ oz (40 g) white bread, crusts removed
3 tablespoons red wine vinegar
1 handful fresh tarragon
2 cloves garlic, peeled and cut in half
8 tablespoons finest-quality olive oil
salt and pepper

Soak the bread in the vinegar. Chop the tarragon finely with the garlic, then transfer to a bowl. Stir in the soaked bread, then sieve the whole thing into another bowl. Stir in the olive oil a little at a time, until you have a smooth, even sauce. Season with salt and pepper and use as required.

CENTERBE
Liqueur of a Hundred Herbs

There are not, of course, one hundred herbs in this very strong Abruzzese liqueur, but then nobody really knows what the commercially sold drink contains. The recipe is a very closely guarded secret, held by a kindly old man who runs the business in a tiny mountain village – I reckon when he goes, the secret might well go with him! His Centerbe is produced in an old family house which was built on the proceeds gained from selling Centerbe to sufferers of cholera whenever the south was hit by an epidemic.

It is strange to think that such a lovely house was built on money made from a drink that hardly anybody buys any more, and almost nobody outside Italy has even heard of – but what I want to know is, does it cure cholera?

Here is a very simple, home-made version.

MAKES ABOUT 18 fl oz (500 ml)

3 bay leaves
3 orange leaves
3 basil leaves
3 camomile flowers
3 Melissa leaves
3 juniper berries, crushed
3 lemon leaves
3 marjoram leaves
3 tangerine leaves
3 mint leaves
3 rosemary leaves
3 sage leaves
3 lime flowers
3 thyme flowers
1 stick cinnamon
3 cloves
6 juniper berries, crushed
3 toasted coffee beans
6 saffron threads
large pinch Indian tea
14 fl oz (400 ml) aquavit
11 oz (300 g) sugar

Put all the herbs and flowers in a wide-necked bottle, add the spices, juniper berries, coffee, saffron and tea. Pour the alcohol over all these ingredients, cork tightly, shake the bottle vigorously and leave to infuse for between 10 days and 1 month. After this time is up, filter the liquid into a large bowl. Boil 12 fl oz (350 ml) water with the sugar until a syrup is formed. Cool it, then pour it into the alcohol mixture, stir and strain again. Bottle it, cork it and leave for about 2 months, after which it will be ready for drinking as an after-dinner drink. It should be a pale greenish colour, rather like lime cordial in appearance.

Soffiato alla Trentina (page 257)

Above: Coffee is more than just a passion for the Neapolitans – they even have a special pot to make it in. *Below:* Midday aperitivo time – there are so many types of vermouth to choose from!

BASIC RECIPES

IL BRODO
Broth

---

*Because soup is such an integral part of Italian cooking, second only to
pasta, I cannot overemphasise the importance of broth. Many soups are
clear, basic meat or chicken broth, with pasta or rice added to it in a second
stage. An example of this type of soup is the classic Tortellini in brodo. Broth
has to look good as well as taste good: it must be clear and of an attractive
colour. A few basic rules should be followed to achieve the desired effect:*
1. Always put the meat or chicken into cold *water with the salt and bring
to the boil very, very slowly.*
2. Add the flavouring vegetables only *when it starts boiling.*
3. Strain it carefully while it is still hot.

SERVES 2

7 oz (200 g) raw shin or
   similar cut of beef *or* raw
   chicken, boned
1¾ pints (1 litre) cold
   water
3 pinches salt
1 onion, peeled and stuck
   with a clove
1 stick celery
1 carrot, scraped and
   halved
1 tomato
4 parsley stalks

Put the meat in a stock pot, cover with the cold
water and add the salt. Cover and bring to the
boil as slowly as possible. As the foam rises to
the surface, skim it off with a slotted spoon.
When the water boils, add the vegetables and
parsley, stir and cover again. Simmer very
slowly for about 2 hours, remove from the heat
and strain. Cool completely and strain again
before use.

NOTE:
To increase the quantity, keep the proportion
of water to meat constant: 4 oz (100 g) meat to
18 fl oz (500 ml) water.

MAIONESE
Mayonnaise

MAKES ABOUT 10 fl oz (300 ml)

By hand
1 egg yolk
pinch each salt and pepper
4 fl oz (120 ml) olive oil
juice of ½ lemon *or* 1
  tablespoon white wine
  vinegar

Be sure all the ingredients are at room temperature before you begin. In a clean, dry bowl, whisk the egg yolk, salt and pepper steadily with a small balloon whisk, fork or wooden spoon. When the egg is pale yellow and smooth, begin to add the oil *one drop at a time* and *very slowly*. Keep dripping in the oil and never stop whisking. When it becomes too thick to whisk easily, begin to alternate drops of lemon juice or vinegar with the oil. Remember that oil will thicken the sauce and lemon juice or vinegar will dilute it. When you have used up all the ingredients, the sauce is ready.

With a food processor
1 egg
10 fl oz (300 ml) vegetable
  oil
salt and pepper
juice of ½ lemon *or* 1½
  tablespoons white wine
  vinegar

Be sure all the ingredients are at room temperature before you begin. Put the egg in the food processor, using the blade attachment. Whizz until the egg is completely blended and pale yellow. Dribble in the oil very slowly, but don't stop the machine. Keep going until the sauce is smooth and thick. Add the lemon juice or vinegar, whizz for a few seconds longer to blend it perfectly, then switch off. Transfer the sauce to a bowl or sauce boat and use as required.

Checklist
If the mayonnaise goes horribly wrong, it may be for one of these reasons:
1. The oil was too cold.
2. You added too much oil in one go.
3. There is too much oil in the sauce compared to the amount of egg yolk – remember that 5 fl oz (150 ml) per egg yolk is the absolute maximum.
4. The oil is either too dense or not dense enough to hold the sauce together.

If despite all these efforts your sauce curdles, don't panic. Put another egg yolk into a separate, clean, dry bowl. Whisk it steadily and rythmically without stopping and gradually add the wild sauce, *one drop at a time*! If you do this carefully and slowly, you will end up with a perfect mayonnaise.

BESCIAMELLA
White Sauce

MAKES ABOUT 10 fl oz (300 ml)
18 fl oz (500 ml) milk
**2 oz (50 g) butter *or*
   margarine**
2 oz (50 g) plain white flour
pinch salt
pinch grated nutmeg

Put the milk into a saucepan, place it on a medium heat and bring to the boil. Melt the butter or margarine until sizzling but not brown in a second saucepan. When it is sizzling, pour in all the flour in one go, remove from the heat and stir vigorously to a smooth paste. Pour in the hot milk, stir and return to the heat. Continue to stir and cook the sauce until it is thickened and no longer tastes of raw flour. Season with the salt and nutmeg and add other flavouring, such as cheese, as required.

STOCKS

Stocks can be made with beef, chicken, fish or vegetables. They are not as fiddly as broth and in general are less rich and their appearance matters less. Their flavour, however, is very important.

Vegetable Stock

MAKES ABOUT 1½ pints
(900 ml)

2 lettuce hearts (this is a
  good way of using up
  lettuce which is past its
  best)
2 carrots, scraped and
  halved
1 large onion, peeled and
  quartered
2 sticks celery, halved
2 tomatoes, halved
8 parsley stalks
1 medium leek, quartered
1 handful fresh spinach
1 large cabbage leaf,
  shredded
2 pints (1.2 litres) cold
  water
2 pinches salt

Put all the ingredients into a stock pot, stir once and place over a medium heat. Bring to the boil slowly and simmer for about 1½ hours. Remove from the heat and cool completely, then strain into a bowl or jug. Keep in the refrigerator for up to 5 days or in the freezer for up to 8 weeks.

Chicken Stock

MAKES ABOUT 1½ pints
(900 ml)

1 cooked chicken carcass *or*
  ½ raw chicken, jointed
2 pinches salt
1 onion, peeled and
  quartered
1 stick celery, halved

Put all the ingredients into a stock pot, stir once and cover. Bring to the boil slowly and simmer for about 2 hours. Remove from the heat and cool completely, then strain into a bowl or jug. Keep in the refrigerator for up to 4 days or in the freezer for up to 6 weeks.

1 carrot, scraped and
  halved
2 pints (1.2 litres) cold
  water

Fish Stock

MAKES ABOUT 1½ pints
(900 ml)
6–7 raw or cooked heads of
  any small fish (such as
  whiting, plaice, mackerel,
  sardines, etc.)
7 oz (200 g) assorted skin
  and bones from raw or
  cooked fish
1 medium leek, quartered
5 sprigs parsley
2 pinches salt
2 pints (1.2 litres) cold
  water

Put all the ingredients into a deep stock pot.
Cover and bring to the boil very slowly. Simmer
for about 1 hour, remove from the heat and
cool completely. When it is cold, strain it into a
bowl or jug. It will keep in the refrigerator for
about 2 days or in the freezer for 1 month.

Meat Stock

MAKES ABOUT 1½ pints
(900 ml)
6½ oz (185 g) leftover
  cooked meat *or* raw meat
  trimmings *or* 4–5
  medium-sized beef *or*
  pork bones
1 onion, peeled
1 carrot, scraped
1 stick celery, quartered
1 tomato, quartered
2 pinches salt
3 sprigs parsley
2 pints (1.2 litres) cold
  water

Put all the ingredients into a deep stock pot,
cover and place on a low heat. Bring to the boil
and simmer for about 1½ hours. Remove from
the heat and cool completely, then strain into a
bowl or jug. As it settles, the fat will rise to the
surface. Skim it off if you prefer to do so. Keep
the stock in the refrigerator for up to 4 days or
in the freezer for 1 month.

PANE COMUNE
Bread Dough

For this recipe you will need to use the freshest possible yeast for the best results. I promise you, you will never have tasted home-made bread so good!

MAKES 2¾ lb (1.35 kg) BREAD

1¼ oz (30 g) fresh yeast

2¼ lb (1.2 kg) strong white bread flour plus extra for dusting

¼ oz (10 g) coarse sea salt

3 tablespoons olive oil plus extra for brushing

Put the yeast in the bottom of a deep bowl. Using the tips of your fingers, blend the yeast with about 3 fl oz (85 ml) warm water. Add 4 oz (100 g) flour and knead all this together on a work-surface.

Place 1 lb (450 g) flour in the bowl, place the kneaded ball of dough on top of the flour, then cover with the remaining 1 lb (450 g) flour. Cover the bowl with a clean white teacloth, then cover it with a woollen blanket or old sweater. Put it in a warm, draught-free place and let it rise overnight.

The following day, boil 18 fl oz (500 ml) water with the salt for about 6 minutes, then allow it to cool. Take out the bowl. You will see that the rising dough has created a crater in the flour. Tip the flour out of the bowl on to the work-surface, then blend the risen dough with the flour, working gradually and adding some of the warm, salted water to blend it as you work. You should end up with a light, elastic dough which doesn't stick to your hands or the work-surface. Put it back into the bowl, cover it again and return it to a warm place. Let it rise for about 3 hours, then take it out again and work 3 tablespoons oil into the dough.

Flour several baking sheets, shape the dough to the desired roll shapes and arrange them on the sheets, making sure they are set well apart. Cover with a tablecloth and put them somewhere warm to rise for the last time, for 2 hours. (It would be preferable if they could be put somewhere damp. I usually put them on top of an unlit stove, with a metal basin of water in the oven on low and the oven door left open.)

Pre-heat the oven to gas mark 7, 425°F (220°C). Brush the rolls with a little olive oil and bake for about 20 minutes. They will be better still if you leave a roasting tin full of water in the bottom of the oven as they bake.

PIZZA DOUGH

MAKES 4 PIZZAS
14 oz (400 g) plain white strong flour
1 cherry-sized lump fresh yeast *or* 1½ level tablespoons dried yeast
1½ fl oz (30 ml) water and milk in equal quantities, mixed together
2 tablespoons olive oil
½ teaspoon salt

Put the flour on the table top in a mountain shape. Make a hole in the centre with your fist. Mix the liquid with the yeast until completely dissolved, then pour it into the hole. Add the oil and the salt, then knead this dough very thoroughly, adding a little flour if it appears too tacky. Knead it energetically for about 15 minutes. Put it in a bowl, cover with a napkin and put it somewhere warm and draught-free to rise for 1 hour. Remove it from the bowl and use as required.

HOME-MADE PASTA

Before I tell you exactly how to make pasta in your own home, let me clarify the whole confusing subject.

Durum wheat factory-made pasta lies at the basis of *all* Italian food. No Italian household is ever without at least 6 packets in various shapes. It must be of good quality and kept in sealed packets until required. You can tell if the quality is good by checking the colour and texture: the best pasta has a rich yellow colour, and even whilst raw has a slight spring about it. When you plunge it into the boiling water the water will remain clear – *not cloudy*. If it clouds the water you might as well throw it all away; it has too high a flour content and will be thick on the palate when you eat it.

If kept in dry, clean conditions, pasta will last almost indefinitely. No product in the world, not even bread, is as pure and perfect as dried durum wheat pasta. I have been to many factories to see the wheat turned from grain to every conceivable shape of pasta and I have felt quite emotional at just how wonderful this foodstuff is. It constantly amazes me that a country that has known poverty, like mine, can have produced something so very special, using only flour and water – and lots of imagination.

At the last count there were over one hundred different varieties of pasta on the market, and every so often a new shape emerges. The factories I visited while researching this book all produced about 40 varieties each. Various manufacturers think up schemes to sell more packets – they bring in famous designers like Giuggiaro and Trussardi to design pasta shapes, they organise competitions and give away free gifts. Despite all these efforts, the king of all the pasta shapes remains the humble spaghetto!

Fresh pasta, so called, is actually pasta made with egg and flour. In Italy it is saved for special occasions, made with infinite love and patience by thousands of women all over the country. You can make this type of pasta at home: by hand, by manual machine, or by electric machine. You cannot make dried durum wheat pasta at home. Egg pasta is used for making stuffed, layered or baked pasta dishes like ravioli, lasagne or cannelloni.

There are a few other types of hand-made pasta which are favoured particularly in the south. They are made of flour and water, tend to be quite thick and heavy when cooked and can also be easily made at home. An example of this type is orecchiette (little ears).

Green-coloured pasta is egg pasta to which spinach purée has been added. I have absolutely no inclination even to discuss pasta made in other colours as they are no more than a passing fashion and this book is concerned with tradition.

Wholewheat pasta (brown pasta) has no real place in my kitchen. In Italy it is on sale at the chemist, which implies there is something wrong with you if you need to eat this. Personally I find boiled bran perfectly loathsome, and I cannot imagine a worse way to waste a good sauce. However, if you like it, please ignore my feelings!

The reason behind serving fresh egg pasta for special occasions is that, in a society which has only recently known overall prosperity, important meals are, by tradition, marked with more nourishing, more special foods. Therefore valuable sources of protein, like eggs and meat, are saved up for special occasions and the corresponding sauce is equally special.

The shape of the pasta has an enormous impact on the whole dish. The shapes are not created out of thin air: their purpose is to blend with the sauce to create a perfectly harmonised dish. For example, there is little point in serving a hot, chilli-flavoured tomato sauce on spaghetti: there is a clash between the shape and the sauce. Far better to serve it with penne (quills) where the marriage is perfection itself. Similarly, a sauce like Carbonara does not sit well on macaroni but is perfect with bucatini and spaghetti. Think about your combination of sauce and pasta carefully: make sure you put the two together thoughtfully and be prepared to make mistakes. Only by experimenting will you discover what works.

There are many different ways of serving pasta. Lasagne, cannelloni and other baked pasta dishes are always served straight from the dish in which they were baked. Soups with pasta parcels or pasta pieces in them are served from tureens. Pastasciutta (plain boiled pasta, either factory-made durum pasta or fresh egg pasta that has been drained and dressed with a sauce by simple tossing) can be served in individual plates or from a central serving bowl or platter. Some households serve the plain, undressed pasta in individual plates, then hand round the sauce separately. I like to toss the drained pasta and most of the sauce together in the pan in which I cooked it, and then tip it out on to a wide platter or into a bowl, in either case warmed, arranging the last of the sauce and a little cheese, if called for, on the top.

I do hope you will grow to enjoy pasta as much as I do – if you don't already! There is nothing more comforting or healthy, and the permutations and varieties are quite literally endless. Both my sons were eating baby pasta by the age of 8 weeks and pasta is still their favourite food. In Casa Harris we eat it at least 6 times a week; in Italy it is eaten at least once a day in one form or another.

To Cook Durum Wheat Pasta

1. Always buy an Italian brand of pasta or a brand made in Italy: it cooks, looks and tastes better than any other.
2. If you are a generous cook, allow 4 oz (100 g) pasta per person. For 14 oz (400 g) pasta you will need 7 pints (4 litres) water so that the pasta will not stick together.
3. Wait for the water to be really boiling before you throw all the pasta in at once. Don't be impatient!

4. A tablespoon of olive oil in the boiling water helps to prevent the pasta from sticking.

5. Stir the pasta well once it is in the water and don't leave it while it cooks. Cover it until it returns to the boil, then keep stirring it occasionally to prevent sticking.

6. It is impossible to give precise cooking times for factory-made, dried pasta. Each brand and shape will vary and the cooking times are always printed clearly on the packet. Time the pasta from the moment the water resumes boiling. Test a small piece every now and again while it is boiling: this is the only way you can tell if it is cooked as you like it. Bear in mind that the bigger or thicker it is, the longer it will take to cook.

7. When pasta is cooked it should be *al dente*, which means firm to the bite. Not everybody likes their pasta like this, but it certainly should not be cooked for so long that it begins to lose its shape. If you cook it to the correct consistency, you will digest it better and it will provide excellent roughage. Overcook it and your stomach receives a gooey, glutinous, impossible-to-digest lump.

8. While the pasta is cooking, get ready to drain it and dress it. Put a colander in the sink, make sure your sauce is standing by and have a big spoon and fork ready to toss it all together. The object of the exercise is to get it from boiling water to serving bowl (with sauce) and on to the table in a matter of seconds. There is nothing worse than cold pasta. If you like, you can pour a glass of cold water into the pan as soon as the pasta is ready, before draining it. This stops the cooking process. Remember that otherwise it will continue to cook even after you have drained it.

Fresh or Egg Pasta

You can make this very easily by hand, as long as you have the time and patience to work at it a little. Very good machines are available on the market to help you; the cheapest is a small hand-turned model that you attach to the side of your table. There are also electric machines which give excellent results.

SERVES 4 VERY GENEROUSLY

14 oz (400 g) plain white
  flour
4 fresh eggs
pinch salt
½ tablespoon olive oil

Put the flour on a work-surface in a mountain shape. Make a hole in the centre with your fist, break the eggs into the hole, add the salt and the oil and begin to knead it together. Use only the tips of your fingers and gradually blend in more and more flour. Finally work with both your hands, energetically rubbing and rolling.

This is a very sensual and wonderful feeling, so please try to enjoy it!

When you have a smooth and elastic dough, begin to roll it out. Roll it out as far as you can go, fold it in half and roll it again. Do this over and over and over again, until you hear a 'popping' sound. This is when the air pocket in the fold releases the air it is holding as the rolling pin goes over it. Only now is the pasta ready to cut and use.

Roll it out as thinly as possible or as required by the recipe, then cut it into the required shape before using. Don't let it dry out for too long before cooking it. Practise a few times before you attempt home-made pasta for an important occasion. Remember that all fresh or egg pasta takes much less time to cook than the hard factory-made variety. Generally speaking, it is more difficult to time fresh or egg pasta so check it frequently.

PASTA FROLLA
Basic Sweet Pastry

MAKES ABOUT 1 lb (450 g) OR ENOUGH TO LINE A 10 inch (25 cm) FLAN DISH

1 lb (450 g) plain white flour
9 oz (250 g) caster sugar
pinch salt
grated rind of 1 lemon
9 oz (250 g) softened butter, cubed
5 egg yolks
a little white wine *or* water

Put the flour on a work-surface in a hill shape, make a hole in the centre with your fist and put the sugar, salt, lemon rind, butter and egg yolks in the hole. Blend all these ingredients together with your hands, kneading the pastry as little as possible. When you have amalgamated everything (if the pastry is too stiff, add a little white wine or water), wrap it in buttered baking parchment or foil and chill for 1 hour before using.

VARIATION
For savoury pastry, proceed as above but omit the sugar and the lemon rind.

PAN di SPAGNA
Basic Sponge Cake

MAKES 1 × 9½ inch (24 cm)
CAKE
3½ oz (90 g) butter *or*
  margarine
4 eggs
2 egg yolks
5 oz (150 g) caster sugar
grated rind of 1 lemon
3 oz (75 g) plain white
  flour, sifted
3 oz (75 g) potato or corn
  flour, sifted

Pre-heat the oven to gas mark 3, 325°F (160°C).

Measure out about 2½ oz (65 g) of butter, put it in the top half of a double boiler and melt it completely. Remove from the heat and let it cool without hardening.

Beat the 4 eggs with the 2 egg yolks and the sugar until light and fluffy in the top half of the double boiler. Whisk in the lemon rind, then sift together the flours and whisk that in also. Whisk the melted butter into the cake mixture and continue to whisk, incorporating as much air as possible. The longer you whisk it, the lighter the cake will be!

Butter a 9½ inch (24 cm) cake tin thoroughly with the rest of the butter. Pour the mixture into the cake tin and bake for about 40 minutes. Remove the cake from the oven and let it stand for 3 minutes, then turn it out on to a rack to cool. Use as required.

CREMA PASTICCERA
Egg Custard

MAKES ABOUT 18 fl oz (500 ml)
18 fl oz (500 ml) milk
1 vanilla pod *or* 1 teaspoon
  vanilla essence
4½ oz (120 g) caster sugar
5 egg yolks
1 tablespoon plain white
  flour

Set aside about 6 tablespoons of the milk. Pour the rest into a saucepan and bring to the boil with the vanilla and the sugar.

Meanwhile, whisk the egg yolks with the flour until pale yellow and thick. Gradually add the reserved 6 tablespoons cold milk, stirring constantly, then slowly pour in the hot milk, still stirring. Strain this mixture back into the saucepan that contained the milk. Bring back to the boil, stirring continuously, and cook slowly until thickened. Transfer to a clean bowl or jug and use as required.

INDEX